The Wind Beneath My Wings

# THE WIND BENEATH MY WINGS

## JOHN HUTCHINSON CONCORDE PILOT

# SUSAN OTTAWAY

LUME BOOKS

LUME BOOKS

This edition published in 2021 by Lume Books
30 Great Guildford Street,
Borough, SE1 0HS

ISBN 978-1-83901-432-1

Typeset using Atomik ePublisher from Easypress Technologies

www.lumebooks.co.uk

*For Nick*

# Contents

# Foreword

# by The Right Honourable Lord Tebbit

John Hutchinson and I are united in our love of flying, although I jilted that love when I was not quite forty for that even more demanding mistress, politics.

We also have it in common that our shared passion for flying almost cost each of us our lives and then he, whilst sailing, and I, whilst politicking again, came all too close to death again. Indeed as I read *The Wind Beneath My Wings*, I realised that John, who is a few years younger than I, had as a ten year old seen even greater savagery following the partition of India in 1947 than I at the same age had seen in the bombing of Cardiff and London.

We have even shared the pain and outrage at violence wrought on our wives although thankfully I have not suffered as he has done, the loss of a child. All that sounds as though John's life has been a sad burden, but far from it. He has risen above every challenge, great or small, which he has faced. Perhaps no one has fully tasted the flavour of life until he has met death and tragedy at close quarters.

I still regard it as a privilege to have been one of John's instructors in the art of navigation, although I regret that I failed to impart to him the immense pleasure and pride which I took in the ability to navigate solely by astro across the great oceans and deserts.

Aviators of all kinds and classes will enjoy the accounts of John's flying career – even if many will, as I did, suffer a twinge or two of envy at the list of types he flew over such a long career. Certainly I regretted that I have only been supersonic as a passenger.

However, this is not just a boy's book of adventures. This is a book about a man of skill, courage and common (or perhaps uncommon) decency. It is also a vignette of history, of a period the like of which we will never see again in aviation.

John Hutchinson was lucky to have been born and lived in such a time. He rode his luck, he took his chances, lived to the full and even today through GAPAN and RAeS he is still returning with interest what he took from his life.

*Per Ardua Ad Astra* indeed.

# Introduction
# by John Hutchinson

It is a strangely disconcerting experience to have a book written about one's life and I must say that to start with it left me feeling rather uncomfortable. Having it written by a meticulous author whose research skills are quite remarkable has resulted in my being reminded of all sorts of things about my childhood and upbringing that I had long since forgotten (or chosen to forget!).

Sue and I have enjoyed a long marriage which has weathered various storms over the last 53 years and our lives have encompassed the full range of emotions. The unimaginable tragedy has been the death of our eldest son Tim in 1977, at the age of 17. This has cast a long and permanent shadow over our lives. It is an appalling and unnatural thing to lose a child on the threshold of adult life; as a parent all you can do is learn to live with the bleak reality. At the other end of the spectrum, we have a wonderful son Chris who has given us three equally wonderful grand children, Tim, Rafaella and Tigerlily. They are the source of great pride and pleasure and we were very touched when his mother, Sally, asked us if we would mind if our grandson was christened Timothy as a memorial to his uncle. So, in our private lives we have lived through great sadness and sublime happiness.

In terms of my working life, there have never been highs and lows; it has been one terrific high from beginning to end. I have never worked in my life, I've been paid to enjoy my hobby and to do it in the company of some of the finest people I have ever met; my fellow aircrew. Thanks to the Royal Air Force, I received the very best flying training available and if anyone had told me when I started that training in Canada on the Harvard that I would spend the last 15 years of my professional flying life driving people across the Atlantic at twice the speed of sound I would have told them that they were barking mad. Yet that is exactly what happened. As far as aviation is concerned I have lived and worked through nearly four exciting decades and have seen some truly fantastic changes. I was lucky enough to miss the Second World War and I have missed all the worst excesses of modern security procedures that have been in place since 9/11. I would have hated flying in an environment where I was locked up in my flight deck for the duration of the flight; one of the great privileges of flying during my working life was that we kept an open flight deck door and were able to invite passengers to come up and visit us during the flight. On Concorde, of course, that meant that I was able to meet some rather special people.

Retirement at the age of 55 was a huge shock to my system and I know that I became extremely grumpy for a year or two as I adjusted to the shock. But retirement has brought its own rewards and the greatest of these was the immense privilege of being elected Master of the Guild of Air Pilots & Air Navigators. This wonderful City Livery Company embraces all aspects of piloting within its membership and we meet because we all share a common passion; a love for flying. That year as Master was my opportunity to give something back to the profession that has given me everything. Sue and I had an incredible year and made many new and lasting friendships. I commend membership of the Guild to all pilots. Election to Fellowship of the Royal Institute of Navigation and the Royal Aeronautical Society was also a source of great pride. I am still flying to this day in an Auster Aiglet which I share with three great friends of mine. I get just as much pleasure being in the air today as I have ever done and I am able to enjoy that pleasure with fellow members of a splendid flying club which I was invited to join a few years ago; the Air Squadron. On top of all that I am lucky enough to be invited to lecture on cruise ships so life is still rewarding and very full and the luckiest thing of all is that we both enjoy good health. Long may that last.

I feel very humbled by the research and sheer hard work that Susan Ottaway has put into writing this book and I hope that you will get some pleasure from reading an account that takes us from the last days of the British Empire to the present day. I hope I will see you on a cruise ship one of these days!

# Chapter 1

# Concorde – a Beautiful Creature

*Lovely! An absolutely gorgeous sight when she comes in to land. She always reminds me of a swan touching down on a lake – elegant and long-necked; a beautiful creature.*

John Hutchinson, Concorde pilot and broadcaster

In the late afternoon of Friday, 24 October 2003 three Concorde aircraft belonging to British Airways landed at London's Heathrow Airport. Arriving within minutes of each other, they were to be the last ever to land at Heathrow and their appearance marked the end of the supersonic era for transatlantic passengers.

Following its decision to ground the Concorde, British Airways organized a Concorde Farewell Tour with one part of the excursion visiting Belfast, Birmingham, Cardiff, Edinburgh and Manchester while the other flew in to Boston, Toronto and Washington during the week before the last commercial flight.

Then came the final departure with fare-paying passengers from Heathrow Airport. At 19.20 on 23 October 2003, Concorde G-BOAG under the command of Captain Adrian Thompson took-off on flight BA001 to New York. His last message to air traffic control was to thank the controllers, and the aircraft enthusiasts gathered beyond the end of the runway, for their support over the years. The aircraft landed at Kennedy Airport at 22.44 London time; 17.44 in New York. As it taxied towards the terminal building the crew waved flags from the open cockpit window.

The next morning Concorde G-BOAE took-off from Heathrow at

10.30 for Edinburgh, with Captain Andrew Baillie at the controls. On board, the 100 passengers comprised competition winners, VIPs and other invited guests. The flight took just under an hour and a half, flying supersonic over the North Sea before turning over Aberdeen, Perth and Stirling for the approach into the Scottish capital. Before it landed one passenger, travelling with his girlfriend, had proposed marriage and been accepted; others told of their excitement at having been able to experience the flight of a lifetime. After landing the crew flew the blue and white Scottish flag – the Saltire – from the cockpit window as the aircraft was taxiing towards the stand. For the return journey to Heathrow Captain Baillie relinquished his seat to Captain Christopher Norris.

In New York passengers, crew, air traffic controllers and aircraft enthusiasts were getting ready for Concorde's final departure from the city's John F. Kennedy Airport. For its last commercial flight, G-BOAG was under the command of Chief Concorde pilot, Captain Mike Bannister, who spoke to the gathering of VIPs, passengers and media in the Concorde lounge before the flight departed:

> We're going to take you to the edge of space, where the sky gets darker; where you can see the curvature of the earth; faster than a rifle bullet, 23 miles every minute. We're going to travel so fast, we're moving faster than the earth rotates – and the world will be watching us.[1]

Sir David Frost, who had made hundreds of supersonic flights across the Atlantic, commented:

> If the Jumbo Jet were being taken out of service it wouldn't mean very much at all but with Concorde there's real emotion.[2]

Businessman David Springbett declared in an angry tone:

> It's a bad decision. I don't care if it loses money. This is something which Britain should be proud of – it's something the world should be proud of – and this is a step backwards in history. It's not a step forward.
> I've done a lot of Concorde flights in my time – over 200 – and I

also have a few Guinness World records using Concorde, including fastest round the world and, in the early days, I tried to promote this wonderful flying machine. And today it's a disgrace that we are having this so-called party. To me it should be a wake.[3]

On Rockaway Beach, a mile or so across the bay from Kennedy Airport, a group of Concorde enthusiasts had gathered, as they had done so many times before, to watch and photograph their favourite aeroplane for the last time. The group was referred to by some as the Concorde Cult and one member had told a reporter why Concorde was so important to him:

I feel as if I'm losing a part of my history because it's what I grew up with. My father would spend his weekends and take us out to the airport; I was a little guy of maybe three, four years old … Since then, whenever I get a chance, if I have a day off, I still try to get over there and catch it flying still. Some people are going to be a millionaire, they want to do that. You know, be a big doctor in Manhattan with a big office. I had a very, very small goal for myself. I wanted to experience the flight and I didn't want to live my life without finally being the person to look out the window.

He then described how he had eventually realized his ambition and flown on the supersonic airliner:

I get chills about it every now and then. I do get teary-eyed still, I can't believe I've done it. To me I still feel like it was a dream.[4]

Another of the group told how he had been filming the aircraft taking-off and had had to put the camera down to watch it:

You know, just the noise and the sea … . It's just so beautiful you know what I mean. It doesn't get much better.[5]

A third Concorde fan said:

I'm just absolutely in awe, when you're underneath it and get the full vibration and noise factor and you watch it go right overhead …

I love the 747 OK, but it doesn't compare to what that Concorde does to you.[6]

Some of those waiting at the beach had air band radios and were listening out for the words that would tell them that flight BA002 was about to leave. As the aircraft left its stand and began taxiing towards the holding point at the end of runway 31L, the JFK firemen sprayed it with jets of water, coloured red, white and blue.

Crews of several other airliners broke air traffic control protocol by asking if they could hold, so that they could watch the mighty bird leave New York for the last time; others sent good-luck messages to the Concorde over the radio, including one from the crew of an American Eagle aircraft, who said:

… if Speedbird 2's on the radio, we just wanted to pass along a 'Best Wishes' and 'Godspeed' and we're gonna miss you there. We just departed La Guardia – wish we were over at Kennedy.

Concorde replied:

Speedbird 2 here: Thanks for that, we're gonna miss you all.

Then the words of air traffic controller Sam Kohn, speaking from Kennedy's control tower, were heard:

Speedbird 2 Heavy, be advised I happened to have the good luck of being here and issuing the first landing clearance to the Concorde here at JFK back in '77. Just want to say it's been wonderful working with your aircraft and I wish good luck to all the crews, and er, we're gonna miss you.

Concorde responded with the words:

Well, we're very, very grateful indeed for all your help, especially over such a long period. It's been great knowing you, and we're gonna miss you a lot.[7]

With that BA002 was given clearance and began its take-off run. As it picked up speed some of the Concorde Cult, standing by the water's edge, pulled out their cameras to take photos and film of the last take-off they would ever witness of this beautiful aircraft; others began to cry. A young woman with tears streaming down her face declared that she was:

… heartbroken; I can't believe that it is all over.

The group watched as the object of their affections for so many years, took to the air and climbed gracefully out over the water. They kept watching until it was a tiny speck on the horizon and then they could see it no more. Their supersonic dream was over.

On board the aircraft the cabin crew were starting to serve drinks to the VIP passengers who included American poet Maya Angelou, broadcasters Sir David Frost and Jeremy Clarkson, models Jodie Kidd and Christie Brinkley, actress Joan Collins and her husband, Formula One chief Bernie Ecclestone, politician Tony Benn and British Airways chairman Lord Marshall.

From her comfortable seat 60,000 feet above the earth, hurtling towards London at Mach 2 for the last time, Maya Angelou reflected:

It's poetically sad because this shows us how far the human being has gone; how far the mind takes us, and withdrawing it tells us, in effect, that we are retrogressing and we should never retrogress. We must go forward.[8]

As BA002 headed towards its home base, G-BOAF, the last Concorde to be built, took-off from Heathrow on a supersonic non-stop journey to the Bay of Biscay and back, carrying more VIPs including John Cochrane who had been the co-pilot on the maiden flight of Concorde 002 in 1969, and several other retired Concorde pilots.

The crowds, anxious to catch sight for the last time of the three aircraft that were coming home, had been building from earlier in the day. The BAA had erected a stand that would seat 1,000 people but many more were expected to make the journey to Heathrow and the BAA were advising them to stay at home and watch the arrivals on television. This advice was clearly no good for some people who had travelled to Heathrow from places as far afield as France and South

Africa. One of the 60 French visitors was former Air France Concorde pilot, Jacky Ramon, who had made his last flight from New York to Paris on 30 May, one day before the airline ceased its own supersonic service. Captain Ramon commented that:

> This is a very sad day for me, but it's also a very happy day because I want to congratulate the British for celebrating this with some honour. Our response was shameful.

There was one retired Concorde pilot who was not among the passengers onboard G-BOAF. His role that day was as a broadcaster when, with veteran aviation commentator Raymond Baxter, he spoke about his feelings for the aircraft and gave his final observations about the Concorde era in a BBC television programme which was watched by millions.

The first Concorde to arrive bounced slightly before settling down onto the runway, which led him to comment: 'Oh well, I think we'll say that a little gust of wind caught it. Oh, dear. He won't be pleased.'

As the second Concorde made its approach, Raymond Baxter spoke of the worldwide prestige which the aircraft had won for British aviation and engineering, and how the cooperation of the British and French had led to the formation of the company that also built the Airbus. Then the wheels touched the runway and the former Concorde pilot could be heard saying:

> Lovely! An absolutely gorgeous sight when she comes in to land. She always reminds me of a swan touching down on a lake – elegant and long-necked; a beautiful creature.[9]

It was an opinion that would be echoed many times amongst the thousands of people who were watching the historic event, either in person or on the television.

Directly behind was the final passenger flight from New York. As it approached Heathrow the crew spoke to a controller at the London Air Traffic Control Centre at West Drayton. Information was passed to them about the other two Concordes and about the arrangements that had been made so that they could land, one after the other. Then the controller signed off by saying:

Speedbird 2, contact Heathrow Director now … and welcome home for the last time.

He received the reply:

Thanks very much indeed for all your help and your colleagues' help over all the years. We couldn't have done it without you.

The aircraft then contacted Heathrow Director with the words:

Good afternoon, for the last time, Speedbird Concorde 2 is out of one-zero-zero descending nine-zero to Ockham.

This message was acknowledged:

Speedbird 2, roger, enter the hold, but there's only going to be a very, very short delay.

Then a few moments later, before the aircraft was handed over to the control tower, the Heathrow Director said:

Speedbird 2, there's only meant to be me and you on this frequency, but I'm sure there's a lot, lot more people listening to what's going on at the moment. Would you like to say something to them on the R/T? It's all over to you.

BA002 replied:

If there are, then it's an opportunity to say thank you to everyone in the UK that supported Concorde over all the years. We realize that Concorde has been a very popular aircraft; an icon of the twentieth and twenty-first centuries and she's been successful and popular because of the support of the general public – particularly those who've taken the time to come out and watch her as she's taken-off and landed during the last six months and we're very privileged and proud to be part of the British Airways team that's flying Concorde today.

BA002 then contacted the tower and was given clearance to land on runway 27R. As it touched down for the final time the controller said:

> Speedbird 2, left turn at the first taxiway. We've all enjoyed you over the years at ATC. Best wishes from us all.[10]

And so the supersonic passenger era was at an end. As the *New York Times* reported the following day:

> Imagine a world where Porsche came out with its 911 series shortly after Henry Ford invented the Model T, only to take its sleek roadsters off the street because they became expensive to maintain and appealed to only the most elitist of drivers.
>
> That is essentially what transpired Friday morning when the final Concorde flight touched down here at Heathrow International Airport. With the shutdown of the service by British Airways, and by Air France last May, supersonic commercial travel became a thing of the past. Technology took a step backward. Tears flowed freely, from the tarmac here to boardrooms in Manhattan.

Many years before, when passengers travelled on aircraft that were driven by piston engines not jets, and a flight from New York took over 12 hours to reach the United Kingdom,[11] the retired Concorde pilot who had been commentating on the arrival of the three aircraft, then a small boy, announced to his parents, Viola and Wynne, at their home in India that when he grew up he was going to be a pilot. His bemused father enquired of him:

> Why on earth would you want to be a pilot, boy? You've never even seen an aeroplane.

The child, whose name was John Hutchinson, could not explain; he just knew he had to fly.

# Chapter 2

# Home from the Earliest Days

*If there is one place on the face of earth where all the dreams of living men have found a home from the very earliest days when man began the dream of existence, it is India!*

Romain Rolland, 1866–1944, French scholar

When Donald Bertram Wynne Hutchinson and Viola Mabel Radcliffe Ekins married in London, in the summer of 1935, two families with strong links to India were united.

Donald, or Wynne as he was known to his family and friends, was born on 5 March 1910 in the most easterly town in the United Kingdom, Lowestoft. He was the younger of the two sons of Donald Hutchinson and his wife, Constance Walley. Several of Wynne's forebears had served in the British Army in India including his great-great-great grandfather Colonel George Hutchinson and his great-great grandfather – also George – who became General Hutchinson and served with great distinction in the British Army in various campaigns in India, including at the Siege of Lucknow in 1857-58.

Wynne's father had broken with the family tradition of joining the Army and had, instead, elected to serve the people of Lowestoft, as a GP. He worked for the community in many more ways than that of general doctor, devoting his time and efforts to surgery and research into a cure for cancer, as well as looking after the religious, educational and social needs of his patients.

No doubt hoping that his two sons would follow him into medical professions, he sent them to Epsom College in Surrey which had long associations with medicine. Sadly for Dr Hutchinson, both sons preferred the Army and completed their education at Sandhurst.

George, the elder son, was commissioned in the British Army and was sent out to India at the end of 1927. Wynne began his Army career two and a half years later.

On 1 February 1930 Dr Hutchinson died after an illness which had lasted for several months. He was only 56 years old and was survived by his wife, his two sons and his mother. His life and work was the subject of a long article in the local Lowestoft newspaper which spoke of his devotion to duty and said: 'It is not exaggeration to say that his death has occasioned profound regret, and this was shown in marked degree at the funeral on Wednesday.' There followed a list of the mourners – nearly 400 – along with details of the representatives of various organizations to which Dr Hutchinson had devoted his energies and who were also at the funeral.

The vicar of Dr Hutchinson's church, St John's, wrote in the parish magazine of March 1930:

> *The death of Dr. Hutchinson, after a lingering illness, has left a sense of personal bereavement in very many homes in the town and neighbourhood ... At the meeting of the Church Council, held on Monday, February 24th, it was unanimously resolved to place on record the keen sense of the loss sustained through his death. The resolution expressed thankfulness to God for Dr. Hutchinson's many gifts of heart and mind, for his devotion to his profession and for his widespread influence in the service of Christ among the people of Lowestoft ... I was privileged to take the burial service at St. Margaret's Church ... . I cannot remember being present at a more impressive service. The beauty and profusion of the flowers, the overflowing congregation, the atmosphere of devotion, the note of humble thankfulness which was felt rather than heard, all made the occasion one that will live in the memory of all who were present.*

Dr Hutchinson was clearly a well-liked and respected member of the community and one who worked tirelessly for the people of Lowestoft. His early death robbed his family of a much loved son, husband and father, and his elder son, George, was not even able to attend his father's funeral as he was already with his regiment at Kirkee (Khadki) in India. Wynne was in Lowestoft to support his mother and grandmother but not for long. Just over a month after his father's death he, too, left his native shores, having received a commission in the Royal Indian Army, and sailed for Bombay (Mumbai) to join the Sikh Pioneers, also based at Kirkee near Poona (Pune). He arrived at 07.00 on 18 March 1930 and was met by his brother at Ballard Pier, south of the Indira Dock, when his ship berthed. He quickly settled into his new life in India and, by the following year, Wynne had met the woman who would become his wife.

Viola Ekins was born on 11 December 1908 in Sylhet which was then part of India but is now in Bangladesh. She was the elder of the two daughters of George William Beaufield Ekins and his wife Florence Mary Mabel Haynes Hutchinson, known as Mabel. The couple had married in 1905 in Barrackpore, West Bengal, now part of the greater urban district of Calcutta (Kolkata) east of the Hooghly River. It is interesting, and slightly confusing, to note that Mabel's maiden name was the same as that which her daughter would take when she married Wynne Hutchinson in 1935, although investigations revealed that the two families were not related. Mabel's greater claim to fame was that she was a descendant of the Royalist Haynes family who fled to Barbados to escape the wrath of Oliver Cromwell and who went on to own vast sugar plantations, and countless slaves. There are still many people with the name Haynes, including the famous West Indian cricketer Desmond Haynes, who come from Barbados and who are, no doubt, descendants of those who fell foul of Oliver Cromwell or of the slaves who took their name.

Viola's father, George was part of the wealthy Ekins family of Northamptonshire. In the seventeenth and eighteenth centuries a number of his forebears had been clergymen but his grandfather, Charles Ekins, had joined the Army and had been sent out to India in 1826 where he became a major in the 7th Bengal Light Cavalry. There he met 17 year old Julia Maxwell, the daughter of Brigadier William Maxwell of the Honourable East India Company. The couple married in Keitah, West Bengal, on 27 March 1830, their marriage lasting for 19 years until Charles was killed at the Battle of Chillianwallah in the Second Sikh War, on 13 January

1849. He was obviously a well respected officer and an inscription in St Luke's Church, Jullundur, says of him:

*Sacred to the memory of Major Charles Ekins of the 7th Bengal Light Cavalry and Deputy Adjt. General of the Army, who fell in action at Chillianwallah on the 13th January 1849, aged 39 years. Cut off by a glorious death in the fullness of his career, whilst in the zealous performance of his duty, he has yet left a bright example in his life in the high esteem in which he was held by the army to which he belonged, as a gallant soldier, a kind warm hearted friend and an honourable upright and good man.*[1]

During their 19 years together Charles and Julia had five children, all born in India, the eldest of whom was George Ekins' father, Charles Chester Ekins who married George's mother, Emily Mary Taylor in 1869.

The couple had four children, a daughter Mary Emily Radcliffe Ekins born in 1870, and three sons, the first of whom was George, born in Kussowlie, West Bengal on 5 June 1871.[2]

George, rejecting the family tradition of either entering the Church or taking a commission in the Army, became a tea planter at Luskerpore tea garden in Sylhet. He worked as the assistant to the manager Bill Lennox and, according to W.M. Fraser, another tea planter to whom he was known:

… was stationed at Kaphaicherra in a comfortable basha. He … was a clever chap, and he had the knack of using a free tongue with such good humour that he was a general favourite with young and old. In some works of reminiscence the writers have a way of telling stories about people that fit in with their subject, and add interest and amusement to their authorship. If I had that gift I could fill some pages with Ekins' tales about his neighbours, for he saw the funny side of life in the Luskerpore Valley, but I shall pass on, merely remarking that if laughter is good for the soul, then Ekins was a public benefactor.

Some years later he was promoted to the management of Silloah, one of the divisions of the Surmah Valley Tea Company in the Juri Valley.[3]

Mabel had a brother, William, who was also a tea planter. Since she, herself, had no other connections with India, it is likely that she was visiting her brother when she met and married George Ekins.

In the summer of 1910 Mabel, George and Viola came to England to visit Mabel's relations in Bournemouth and await the birth of a second child. It was in nearby Christchurch that Viola's sister, Sybil Muriel Haynes Ekins, was born on 21 July 1910. Tragically the birth was not straightforward and Mabel contracted puerperal fever and died a month after the arrival of her second daughter. She was two months short of her 33rd birthday. Her untimely death left George with a problem. He had a 2 year old child and a newborn baby to care for and he was thousands of miles from his home in India. In his grief the widower turned to his sister Mary for help.

Mary had come to England some years before and, in 1889, had married a London solicitor, Charles Ford who was 20 years her senior. The couple lived in some style in a large house in Highgate and, in the year of her sister-in-law's death, Mary gave birth herself, to her twelfth and last child. Although their house, Brookfield, was substantial, it was home to a very large family and at least six servants. Mary, however, did not refuse the help her brother requested and Viola and Sybil were taken in. They were placed in the care of a nurse, Annie Halsey, and lived with her and her family in their house in the grounds of Mary's own home. George returned to India and:

> … went out to rubber in the Malay States, only to return to tea again as manager of his old garden, Luskerpore, in 1912 or 1913. He came back in bad health and, with a weakened constitution, died shortly afterwards. Ekins, though well provided with brains, and likely to have been a success as a schoolmaster or a writer for Punch, was not made for tea planting, a profession which requires practical commercial sense rather than artistic qualities.[4]

George Ekins died on 6 October 1913 at the age of 42 and was buried the next day in the Lower Circular Road Cemetery in Calcutta. After he had left the girls in the care of his sister and returned home, Viola was told that he had fallen overboard from the ship taking him back to India and had been lost at sea. She later thought that she was meant to believe that in his depressed state he had taken his own life. It is unclear whether it was Mary Ford or the nurse employed to look after the children who had told this monstrous lie but Viola never knew anything different and believed to her dying day that her father had died three years before the actual date of his death. None of the money that had belonged to the family was inherited by the two girls and nothing was discovered about who it was that had appropriated it. There was, however, a belief that either the nurse, or Mary Ford herself, was a gambler and that the children's inheritance may have been used to further the habit.

Mary Ford did not have an easy life. In the actual year of her brother's death, 1913, her husband also died, leaving her with her youngest five children, still not in their teens, and Viola and Sybil to look after.

In a very strange twist of fate, Viola's uncle – her mother's brother, William, the tea planter – did die at sea. At the beginning of 1915 he was returning to India on board the SS *City of Paris* after visiting his family in England, when he disappeared from the ship while it was in the Bay of Biscay. The reason for his loss was never established.[5]

Viola grew up with only hazy memories of her parents and Sybil had no memories of them at all. As soon as they were old enough to go to school, their Aunt Mary sent the sisters to St Mary's School in Wantage, Berkshire, where they became boarders. Their family life was virtually non-existent as, although they did occasionally return to their aunt's home, they often remained at the school during the holidays. Viola thrived in the academic atmosphere of St Mary's but Sybil disliked it and left as soon as she was able, to take up a career as an actress. It was a strange childhood for the two sisters but both survived to make successes of their lives.

After finishing her schooling, Viola went on to gain a degree at London University and decided that she would like to become a teacher. In the early part of the 1930s she returned to the land of her birth, settled in Poona and began her teaching career.

In November 1930 Wynne Hutchinson's brother George became engaged, returning to England in the spring of 1931 to marry his fiancée Betty. His diary records trips made during his home leave, taking his mother and her friend to Scotland, playing tennis and bridge and visiting friends, before he and his new bride boarded the SS *California* in Liverpool on 20 October 1931. They arrived in Bombay on 9 November 1931 and were met by Wynne who whisked Betty off to the Taj Mahal Hotel to wait while George battled with their baggage and the Indian Customs' procedures before joining them for lunch.

It would appear from the diary entries that life in the British Army in India during the 1930s was fairly relaxed, with plenty of social events and sport. Shortly after George and Betty arrived in Bombay there is an entry in George's diary for Saturday 28 November 1931, in which he says:

> *This afternoon Wynne and Betty and I went in to Poona in Mess car and played tennis with Miss Ekins.*

This was the first time that Viola was mentioned; in subsequent entries George always referred to her as Vi and it was clear that not only was a romance developing between Wynne and Viola but also a great friendship between the two couples. Wynne brought Viola to visit George and Betty frequently and she sometimes stayed all day. When, in 1932, she had a brief stay in the Sassoon Hospital in Poona, they visited her in the hospital and then invited her to stay with them for a few days to convalesce. When time permitted they went out to visit local places of interest such as the ancient Buddhist rock-cut Karla Caves with their intricate carvings; the town of Dehu with its many temples where they watched the sacred fish being fed or the dam at Khadakwasla where they swam and had picnics under a large mango tree.

In 1932 the three Sikh Pioneer regiments were disbanded and Wynne was transferred to the Royal Indian Army Service Corps (RIASC). In this role he travelled around the country a lot, visiting places such as Belgaum in the Western Ghats, midway between Bombay and Bangalore, and Waziristan, a fierce tribal area on the border with Afghanistan.

On 31 May 1935, in the early hours of the morning, the vibrant, bustling city of Quetta, capital of the province of Baluchistan and home to over 12,000 soldiers of the Army garrison, was devastated by an earthquake measuring 7.5 on the Richter scale. At least 30,000 people died; some estimates put the death toll as high as 65,000. A tent city was erected to house the survivors and to provide shelter for the Army units who had been drafted in to help. Wynne was sent to assist in the rescue operation and the clearing of the tons of rubble from the destroyed buildings. The city had been completely destroyed. Hardly a building remained standing and those that did had been so badly damaged that they had to be demolished. The search for survivors quickly became an operation to remove decaying bodies from the ruins, and first-aid posts and mobile canteens had to be set up to care for those who had lost everything.

When he returned from Quetta Wynne had little time to consider the horrors he had witnessed as he and Viola were busy, getting ready to sail for England to be married. They became Mr and Mrs Hutchinson at a service held at Holy Trinity Church, Brompton in the summer of 1935 and spent some time visiting family and friends in the weeks after the wedding. They ended their leave at the home of Wynne's mother in Lowestoft and then went to London where they boarded the P&O ship *Chitral* on 6 December 1935 for their return voyage to India. Viola celebrated her 27th birthday on board ship, five days later.

When considering where they would make their home and bring up the family they hoped to have, they had rejected the idea of returning to England when Wynne's time in the Royal Indian Army was over and decided that their future would be in the country they both loved – India.

# Chapter 3

# Suffering and Sacrifice

*That freedom can never be attained by a nation without suffering and sacrifice has been amply borne out by the recent tragic happenings in this subcontinent.*

Muhammad Ali Jinnah, 1876–1948, Quaid-e-Azam (Great Leader)
and first Governor-General of Pakistan

In 1849, at the end of the Second Sikh War, which had claimed the life of Major Charles Ekins at Chillianwallah, the British victors occupied the ancient Punjabi city of Rawalpindi. By 1851 it had become a garrison for the British Army and went on to be the headquarters of the Northern Command and the largest military garrison in British India. Thirty years later the British built the railway whose lines still serve the city to this day.

It was in Rawalpindi that Viola and Wynne were living while they awaited the arrival of their first baby although Wynne was not at the hospital nor even in Rawalpindi for the birth, having gone away on Army business. Their son, John, took his first breath at the Holy Family Hospital on Murree Road, Rawalpindi at 18.41 on the evening of Saturday 17 April 1937 and Wynne learnt of the arrival in a telegram sent by his wife. Viola herself described the birth of her son as:

24 hours of pain before membranes ruptured. After that 44 hours of pain. 2 days early.

She also made a note of the cost of her firstborn, listing items such as

17

clothes, bedding, hospital expenses and the fees for registering him at both Wellington College and Epsom College. Although the family home was in India both Viola and Wynne wanted him to have a British education and intended to send him to the United Kingdom where he would attend a boarding school, in common with many British children who had been born in India. By the time that John was old enough to go to a boarding school, however, their lives had changed dramatically, in ways they could never have imagined in the more peaceful days of the late 1930s.

The family remained in Rawalpindi for only 20 days after John's birth when they moved to Murree, a hill station 7,500 feet up in the foothills of the Himalayas where the air was cooler than in the city.

It had been planned that John's christening would take place in Murree on 8 June. This was the anniversary of the death of Colonel Charles Chester, the Adjutant-General of the Army, who had been killed at the Battle of Badli-Ki-Serai (Badlee Suraie) 80 years before during what was known as the Indian Rebellion of 1857. He was a distant relation of John's mother and she wanted her child to have the name of Chester in his honour. However, the Army had no respect for family celebrations and, on 8 June, Wynne was in Waziristan and was unable to return home. In fact he didn't arrive until the following month so the christening had to wait until 11 July when, at Holy Trinity Church in Murree, it was conducted by the Revd L.M. Gorrie. It was a joint ceremony with another baby, Rosemary Rash, whose father was also in the Army and, after the service, a reception was held at the George Hotel.

Throughout the summer of 1937 the family remained in Murree. Although John's health at the time of his birth was recorded as being good, his mother worried that during his first few weeks he lost a lot of weight and, at the age of one month, developed a boil on his right wrist which required minor surgery by an Army doctor at the British Military Hospital.

After the operation he gradually regained his birth weight of 7 lbs 4 ozs and thereafter his health improved considerably.

The life of Army families in India could be somewhat nomadic and that of the Hutchinsons was no exception. When John was 6 months old he and his parents returned to Rawalpindi for a few days before going on to Bannu in the central part of the North-West Frontier Province in what is now Pakistan, where they remained for 7 weeks prior to moving on to Dera Ismail Khan on the banks of the Indus river for a week and then returning to Rawalpindi for another 4 months. This pattern of constant moves was repeated throughout John's early childhood with periods of some months being spent in various hill stations during very hot weather before returning to the plains as they became cooler.

Wynne and Viola had employed some servants, including an ayah for John who looked after him for the first four years of his life. They then decided that he was too old to have a nurse and Viola took over his entire care herself. In the records that she kept about her son's first years, she noted that John was rather shy with English adults but that he was very friendly towards Indians, and all children. His first words were a mixture of English and Urdu.

Wynne had been taking legal training in the years following the disbanding of the Sikh Pioneers and, the year after his son's birth, he sat exams that would allow him to leave the RIASC and join the Department of the Judge Advocate General. On 19 July 1938 he received the telegram that told him he had been successful. This change in the path of his Army career meant that Wynne had to travel around the country even more, often being away for days, and sometimes weeks, at a time. When John was about 6 years old and his father was away once again, he remarked to his mother: 'I wonder if daddy has become an office boarder.'

At the age of two John learnt to ride. On two or three evenings each week, when the fierceness of the Indian sun began to diminish and the air became cooler, he rode a little donkey and he loved it. The following year he started to ride a pony every morning and refused to have anyone hold the reins. When he fell off he remounted immediately and quickly learnt how to get the pony to trot. His mother described him as a very plucky, fearless boy who loved animals, especially cats and dogs, but who was very destructive with his toys:

> So far his one idea is to tear them to pieces; most eyes and tails etc. have been removed! … A top has always been a favourite toy; he has broken four to date! His latest acquisition is a swing, which gives much pleasure.

In October 1940 when John was 3½, his brother Michael was born. By then the family was living in Nainital, a beautiful town surrounding Lake Naini in the wooded hills of the sub-Himalayan Siwalik Range of northern India. John was said to be 'very sweet' to Michael although, having been the centre of his parents' attention until then, he was jealous of the new baby. This feeling did not last long however, and John soon began to play with his brother and tried to entertain him by telling him, 'Time to laugh, Mick'.

No doubt because Wynne was a soldier, John took an interest in soldiers and fighting. His parents bought him a toy Howitzer, and some bricks so that he could build a fort and he enjoyed this activity so much that he demanded to be dressed in khaki like a real soldier. His demand was rejected by his mother and he forgot the soldier's uniform and pretended to be an engine driver instead, using his bed as the train. Thereafter his imagination led him to try out a number of different 'occupations', including that of a dudh wallah – a seller of hot, sweet milk who poured the liquid from one container to another from a height, so that froth was generated on the top – and, bizarrely, a mourner at a funeral which involved a lot of loud wailing and beating of the chest.

Although John was growing up in an age when boys were not encouraged to show an interest in anything traditionally regarded as feminine, Wynne and Viola were very forward-thinking and didn't baulk at any of their son's more out of the ordinary pastimes. When, the year after his birth, Michael had to have a short stay in hospital, John went to visit him and was fascinated by the nuns who nursed the patients. Upon returning home he insisted on wearing a veil and being called 'sister'. He also tied handkerchiefs to his back and informed his amused mother that he was an angel and that they were his wings. Because he was allowed to explore whatever took his fancy in a natural way, he developed interests in things that might otherwise have been lost to him such as poetry, religion, animals, birds, flowers and trees; he regarded people as equal and had many more friends from the Indian community than from the British and, at a time when most boys of his age regard girls as alien creatures, he was quite happy in their company. He was taught by his mother while in Nainital and could read and write by the time he was 5 years old. When asked where his school was he amused everyone when he replied, very seriously, 'My school is by my bed'.

Viola had a strong religious belief and John started asking her about religion when he was still a very small boy. He liked to look at the Bible and prayer books and, while having their morning tea, Viola would read to him from the Bible while he looked at picture cards. She also took him for walks in the hills so that he could look for wild flowers and birds and he would come home and draw pictures of the flowers he had seen. He often told her that she was, '… looking after me wery, wery nicely, Mummy.'

By April 1943 the family had moved to Simla, the summer capital of British India, and it was here that 6 year old John first went to school. He was enrolled in the Bishop Cotton Preparatory School in Simla which had been opened in 1937 and was part of the first public boarding school in Asia, founded in 1859 and called at that time both Bishop's School and Simla Public School. Its founder was Bishop George Edward Lynch Cotton, the son of an Army captain. He had been a master at both Rugby and Marlborough before being ordained a bishop and, in 1857, had been personally selected by Queen Victoria to be Bishop of Calcutta and Metropolitan Bishop of India, Burma and the Island of Ceylon.[1] In 1866, two weeks after the foundation stone was laid for a new purpose-built school, Bishop Cotton drowned in a boating accident and, in his honour, the school was renamed Bishop Cotton School, the name it retains to this day.

While at his prep school John saw one of the masters wearing a mortar board and came home, anxious to tell his mother about it. He described it as being, 'A topee with a flag on it!'

At 6 years old John had mastered multiplication tables, learnt two poems – *The Fairies* by Rose Fyleman and *A Boy's Aspirations* by Menella Smedley – some hymns, and some passages from both the Old and New Testaments, which he could recite. He had also begun to learn French and, within six months of enrolling in the school, had won the Kindergarten Form Prize – a copy of Kenneth Graeme's *The Wind in the Willows*.

John had been at Bishop Cotton School for only nine months when the family had to move again. This time they went to Agra where, in the seventeenth century, the Muslim Emperor Shah Jehan had built the beautiful white marble Taj Mahal on the banks of the Jamuna river, as a memorial to his beloved wife Mumtaz. John remembers Agra as being stiflingly hot; a condition made worse by the entire family having to live in a tent during the whole of one summer. It was, as he says, not to be recommended.

Having learnt to play football, which he loved, and to box while at Bishop Cotton Prep School, John learnt to swim in Agra and taught himself to dive. He also started to ride a bike which was too big for him at the time and had to have blocks put on the pedals so that he could reach them. He was soon a proficient cyclist completing a 12-mile ride on a main road when he was only 7 years old.

It was while the family was living in Agra that, in December 1944, Viola gave birth to her first daughter, Mary. Having quickly recovered from the jealousy he felt at the birth of his brother Michael, John seemed to harbour no such feelings when his sister arrived and Viola was happy to report, a month after the birth, that John 'loves and admires Mary'.

During the First World War 43,000 Indian soldiers had given their lives in the service of the King Emperor, George V.[2] There were many in India who believed that the sacrifice of those who had died, entitled the country to its independence and the end of British rule which had lasted for nearly a century and a half. They were to be disappointed.

In September 1939 when Germany invaded Poland and Britain once again went to war, the Indian people were left in no doubt as to how they were regarded by the British government. Without bothering to consult any Indian political representatives at all, the Viceroy, Lord Linlithgow, declared war against Germany on behalf of the Indian people. Despite being treated in such a cavalier fashion India, once more, gave sterling service to the Mother Country and the sovereign, King George VI, but the question of Indian independence had become more urgent and, with the passage of time, it was clear that not only did the Indians want to throw off the British yoke, they also had issues about who should be in power when the British left.

Two of the aims of the Atlantic Charter,[3] the result of discussions between US President Franklin D. Roosevelt and Prime Minister Winston Churchill in the summer of 1941, were that their respective countries:

> … desire to see no territorial changes that do not accord with the freely expressed wishes of the peoples concerned [and that they] … respect the right of all peoples to choose the form of government under which they will live; and they wish to see sovereign rights and self government restored to those who have been forcibly deprived of them.

Perversely, when questioned about how this would affect Indian independence, Churchill declared that it would not affect it at all, as the terms that had been discussed were not applicable to India.[4]

His obduracy in the matter of Indian independence was particularly hard to understand and served only to harden the resolve of the Indians to free themselves from British rule at the earliest possible opportunity.

When, in 1942, the Japanese invaded and captured Singapore, they took Indian, as well as British, prisoners of war and tried to turn them against the British, with some success. This cause had also been taken up enthusiastically by Subhas Chandra Bose of the Indian National Army (INA), a separate fighting force whose main aim was to rid India of the British. He and his cronies, with the encouragement of the Japanese, hoped to recruit defectors from the Royal Indian Army thus weakening the security of India and allowing the Japanese to take the country as they had taken Singapore. Some did defect and were regarded as heroes by those who wanted their freedom from the British but defection to an enemy force is, of course, treason and a large number of courts martial were convened to deal with those who had defected.

In the offices of the Judge Advocate General everyone was kept very busy during the war, including Wynne Hutchinson, as the numbers of courts martial, for these and other offences, increased. Wynne was often away from home for long periods but would not speak about his work during this turbulent period of Indian history and, even in the years after the war, never discussed it.

Viola, meanwhile, as well as caring for her baby daughter, had also taken over her sons' education. With so many moves, it was almost impossible for the boys to have any consistency in their education and since she was a teacher anyway it was logical that she should teach them. She used material obtained via the Parents' National Education Union (PNEU), an organization that had been set up in the latter part of the nineteenth century by educational reformer, Charlotte Mason, who believed that children needed a broad curriculum including art, literature and sciences and should not be restricted to the traditional three Rs.

When war was declared the chance of a traditional long home leave for Wynne and the family had gone and so, once it became clear that the conflict was coming to an end, plans were made to take the long overdue break and visit relatives and friends in England. It had been 10 years since Viola and Wynne had been there and the three children had never set foot outside India. Having gone to Nainital after VE day, when the temperature in Agra became too hot for comfort, Viola and the children remained there where they stayed at the Hallett War School, a public school set up for British children who had been unable to return to the United Kingdom because of the war. The school's last term had been that of December 1944 and it reopened in 1947 as an Indian senior residential secondary school for boys. In the intervening period it seems to have been used as a place for British families to stay while in Nainital. Wynne remained in Agra and, in July 1945, wrote a letter to John telling him:

> *Darling John,*
>    *Thank you very much for your letter and the French writing. I think you are doing very well.*
>    *There is still no news of our journey home, so it's just as well that you stayed in the hills as it's very hot down here.*
>    *The tamarind trees are in flower now, but it is an insignificant flower and you have to look closely to see them.*
>    *Much love old boy and be good.*
>    *Daddy.*

A few weeks later the holiday plans were confirmed and the sea passage booked. On Saturday 4 August 1945 they sailed from Bombay onboard the Union Castle ship *Arundel Castle*. During the voyage John remembers hearing the news that the war was finally over when, on 15 August, Japan surrendered.

The *Arundel Castle* docked in Liverpool on 24 August and the family made their way south, across a war scarred England to the village of Crockerton, near Warminster in Wiltshire, where Viola's sister Sybil lived with her husband Thomas Gill, land agent for Lord Bath (the 6th Marquess of Bath) at nearby Longleat. They stayed there for a month and then went to Lowestoft to visit Wynne's family before returning to Crockerton for another two months. For 8 year old John the time spent in Crockerton was a great success. He remembers it with great affection as being a 'wonderful holiday' and particularly enjoyed being taken out by the gamekeeper who taught him the rudiments of shooting.

The children spent another short time with their grandmother in

Lowestoft at the beginning of 1946 and John appears to have been suffering from homesickness. He wrote a letter to his mother in which he said:

*Please Keep this Letter*
*Darling Mummy,*
*I miss you terribly.*
*Please write to us.*
*With love from*
*John*

He finished the letter with lots of kisses and a picture he had drawn.

The final trip the family made was a seaside holiday in the Isle of Wight where they stayed at Rock Cottage in Seaview near Ryde, the home of Viola's cousin, Etta Ford. It was Etta's mother, Mary, who had been Viola's childhood guardian. Despite the cold winter weather they all enjoyed their stay there and in later years Seaview became a favourite holiday destination for the family.

On 28 February 1946, with the long break finally at an end, they returned to the docks at Liverpool where they boarded the Cunard White Star liner SS *Britannic* for the return voyage to Bombay via Port Said. *Britannic* sailed on 1 March and upon arrival they went directly to the hill station of Simla. It was to be their last family home in India.

In July 1945, after the Allies' victory in Europe, a general election was held in the United Kingdom. All three of the main political parties recognized in their campaign promises that the question of Indian independence was a major issue that could be ignored no longer. Even Winston Churchill who had declared in 1942, 'I hate Indians. They are a beastly people with a beastly religion'[5] pledged, on behalf of the Tories, support for Indian independence:

> We shall base the whole of our international policy on a recognition that in world affairs the Mother Country must act in the closest possible concert with all other parts of the British Commonwealth and Empire. We shall never forget their love and steadfastness when we stood alone against the German Terror. We, too, have done our best for them.

The prowess of the Indian Army must not be overlooked in the framing of plans for granting India a fuller opportunity to achieve Dominion Status. We should remember those friends who stood by us in our hour of peril, and should be ever mindful of our obligations towards minorities and the Indian States.[6]

When the election results were declared a stunned Churchill found that he had been deposed and that the Labour Party had won what was only its third election victory ever, with a record majority of 146. Its leader, Clement Attlee, Churchill's wartime deputy, became Prime Minister.

Clementine Churchill told her husband, 'It may well be a blessing in disguise', to which he is said to have replied, 'At the moment it seems quite effectively disguised'.[7] His surprise must have been reflected in India where it was, no doubt, greeted with more enthusiasm than the man himself felt. Having earlier had their hopes dashed by Churchill, the change in government in Britain led the Indian people to hope that perhaps their aspirations for self-government might, at long last, be fulfilled.

The Labour government was anxious to keep its own election promise to the Indian people as rapidly as possible and it soon realized that it would be a formidable task. In the days following the end of the war in Europe, unrest in the Indian sub-continent continued unabated and against this backdrop the Viceroy, Viscount Wavell, who had succeeded Lord Linlithgow in 1943, was endeavouring to broker an agreement between Jawaharlal Nehru's Hindu Congress party and the Muslim League of Muhammed Ali Jinnah so that a transfer of power could be peacefully completed, to the mutual satisfaction of all concerned. By the summer of 1946 they had reached a stalemate and Wavell was despairing of ever finding a solution. Then, in August, violence erupted between the different factions in Calcutta and, in a period of only three days, thousands of the city's inhabitants had been killed or injured. The violence continued, spreading across the country during the autumn and winter of 1946.

At the end of the year Prime Minister Attlee decided that Wavell had had long enough to come up with a way to stop the carnage and allow a smooth transition of government and asked Lord Louis Mountbatten to take over as Viceroy. Mountbatten, although reluctant at first, gave Attlee an affirmative answer at the beginning of January 1947. He had been told that the transfer of power from Britain to India must be completed by June 1948[8] but he didn't want to stay in India for a moment longer than was absolutely necessary and resolved to cut the time allowed by as much as he could. He assembled a large group of people who could assist him with the task he had been set, including those with legal expertise.

Wynne was seconded to Mountbatten's group but did not enjoy the work; he disliked the Viceroy intensely, finding him to be an extremely arrogant man. John recalls social occasions at the family home when he was supposed to be in bed but got up to eavesdrop on what was happening. He remembers the adults talking about the Viceroy's wife, Lady Edwina Mountbatten, and not understanding what was being said about her. With hindsight he believes it is likely that they were discussing the scandal of her affairs, one of which was said to have been with Nehru.

Despite the turmoil in India, Simla remained relatively sheltered and the children were not unduly troubled by what was happening in the rest of the country. The boys continued to be taught by their mother and enjoyed their lessons. John made friends among the Indian community and joined the Simla Ice Skating Club which had the only outdoor skating rink in India. He learnt to ice skate and played ice hockey and then, when the weather became warmer and the ice melted, he took up roller skating. For his 10th birthday he received a red photo album from his friends Salim, Rashid and Asad and used it to display his photos of the ice rink and the members of the club, along with pictures of his family and places he had visited. He still has the album to this day.

Independence talks continued but the more they talked the wider the gulf between the opposing factions became. Nehru wanted to find common ground for an agreement to ensure a united India; Jinnah believed that the country should be divided into two countries, a predominantly Hindu country he called Hindustan and a Muslim land called Pakistan; the minority Sikh community wanted their own homeland, Khalistan, in Punjab. Eventually it was decided that India would be partitioned, forming the new country of Pakistan while the remaining territory would still be known as India.

The man chosen to define the boundaries of the two countries was a lawyer; not one of the legal team from the Department of the Judge Advocate General or anyone with experience of India at all, but a London lawyer, Sir Cyril Radcliffe, who set foot in India for the very first time when he arrived to partition the country. The boundaries were drawn with inordinate haste in order to be ready for the independence ceremonies, the dates of which had been set as 14 August for Pakistan and 15 August for India, 10 months before the deadline given to Mountbatten by Attlee. The exact details of the new frontiers were not disclosed until after the celebrations but it must have been clear to anyone with even a tiny knowledge of India that there would never be a smooth transition of government when hotly disputed areas such as Bengal and Punjab were being dismembered, to the dismay of all and the satisfaction of none.

On 14 August 1947 the new state of Pakistan came into being; two separate areas, one in the west comprising much of Punjab, the other in the east, which divided Bengal but did not include the cosmopolitan city of Calcutta. In between was the great land mass of India. That night, as evening vanished and the first light of morning appeared, India gained the independence for which she had struggled so long. Jawaharlal Nehru, the country's new Prime Minister, made a moving speech to celebrate the occasion which began:

> Long years ago, we made a tryst with destiny and now the time comes when we shall redeem our pledge. At the stroke of the midnight hour, when the world sleeps, India will awake to life and freedom.

Sadly the life and freedom of which Nehru spoke, did not extend to the thousands who had died in the battle for independence nor to the millions who would die after the battle had been won.

Four of the five members of the Hutchinson family had been born in India and a fifth was due to arrive shortly, as Viola was expecting another baby. After 14 August the birthplaces of two – John and his mother – were ceded to Pakistan; a quarter of a century later when the Indian subcontinent was still suffering the repercussions of the hurried settlement, Viola's birthplace became part of the new nation of Bangladesh.

Although Mountbatten had achieved what he had been sent to do, it had been done at a colossal price. His work was then practically over, although he remained in India for a further 10 months as the country's Governor-General, while the duties of those who had to make the independence work were just beginning. They had enormous responsibilities;

ensuring the smooth running of public facilities, providing transport to allow the transfer of millions of people who, because of their religion, felt they could no longer live in the villages, towns and cities that had been their family homes for generations; dividing the Indian Armed Services and the assets of what had been one country into two and keeping the peace between the various warring factions, to name but a few.

In the weeks following partition the rioting and violence escalated to a point where many believed war would soon be declared between the two new nations. Simla was no longer the peaceful mountain retreat that it had once been and Wynne and Viola realized that India was not going to be a safe place in which to bring up their growing family, and that they would have to leave. With great sadness they began to pack their belongings while trying to maintain a semblance of normality for the sake of the children.

At the beginning of September the violence hit Simla with a vengeance when Sikhs went on the rampage killing and injuring any Muslim who happened to get in the way. The life of Wynne's office supervisor – a Muslim – was threatened, along with those of his wife and children and an appeal for help to the Army OC, Simla, was ignored. Nothing at all was done to help the terrified family and so Wynne advised the man to take them to Corstorphan's Hotel, where he thought there would be safety in numbers. His advice was accepted but on the day the family moved, Wynne and Viola received an urgent note asking them to come to the hotel. When they got there they found the distressed man in his pyjamas and dressing gown. In the next room his three sons were playing cards, there were three other people, all Muslims, and the man's wife who was in bed, having suffered a heart attack. There was very little that Wynne could do to help but, in the days to come, he would be called upon many times to assist friends, neighbours and servants alike as brutality swept like wildfire, through the small mountain community.

On 9 September the Hutchinsons' bearer, a Muslim, asked if he might be permitted to sleep in the house and although they were concerned that they would be putting themselves and the children at risk, Wynne and Viola did not feel that they could refuse to help him. Their home was in an area very close to the busy Lukkar Bazaar and later that evening, when Wynne took their dogs out for a walk, he discovered that there was trouble in the bazaar. He called for the police to attend and he and Viola stood in their garden watching rickshaws being hurled over the khud (hillside or deep valley) by marauding Sikhs who went on to loot the Muslim shops in the bazaar, killing the shopkeepers. The rioting continued into the small hours of the next morning.

The following lunchtime Viola took John and Michael into town to do some shopping. After their morning lessons had been completed, they walked to the shops, counting at least eight smashed rickshaws on the way. There were numbers of Sikhs, armed with long curved knives called kirpans, wandering the streets, looking for trouble and, although some shops were still open, they had their shutters up and it was already difficult to find food. Viola was surprised to be met in the town by Wynne who had heard that there was shooting in the Lower Bazaar and had come to fetch them before they were caught up in the fighting. He wanted Viola and the children to leave their home and go to the United Services Club where he felt they would be safe but unless they were willing to lose all their belongings to looters, they could not leave their home empty and Viola didn't want to leave Wynne in the house alone. Wynne argued that he would be in a better position if he did not have the family to defend should anyone try to break into their home. The United Services Club was contacted but was unable to accept any more people and they decided that they would be safer at home than in a hotel, most of which were Muslim owned and, therefore, targets of the Sikhs. Although a lot of their possessions had already been packed, there was no one to help them transport their boxes to the railway station and, even if there had been, the railway company was not taking any bookings for freight.

That same afternoon, while John, Michael and Mary were in the garden with their parents, two Muslims were accosted by Sikhs and, while fleeing for their lives, were caught and murdered in front of the house. One did not die immediately, having been stabbed in the neck and badly injured, but within a short while gunshots were heard as the murderers finished off their victims. The police, who were mostly Sikhs, just stood by and watched. Viola wrote of the event in her diary:

*Fortunately we got the children into the house in time to prevent them seeing anything. After tea, tho' our nerves were in shreds, we endeavoured to watch a play the boys had made up. A fairly quiet night but some shouting and shooting. Curfew is not properly enforced.*[9]

After their horrific experience the day before, Viola decided that she should get on as quickly as possible with their packing and told the boys that she would not be taking their lessons that day. They were both disappointed but decided to work alone and finished everything that had been planned for them to do, with John helping Michael. Viola continued:

> *It was a dreadful morning. At about 11 o'clock we heard that a party of Sikhs were searching Aberfoyle Cottage – just below our house – for Muslim servants. The owner of the house had just gone out, and his wife fled in terror. I suppose she expected to see her servants killed. I said to Wynne: 'Haven't we time to hide the cook and the bearer?' So we dashed along, found them both, locked them up in a bathroom and told them to keep dead quiet. Poor devils, they were shaking with fear. The young bearer begged to be made a Christian on the spot! It was a dreadful morning for them. However, no Sikhs came. They obviously knew Wynne was here, armed. Had we had a visit, we were going to say that the two Muslim servants were out – (curfew was lifted at the time). It was becoming very nerve-racking; it was obviously impossible to keep Muslim servants; we had to get them to safety … Curfew came down at 2 p.m. so we couldn't get them to a refugee camp that day. We told the cook to sleep in the house with the bearer.[10]*

John remembers a day when the Sikhs did come to the house. His father answered the door and when they demanded that he hand over his Muslim servants, he pointed his service revolver at them and said 'Over my dead body!' They left in a great hurry.

Muslims were not the only victims of Sikh violence. Fearing that the Muslims might retaliate for the crimes committed against them, by raping or murdering Sikh women, many Sikhs slaughtered their mothers, wives, sisters and daughters themselves rather than have the womenfolk disgrace the family name by being violated by Muslims.

On Friday 12 September Wynne went to his office, leaving Viola to guard the cook and the bearer. She was terrified that, once the Sikhs knew Wynne was not at home, she would receive a visit from them and was enormously grateful when her Indian neighbour, Dr Rae came to tell her that he was going to give temporary shelter to all the Muslim servants from the surrounding houses and hoped to be able to move them to a refugee camp later that day. It proved to be impossible because they discovered that the feeding and sanitation arrangements at the camp had not been properly put in place and there was a belief that the refugees were being deliberately starved. Faced with this situation Dr Rae kept the 12 Muslims he had taken in and he, Wynne and another neighbour, Mr Narain, armed themselves and patrolled the area until midnight thus ensuring that they were safe for another night.

The following day Viola, unwilling to be intimidated any longer, decided to go into town and keep a hairdressing appointment. She was the only one of the hairdresser's clients to do so that day. While Viola had her hair permed by a very nervous stylist, a Muslim vet was hiding in the salon and five Sikhs, armed with kirpans, waited for him to come outside. When Wynne came to check that his wife was all right, the vet begged him to escort him to his home. Wynne did as he asked and later heard that the vet and his eight children had managed to get to safety in a refugee camp. Viola declared her perm to be one that she would never forget, not least because while she was still in the salon a bomb was thrown in the street outside which killed several people including a police inspector. A curfew was immediately imposed and Wynne had to bring her a curfew pass so that she could get home. She said of the outing:

I got away from the hairdresser at 1.45, having heard many terrible stories; the details of one are so revolting that they have haunted me ever since. Heard that the Sikhs had looted Major Scott's house; I believe he was sheltering a number of Muslims. Capt. Matthews, the staff surgeon, was threatened that his house would be looted and burnt, if he didn't eject Muslims he was sheltering, he told me this himself; a Muslim neighbour rushed in one morning and asked for shelter for his women; 45 turned up! Capt. Matthews got them safely to the Grand Hotel.

On Saturday afternoon Wynne and Dr Rae escorted 12 Muslim refugees (including our servants) to the Elysium [Hotel]. The police refused to do the job, in any case a police escort is not necessarily reliable. Wynne took a good deal of rice and tea to the Camp, but he came back with such dreadful tales of insufficient food. (e.g. one man had had no food for 2 days) that we sent down every grain of rice that we had that evening and our last tin of Klim [powdered milk], as there were babies with no milk. I can't think it was much good among 900 refugees, but Wynne says the gratitude was pathetic. It seems as if they were being deliberately starved by the Government. Owing to Dr Rae's efforts they are now being supplied with food. Gradually all the refugees in all the camps will be sent to Pakistan.[11]

Simla's population was so overwrought that there was panic over normal, everyday occurrences. When the local darzi [tailor] and mistri [handyman], both of whom were Sikhs, called on Viola one morning, asking for work, her Indian neighbours were terrified and thought that they had come to murder her.

The catalogue of horrors was, seemingly, endless.

At the Lady Reading Hospital the doctor, who would be delivering Viola's baby, told her of a 7 year old girl who had been in a tunnel when a bomb was thrown and had seen all her family killed. The traumatized child was taken to the hospital where she received a visit from the police, asking her to identify the bodies. They were sent packing by the indignant doctor. Sikhs began attacking a refugee camp in the Lower Bazaar and killed 15 people; a Muslim rations depot was burnt and even Grindlays Bank was unable to trade, having run out of money. Then the Muslims began to fight back. Viola received another visit from the Sikh mistri who had been badly injured when a bomb was thrown by a Muslim into a group of Sikhs.

John and Michael continued their lessons but in their free time could only leave the relative safety of their home occasionally, and were no longer allowed to go without the protection of at least one of their parents. Mary, by now a toddler, wasn't taken out at all. Viola described their plight when she wrote, 'We are marooned in Simla'.

Food supplies were running out. Poultry and eggs were completely unobtainable and although there had been pork and sausages available, which the Muslims would not eat, on 22 September Wynne was told that the last pig had just been slaughtered and that when the meat had gone there would be no more of any sort in Simla.

By now heavily pregnant and, with no cook or bearer, having to attend to all the household chores herself, with some help from the children's ayah, Viola continued to sort the family belongings in the hope that they would eventually be able to leave Simla for the docks of Bombay and a ship to take them to England:

> We continue packing when there's time – Wynne with a revolver and I with an automatic pistol to hand! Lessons proceed as best they can. Cholera, smallpox and dysentery have broken out in some camps. The only cheerful aspect is the attitude of our neighbours – all Indians, and all most helpful and kind.[12]
>
> Yesterday's 1 p.m. news informed us that a refugee train from Pakistan to India was attacked at Lahore, and 1,000 were killed. Now all refugee trains between the 2 Dominions have been stopped. We all think war is imminent.[13]

It would be another two months, during which time the Hutchinsons' second daughter, also named Viola, was born on 10 October, before the family was able to leave India.

# Chapter 4

# Desire to Fly

*The desire to fly is an idea handed down to us by our ancestors who, in their gruelling travels across trackless lands in prehistoric times, looked enviously on the birds soaring freely through space, at full speed, above all obstacles, on the infinite highway of the air.*

Wilbur Wright, 1867–1912, American inventor and aviator

John said goodbye to India from the dockside in Bombay at the end of November 1947, when he and his family boarded the Canadian Pacific ship, *Empress of Scotland*, for the voyage to England. The atmosphere on this trip was different from the one they had made only two years before. Then they were coming to England for a long holiday and the children were meeting their relations for the first time. This time they were coming to stay and didn't know how they would manage when they arrived. It was a very worrying time for the adults but the children seemed to enjoy themselves on the journey. John remembers that Michael managed to shoot a hole in their sisters' potty with an airgun while onboard the ship. *Empress of Scotland* docked in Liverpool on 16 December and the family went, once more, to Wiltshire to stay for a short time with Sybil and Thomas Gill in Crockerton.

Although Wynne had been given the opportunity to remain in the Indian Army and could, possibly, have returned to India when the violence had subsided, he was doubtful that it would suit him. He felt that, with all the changes that had taken place, he would increasingly become a square peg in a round hole. It was a compromise he wasn't willing to make and so, reluctantly, he and Viola concluded that the only way forward for their family was to settle permanently in England. It was a brave decision. Wynne had gone out to India when he was 20 years old intending to devote his life to the country. At 38 he had spent nearly half his life there; his wife had been born there as had his four children. He knew nothing except the Army but he realized that, with a family to feed, he would have to find a job very soon and, despite the Allied victory, life in Britain in the late 1940s was not easy. The country was suffering housing shortages and unemployment, and many commodities were still rationed – some would remain so until 1954. The outlook in post-war Britain for an ex-Indian Army colonel with a family to support was, by no means, straightforward.

Having left India with whatever possessions they could manage to carry, the family went from being financially secure to a life of relative poverty. John's sisters, Mary and Viola, were sent to stay with Wynne's brother George and his wife, Betty. George was, by then, a brigadier and was stationed in Germany, where the girls remained until their parents were more settled in England. Wynne immediately began searching for work and, through an opportunity brought to him by Thomas Gill, he managed to secure the position of manager of the Cheddar Caves in Somerset which were owned by Lord Bath, Thomas's employer. The family moved into a house called St Vincent in North Street, Cheddar, which came with the job, and a prep school was found for John; not one of those to which his parents had planned to send him but one that, at first, he seemed to enjoy. He started his English school life as a boarder at Tockington Manor in January 1948.

The school was relatively close to the family home; around 30 miles away, to the north of Bristol, in the village of Tockington. It was situated in what is now a grade II listed building, in beautiful countryside and had been founded only a year before by a Mr and Mrs Tovey as a day and boarding school for boys. The school is now co-educational and remains a family run establishment with the son of the founders being the present headmaster.

John settled in immediately and, in one of his first letters to his mother, told her:

*It's lovely here; I think Michael would love it here. We have stories quite often; they are Sherlock Holmes' stories, and they're terribly*

*exciting. I don't play Rugger, but I play football instead. I do all*
*my writing by my fountain pen. Mummy I should have brought*
*a pad with me. I suppose you couldn't bring a pad when I see you*
*again, envelopes too?*
      He closed the letter by saying, in typical brotherly fashion:
*I hope Michael is as fat as usal. [sic]*
*Love and kisses from John*
*XXXX*
*P.S. Those Indian shoes are very thin, they'll very soon be worn*
*out, I'll have to have a new pair soon, what'll we do about it.*

Above the postscript he had drawn a tiny aeroplane.

Ten days later he wrote again to his mother, his worries about his shoes forgotten:

*Darling Mummy,*
      *Thank you very much for the letter. Last Monday I saw a hunt.*
*It was lovely. There were some beautiful hounds. We saw them*
*start off. I am so glad I'm going to see you on Sunday.*
      *If you have unpacked my Stamp Album please send it to me if*
*you can. I go to bed at 7.30.*

He went on to name a few of his new teachers and gave his mother a list of his new best friends – 17 in all – before sending lots of love and kisses to all the family.

John's father was pleased to have found a position so quickly. His first task had been to open up the Cheddar Caves again. During the war they had been out of bounds to the general public having been used by the War Office to store paintings and other treasures. These all had to be removed and restored to the National Gallery and the other museums from where they had been taken. Then the caves had to be made ready to take in tourists to ensure a steady income for Lord Bath who, upon the death of his father in 1946, had had such a large bill for death duties that he had to sell off parts of his estate. Wynne had a genuine interest in the caves and, although the job was very different from life in the Indian Army, found it both pleasant and suitable for his, and his family's immediate needs, although it was not what either he or his wife wanted in the long term.

They remained in Cheddar for two years, however, while they considered what to do in the future.

Five months after the family arrived in England, Viola's brother-in-law, Thomas Gill, died of a heart attack. He was 62. He and Sybil had been married for just four and a half years; years that had already brought great sorrow as their first child, Julia, had died in November 1944 the day after her birth. With the death of her husband, 37 year old Sybil was left with two small children to bring up; a daughter, Louisa, aged 2 and a son Nicholas, who was only a few months old. On hearing the news, John wrote to his mother to tell her that he was, '… terribly sorry about Uncle Thomas'. In truth he hadn't known his uncle very well, having spent only a few weeks of his entire life in his company.

John did well at Tockington Manor and seemed to enjoy his stay there although, looking back to that time now, he remembers feeling very unsettled. A sensitive child, he obviously realized that he had to make the best of his situation and, as he had reported in his letter home, he had numerous 'best friends' to keep him company although he missed his family a lot. He also had many interests including stamp collecting, which kept him busy. He took riding lessons at the school and became quite proficient, building on the experience he had gained while in India. He also played a lot of sport. He enjoyed cricket in the summer and sent home detailed accounts of both the matches and the scores but very little was written about his other lessons.

In the summer of 1948 he wrote to his mother to tell her that he had been hit in the mouth with a cricket ball and had cut his lip badly. He described it in a very matter of fact way and there was no hint of any self pity or desire to use it as an excuse to come home. During his school holidays he worked as a guide in the Cheddar Caves and also took up potholing.

After he had been at the school for several months he, along with several other boys, caught the skin infection known as ringworm and came home to recover. He didn't go back to Tockington Manor as his parents decided to move him to Wells Cathedral School where he attended as a day pupil while they looked for another boarding school. Viola and Wynne were determined to give their children the very best education that they could afford and worked hard to that end, sacrificing much in order to be able to pay school fees.

In January 1949 they managed to secure a place for John at St Michael's

School in the village of Otford near Sevenoaks, Kent. The school was run and subsidized by the Anglo-Catholic Church. Much older than Tockington Manor, St Michael's was founded in 1872 by Father Arthur Tooth for '… sons of the Clergy, officers of the Army and Navy and of professional men whose homes had been marred by bereavement or by some form of domestic unhappiness'. Eleven year old John settled into his new surroundings immediately. In his first letter home he wrote:

> *My darling Mummy and Daddy,*
> *I hope you are well. I love it at school. I got my school cap and tie today. We have quite good meals, but they are not as good as the meals we had at Tockington. The Chapel is absolutely beautiful. They were swinging a censer of frankincense. There are nine people in our dormitory. It is No. 7. There are lots of people who I have made friends with. I got your letter yesterday. I thought it was the nicest letter that you've ever sent me. We are starting lessons tomorrow. They play a lot of Ping-Pong and Billiards here. Matron is so nice to me. I have a bath on Tuesdays and Fridays and go to bed at 7.40 and I get into bed at about 8.0 and we have our lights switched off at 8.30. I'm longing to see you all again. Well, I suppose I had better finish my letter. I hope Michael, Mary, Viola and Daddy are very well and please give them all my love.*

Later that year Michael joined him at St Michael's. John reported to his parents that:

> *I think Michael is getting on very well indeed. He's made a lot of friends all ready … I was awfully sad leaving you although Michael doesn't seem to mind a bit. I am longing to see you … Michael seems to love it at school and is perfectly happy.*

Although Michael may have loved the school he felt that both he and John must have been a great disappointment to their mother who was 'incredibly academic' whereas her sons were not.[1]

John became a prolific letter writer while at St Michael's, writing home several times each month. Although he addressed the letters to both his parents he wrote as if to his mother alone on many occasions and asked

Viola to remind Wynne of his promise that he would send John a letter once a term. All of the communications were full of his school activities, his friends and questions about what was happening back home in Cheddar. Sometimes there were requests for little things such as a new biro. In one letter he asked his mother to send him, '... another packet of cereal as I've finished the Corn Flakes. Could you send a packet of Weetabix, if possible.' Letters were concluded in very affectionate terms and although he always seemed to be very cheerful and enjoyed his life at the school, he quite clearly missed his family and loved them all dearly, especially his mother.

A few days after the request for Weetabix, Viola and Wynne received another request from John:

*Two friends of mine want to come to Cheddar in the holidays for a week in the 1st month of the holidays. Their names are Owen and Dennis. They have never been to Cheddar before. I suppose they couldn't come. They say they are quite willing to clear the table and help washing up. They wouldn't mind that a bit if they can come. I hope they can because they are longing to see the caves and want to go climbing up the gorge and go on the Lion Rock, they also want to recieve [sic] communion at our Church. If they can come could you arrange some way for them to come. If they could catch a train to Bristol from London and catch a bus from Bristol to Cheddar; would that be all right? I hope they can come.*

What parent could resist such an impassioned and well thought out plea?

While at St Michael's John continued to enjoy cricket, especially when a new cricket bat arrived for him from his father. He also began playing rugby and was picked for the school team which had mixed results; in his first match the team lost 45 – 0.

For his 12th birthday John asked his parents for a pair of boxing gloves as he was being coached in boxing by the headmaster, Donald Cormack. Cormack later proved to be a controversial figure. In 2005 actor John Hurt, an old boy of St Michael's, claimed in a newspaper article that he and other boys had been abused by the headmaster.[2] John remembered him as a strict disciplinarian but has no recollections of any abuse; he certainly did not suffer any himself other than a caning which was, of course, regarded as a normal punishment at that time.

Although Wynne's position as manager of the Cheddar Caves had been a godsend, allowing the family to settle into life in England relatively painlessly, it was always regarded by him and by Viola as being a temporary measure while they explored other options. They saved very hard while in Cheddar and, by 1949, had decided that they would like to run a small private school. Viola had a teaching qualification and although Wynne did not – he did not need one for a private school – he had varied interests and was accomplished in subjects such as maths and science.

Eventually after a long search they found a small school in Harpenden, Hertfordshire, that they could just afford. It was called St Hilda's and had been founded in 1891 as a day school for boys and girls by a Miss Craig.

Around 1900 the school moved to a large Victorian house in Douglas Road and had had a number of different headmistresses before being taken over by Miss Hallett and Miss Hanson in the early part of the Second World War. The Hutchinsons bought the school, which had only 20 pupils – all girls by this time – from these two ladies for around £4,000-£5,000. It was a very large investment especially as the school was run down and needed a lot of attention. The house itself was large enough to provide a family home as well as a school and, at the beginning of 1950, John sat an exam for a scholarship to St George's School in Harpenden so that he could finish his education while living at home. On 23 March he wrote to his mother to tell her:

> *I am SO GLAD I PASSED MY SCHOLARSHIP. I thought you would like the bill to my cereals. I have got them, thank you … It was a £40 scholarship in case you do not know. Please excuse my short letter because there is nothing to say.*

In June Viola and Wynne, along with Mary, came to visit St Michael's and afterwards John wrote to thank them for the visit and to clear up a misunderstanding:

> *I do hope you are all well. How I miss you. It was a simply heavenly day and thank you very much for being able to come*

*over … Please remind Daddy to tell those girls that he made a
mistake and that I quite like girls.*

He finished his letter with the hope that they would bring Mary to his
Sports Day and drew a little picture which he called, 'Playing Tennis' at
the bottom of the page.

In order to upgrade the building and the amenities of St Hilda's to
the standard that they wanted, the Hutchinsons had to invest a lot more
money and they struggled for many years while the improvements were
made. Although they couldn't afford even a small car for several years after
moving to Harpenden, each family member did have a bicycle. Holidays
were spent either at Frinton-on-Sea in Essex or on the Isle of Wight with
Viola's cousin, Etta. They travelled to these destinations by bike. Even the
younger children cycled and the journeys, at least 100 miles each way, were
made possible by taking an overnight break when they were halfway there.
It was during a holiday in the Isle of Wight that John first had the chance
to fly when his mother paid for a pleasure trip for him in a Tiger Moth.

John enjoyed the time he spent at St George's, a remarkable school which
was founded in the Lake District but had moved south in 1906 to become
a co-educational boarding school. This was highly unusual in those days
and, according to the school history:

> It was chosen by a number of unconventional, intellectual and
> articulate parents. The careers of their children reflected this diver-
> sity of origins, talents and interests. Old Georgians made their
> ways in academia, medicine, finance, the Church, State and the
> Colonial Service, the Armed Forces, art, music and radio.[3]

It would certainly seem to have been the ideal choice for John although it
is doubtful that St George's provided the discipline that was necessary to
ensure that he worked as hard as he could. He started there in September
1950 at the age of 13. It was the first time he had been at a school with girls
and this was, for him, St George's major attraction. He says of his time there:

> It was absolutely brilliant. I had no interest in working. I did
> know though, that I wanted to fly and I knew how much work I

would have to do to be able to join the RAF. I did the minimum amount of work that was necessary to achieve what was needed to get into the air force.

His sister Mary confirmed that John's main interest at this time was not school work and said that:

He greatly enjoyed his social life and he took a great pride in polishing his dancing shoes for Miss Flecknoe's dancing classes.[4]

The dancing classes were taken at his mother's suggestion as she wanted to ensure that he had social skills as well as a good education. Since his youngest sister Viola, known to all the family as Tinks, thinks that he was a 'ladies man' the classes would seem to have been a rather good idea.[5]

While at St George's John became friendly with a fellow student; a girl called Pippa Roe who was 18 months his junior. Pippa was the second of the three daughters of the Revd George Roe of St Helen's Church in Wheathampstead; a village between St Albans and Harpenden. The girls' mother had died when Pippa was only 7 years old and she and her sisters were looked after by a housekeeper. While her sisters, Sue and Carola, went to St Albans High School, their father had sent Pippa to her mother's old school in Bedford where she was a boarder. He thought that there she would receive the extra care she needed, having had pneumonia when she was quite small. Boarding school did not suit Pippa however, and she returned to the family home, a sprawling eight bedroom Georgian rectory with a leaking roof and huge grounds, and a place at St George's School, where she met John.

When, one day, Pippa invited him home for tea, her elder sister Sue was ill in bed. Since Pippa did not usually bring boys home Sue was curious and decided to keep her bedroom door open so that she could see John if he went to the bathroom. He did and Sue called out to him. She used the pretext of enquiring if he was having a good time and whether or not he was being well looked after, to get a good look at her sister's new friend. John blushed at being summoned to her bedroom but told her that he was enjoying himself. Having inspected him Sue then warned him not to get too close as she had flu.

A few weeks later she was at a dancing class when a young man arrived carrying a pair of gloves and wearing a trilby hat, a tweed sports jacket and a pair of brown brogues. Sue thought, 'What a poncy looking chap' but then realized that it was John. During the part of the class where the boys had to ask the girls to dance, Sue found herself face to face with John. She said to him, 'You probably don't remember me but we have met before'. She jogged his memory by announcing, rather loudly, 'I was in bed at the time'. Everyone in the class heard what had been said and John blushed scarlet. As Sue says, it ruined both his reputation and his dignity. She discovered that his rather odd clothes had been picked for him by his mother who was slightly out of touch with what was in vogue for young men in England at that time. John and Sue met infrequently after that, usually at dances held by the Young Conservatives at the town hall.

Sue had a boyfriend at the time called Andy, who was about to do his National Service in the Navy but it was not a serious relationship; she had many friends, both male and female, John being just one of them. She, like her sisters, was a tomboy and more interested in horses than boys. She had her own ponies and loved to ride. Most of her spare time was spent riding and caring for the ponies but there were occasions when she wanted to present a more feminine picture. One such event was a particularly important dance where she wanted to look glamorous and sophisticated. Her father had recently met a new girlfriend, a high-powered London lawyer, who Sue remembers as being very elegant and who offered to help her choose a new dress for the dance. Sue wanted something black, slinky and, preferably, strapless. What she got was white sprigged organdie with a maroon velvet sash and puffed sleeves which made her look like a Jane Austen character. To make matters worse Kitty, a girl from St George's who was regarded as the school pinup, was wearing a black, slinky, strapless number and John, along with most of the other males present, spent the entire evening making eyes at her. Sue knew that she couldn't compete with the blonde, blue-eyed bombshell.

The friendship between John and Sue continued, however, and John was sometimes invited to the rectory for tea. When he arrived, Sue was invariably still attending to the ponies and John was left in front of a roaring fire, with the family's Dalmatians, and a pile of magazines to read, while Sue changed and washed away the smell of the stables. Her home life was very informal and she realized how different it was from John's home when she visited St Hilda's for the first time.

She had been told by friends that John's parents were quite old fashioned and so she made sure she was neatly dressed and had a clean handkerchief. Her first impression of John's mother was that she was a very elegant lady who did things properly; his father was tall, forbidding and spoke his mind; he was every inch an Army colonel. The Hutchinsons had employed a cook and a parlour maid for the school and, unlike the informality of the rectory teas, afternoon tea at St Hilda's was quite proper, with the food being brought into the drawing room, on a silver tray, by the maid.

There seemed to be lots of children in the family quarters and Sue thought that John had at least five brothers and sisters. She soon discovered that two of the children living there were John's cousins, Louisa and Nicholas.

After the death of Thomas Gill, his widow Sybil had had a difficult time bringing up her two small children alone. Lord Bath had told her that he couldn't afford to give her a pension but in 1949 he opened up his home, Longleat House, to the public and gave Sybil a job as a guide there. Viola and Wynne brought Louisa and Nicholas to the school to look after them while Sybil was working and Louisa became a pupil at St Hilda's. The children spent some part of each of their school holidays with their mother but remained with the Hutchinsons in Harpenden for several years. In the summer of 1956, the children gained a stepfather when Sybil remarried and became Mrs Jack Watts.

In January 1954 John went to the Aircrew Selection Centre at RAF Hornchurch in Essex to begin the process of joining the Royal Air Force and fulfil his ambition to fly. Here he had a medical, filled in countless forms and got his first taste of RAF food and tea which he declared to be 'dreadful'. Having passed all the tests that were set in Hornchurch the successful candidates were taken to RAF Cranwell in Sleaford, Lincolnshire, where John hoped to become a cadet. He thought it was a marvellous place and wrote to Sue to tell her that, 'The cadets live in the most complete luxury'. The few days spent at Cranwell were taken up with leadership courses and a series of interviews to determine whether or not the candidates were suitable officer material. The results of the selection process took some time to come through and, at the end of the summer term of 1954 when John left St George's School, he was devastated to learn that

45

he had been unsuccessful in his attempt to become a cadet at Cranwell. He described this failure as 'a great blow to all of us' but, as always, his parents were very supportive and helped him formulate a plan to ensure that he stood a better chance of success when he got a second, and final, chance at RAF Cranwell which he hoped to take at the beginning of 1955, before his 18th birthday.

It was arranged that he would return to his old school, St Michael's in Otford, Kent, when the new term began in September, the idea being that he would study maths again so that he would be able to re-sit this exam and get better results, and that he would teach science to the fifth form boys. Preparation for the lessons would ensure that he learnt the subject himself. It was also felt that the work he would undertake at St Michael's would help him develop his sense of responsibility and his leadership skills; both vital if he was to be successful at his second attempt with the Royal Air Force.

As is often the case, the plan did not work out quite as expected. At the end of September 1954 John wrote to his parents to tell them how he was getting on:

*I'm afraid it doesn't look as if I am going to teach sciences after all so I shall have to learn it without the additional help of teaching it … I find teaching quite an interesting experience; certainly a worthwhile one. It's also very interesting to see how the staff get on … being a member of staff entitles you to vastly better meals, anyway I seem to manage to get just about as much as I can take.*

*Did I tell you that I teach Geography to the whole of the senior school?! I didn't know until about 24 hours before the lesson was due to begin. I thought it would be a lesson for my fifth only. It turned out to be quite a good lesson – I thought – considering I haven't done Geography since I left St Michael's.*

*It's funny but I can't get used to being called 'sir'. Sometimes I'm walking down a passage and I hear someone shouting 'sir' behind me and it really does take time for me to realise that it's me he's shouting for. I'm afraid that it doesn't look as if I am going to get any sort of pay here at all. I've been here a week now and not a word has been spoken to me about it but perhaps something will happen.*

*I have to take football for the seniors on Friday … . It's rather*

*good fun getting the poor boys in training – running round the
field four times, alternating between sprinting and trotting. The
only drawback is that I'm expected to go round with them.*

Happily for John the subject of pay was discussed three weeks later when
he received his back pay for the time he had already been there and discovered that he would be getting £1 per week for his teaching efforts. He
started to save as much money as he could with the intention of buying
a radiogram and told Sue, 'I've no doubt that my esteemed parents will
help if I approach them with caution and tact'.

Three months into the teaching assignment the headmaster of St
Michael's wrote to John's parents to report on his progress:

*My idea is to give John a definite goal, and to ensure that he works
damned hard to achieve it. The discipline of hard mental effort,
and sustained effort at that, will do him no harm.*

*… He takes my 'chivvying' with a very good grace and I am
really pleased with his efforts so far.*

*We find him a delightful person to have about the place.
Nothing is too much trouble for him to do and he has been a great
help to me personally with the Games and 'odd jobs' – including
Junior P.T!*

*He is getting on well with his Maths class, and by the trouble
he takes in preparing his Geog. lessons, I think he is learning quite
a bit himself!*

*… Anyway, everybody here is well satisfied with his efforts for
us, and the purpose of this scribbled note is to ensure that we are
doing what you consider best for him.*

By the end of January John had the date for his next interview at Cranwell
and wrote to Sue to tell her:

*I shall need plenty of luck to get through this interview. It's a
horrible feeling to think that if I fail this time, I've had it as far as
Cranwell is concerned.*

Having had the interview he wrote again a week later to tell her:

*I had a hell of a rough time at Cranwell. The fellow candidates were a very pleasant crowd, but the knowledge that it was my last chance for entry into Cranwell ruined all the fun of it … It's a bloody awful feeling, this suspense of waiting for a result. There is nothing so conducive to moods of depression as the fear that you have failed – I daren't let myself think that I've passed. God, that must sound like sheer tripe to you, but perhaps you do know what it's like. There is absolutely nothing I want more than to go to Cranwell; if I fail it will ruin me. Hell, I mustn't be so morbid – I haven't even got the result yet. Who knows? I may get in.*

Sue had also been making plans for a career. She wanted to be a stewardess with an airline or, as her father had suggested, a ship's purser. In order to give herself the best possible chance of being accepted in either role when she was old enough, she took a job in Paris, looking after three young children, before enrolling for nursing training. When she had spoken to her headmistress at St Albans High School and told her that she intended to train as a nurse, she had been asked to which hospital she proposed to apply. Sue said that she wanted to apply to St Thomas's in London and received the quite astounding reply from someone who should have been encouraging her, rather than belittling her ambitions, that she shouldn't aim for such a prestigious place as they only took the 'crème de la crème' and Sue would not be accepted. She then asked if Sue had thought about the Luton & Dunstable Hospital. Sue had not, nor did she intend to. She remembers leaving the headmistress's office and stamping her foot in defiance, silently promising herself that she would go to St Thomas's if it killed her – 'just to prove the old bat wrong'. She then applied to and was accepted by St Thomas's to start her training when she reached her 19th birthday.

A month after his interview at Cranwell John received the news he had dreaded – he had not been accepted as a cadet. He was heartbroken and told Sue that he felt, … 'utterly stunned. I wanted to give up and go to some quiet corner where I could die'. He then revealed that of the approximately 300 people interviewed for a cadetship only 40 had succeeded and of the 260 who had failed just six were offered Direct Entry Commissions. He was one of the six and decided to accept the offer the RAF had made him.

He was sent to Kirton-in-Lindsey in Lincolnshire for the first 12 weeks of his RAF career where he did his 'square bashing'. He found it to be a very intimidating experience which was conducted by ferocious drill sergeants and spent most of his time on parade ground drill, polishing his boots and making beds.

There was some doubt as to where he would receive his pilot training and, after changing its mind more than once, the Royal Air Force finally decided to send him to Canada as one of the NATO aircrew students being trained there. In September 1955 he boarded a BOAC Stratocruiser for the flight to Montreal via Prestwick and Keflavik, arriving in Canada on Saturday the 17th. From there he and the other prospective pilots travelled by train to Toronto. After the austerity of 1950s Britain, John was amazed by what he saw in Canada. Everything was clean and bright and the trains, which were air-conditioned, had swivelling armchairs for the passengers, affording them excellent views of the countryside. However, the RAF had treated their students to first class tickets both with BOAC and on the train.

For the first three weeks they were based at the Royal Canadian Air Force Station London, in Crumlin, Ontario, where they were shown instructional films and were taken to nearby places of interest. Before long John thought that the majority of Canadians knew far less about Canada than he and his fellow students knew. The place that impressed him the most was Niagara Falls. He wrote to his parents to tell them about the trip:

*On the way over we stopped at a place called Fort George. This was built during the War of Independence in defence against the Yankees and made a most interesting point of interest. Then we stopped once more at the huge power station at the foot of the falls. But this did not mean much to us as, by this time, we were too keen on getting a view of Niagara itself. At last we could see a vast sheet of spray rising above the ground and there were the falls in front of us. It's something to which no words can do justice. A sight of incredible power and beauty. At the edge, the water starts to topple over the precipice. It seems to hang suspended for a split second, then, the moment of indecision over, it plunges down into the unseen depths at ever increasing speed.*

*During our visit over there, which lasted for about 4½ hours,*

*we visited the States. This was not a particularly enlightening
sight. The town was very dirty in comparison to its spotless
counterpart in Canada. However, it was a wonderful day and the
Niagara Falls will live for a long time in my memory.*

On 3 October 1955 the students were given the news that they would commence their flying training at Moose Jaw, Saskatchewan where, John informed his family, temperatures sometimes plummeted to 40 degrees below zero. He assured them that he had been right to bring his ice skates with him.

# Chapter 5

# Eyes Turned Skyward

*When once you have tasted flight, you will forever walk the earth with your eyes turned skyward, for there you have been, and there you will always long to return.*

Leonardo da Vinci, 1452–1519, Italian engineer, painter and sculptor

Moose Jaw lies on the Moose Jaw River in the central southern part of the province of Saskatchewan, approximately 40 miles to the west of the provincial capital, Regina. Although always known as a city, when John arrived there in the autumn of 1955, its population was that of a small English town.

Moose Jaw's airfield had been built in the 1920s for the city's flying club but had been taken over by the Canadian government in the Second World War. It was used to train pilots for the Royal Canadian Air Force (RCAF) and then the British Commonwealth Air Training Plan (BCATP) used the airfield to train British and other Commonwealth nationals. The facility was closed after the end of the war with the airfield reverting to civilian use until it was again taken over by the RCAF to provide training for Canadian and NATO pilots.

4168600 Flight Cadet Hutchinson's flying training began there with two weeks of ground school, learning about such things as navigation, air rules, meteorology and basic aircraft engineering. Then the great moment arrived when John took to the air for the first time. His flying began, on 25 October 1955, in a Harvard; a rugged, single engined trainer aircraft, with a maximum speed of 212 mph, that traced its origins back to the 1930s and was manufactured by the North American Aircraft company.

He was allowed to start the engine himself and, after the instructor had taken the aeroplane into the air, John took over on the control column and put the plane into a few banks. He declared his first experience of actual flying to have been 'terrific' although he was less enthusiastic about the flying instructor, Flying Officer John Ayres, who was dour and unhelpful and shook his confidence.

He was not impressed with Saskatchewan either: 'This province looks grim anyway, even in the best of weather. But in this snow it looks positively bleak.' It did have one huge advantage for trainee pilots, however. It was completely flat and largely empty. Should there be a problem that necessitated a forced landing, the province presented one vast airfield on which to set down an aircraft and some of the trainees did make use of that facility. John described an incident to his parents in which the engine of a Harvard being flown by a Turkish trainee, cut out due to carburettor icing. The young man made a forced landing, wrecking the aircraft in the process, and was found by the RCAF search team sitting on a detached chunk of the wing, calmly smoking a cigarette and waiting to be rescued. John described the Turks as being 'first-class chaps' and liked them better than any of the other nationalities on the course.

By the beginning of November John had completed 5¼ hours in the air. He told his parents that:

This has included climbing and descending turns, high bank turns, stalls and just one take-off. That was some take-off too!

To get the plane off the ground, there are three things one must do – (a) Build up power. (b) Ease the stick back (c) Use the rudder to counteract yaw. The first two things I can manage beautifully; in fact I even drew a word of praise from the old instructor. But that rudder! During take-off, the plane has a natural tendency to swing over to the left. This, combined with the fact that the wind will also swing you off course, means that the rudders do a lot of work. What happened to me was that I tended to overcorrect for swing (or yaw) and went too far over in a certain direction. So, of course, I had to try and straighten it out and again overcorrected, too far in the other direction. The result of all this was that I managed to trace a glorious zigzag course right down the length of the runway.

Ah well, it will come some day, I suppose.

With the early onset of winter in Saskatchewan a lot of time was lost as the weather conditions made flying impossible. The RCAF found them other things to do when they couldn't take to the air and John reported to Sue in a letter how disgusted he was to be given the task, along with his roommates, of scraping the wax from the floor of their room using nothing but razorblades. It took them over 5 hours and he thought it was a completely pointless exercise.

When he was allowed into the city of Moose Jaw he took the opportunity to buy himself some clothing suitable for Canadian winters. His pride and joy was what he described as a 'leather windbreaker' which was bright red with white slashes on the sleeves and white patches on the front. He relished the thought of wearing it when he returned to Harpenden so that he could show the population how the other half lived.

By the time he had been in Canada for a few days short of two months John declared himself to be sick of the country and wished he could come home. He missed London, the pubs and Sue. Although John knew that she had other male friends he was beginning to regard Sue as his girlfriend and looked forward to the day when they could be together again. When he heard that his father was in bed with a slipped disc he wrote to his mother telling her to contact the Air Ministry and ask for him to be sent home to help her run St Hilda's while Wynne was incapacitated. Viola had no intentions of jeopardizing her son's chances of becoming a pilot and ignored his offer of help, battling on by herself until her husband was fit again and able to resume his duties at the school. Although John still had bouts of homesickness throughout the time he was at Moose Jaw, he enjoyed the flying but never got used to the isolation and lack of facilities in the small city and found life in general there to be exceedingly tedious.

Sue wrote to John quite regularly which cheered him up considerably. She had started her nursing training and had been working hard to pass her first exams before being able to do some practical work on a ward. The first day on the ward coincided with John telling her how fed up he was and, while commiserating with him, she tried to cheer him up by telling him:

You will no doubt be thrilled to hear that I have given my first bed-pan!!!

The flying continued and when the unhelpful flying instructor was replaced for a short while by Flying Officer Ally, who had a completely different approach, John's confidence returned and he began to make much better progress. He longed for the day when he would make his first solo flight.

Christmas was only a few weeks away and he complained that it would be a very boring time as Moose Jaw was 'completely lifeless and dead'; there was nothing there to do except go to the cinema, bowling alley or Western type dances and the girls were awful. They all wore sweaters and jeans and if you passed one in the street you had to look twice to check whether it really was a girl or a man.

The festive season turned out to be better than John had expected however, as he managed to get two Christmas dinners – one in the Mess and the other with his flying instructor – and he and the other English students had a party in the evening, rounding off the celebrations by ice skating on the parade ground.

On 4 January 1956 John wrote to Sue with significant news:

*Well, I suppose I could call today one of the greatest days in my life, although I don't feel it right now. I've at last gone solo. Up till now, the weather has been completely against me, but at last the runways have cleared up.*

*So that's all there is to it. I was up in that aircraft by myself. I can't describe the feeling. It's a combination of exhilaration, relief and an attitude of mind which says 'about time too'. I didn't even feel nervous or tense which surprised me. At least, not during the trip. But as soon as I got out of the plane I started shaking like a leaf with reaction. Right now I've got no other feeling than sheer relief. Relief at having crossed one of the biggest bridges in this flying training.*

*Flying alone is one of the biggest thrills I've ever experienced. Controlling a machine of power is something that sends a surge of pleasure through me. Flying is wonderful!*

After his first solo flight John had to undergo a traditional ceremony where his tie was cut off and pinned to the crew room wall, along with those of other students who had also completed their first solo flights.

The weather improved, remaining good enough for flying and, 10 days later, John was able to report:

*I went solo out of the circuit for the first time. If I said my first solo felt good, this felt terrific. Out alone, with the whole sky to myself. Doing stalls, spins, rolls, loops, lazy eights. I did everything I had been taught and tried a few things I hadn't been taught. That's when flying really begins. I've done 4 solo hours of solid aerobatics now and I've never had such a wonderful time in my life.*

Although John never felt at home in Moose Jaw he continued to love flying and admitted that, with everything he had to do, the time was flashing by. He had mid-term exams to pass if he was to complete his flying training and had been told that there was at least a 50 per cent chance of failing to finish the course which must have played on his mind. By the time he had completed around 35 hours of flying, however, something clicked and he felt that all the problems he had had up until then were now over. He never had any significant trouble with flying after that time.

When their exams were over the students had a two week break and John, with some of his classmates, went to Calgary and Vancouver and then on to San Francisco and Los Angeles. He loved San Francisco and found Vancouver to be a very pleasant city – the best he had visited in Canada up to that date – but he was less than impressed by much of Los Angeles although he enjoyed Beverly Hills, Wilshire Boulevard, Hollywood and a visit to Universal Studios.

Soon after their return to Moose Jaw one of his travelling companions had a night flying accident and crashed his aircraft. Although injured he survived. It gave them all a jolt but, with most of the initial flying training complete and the exams having been dealt with successfully, John was at last beginning to believe that he would pass the course.

On 23 June 1956 he left Moose Jaw and travelled to the RCAF station at Gimli, Manitoba, for the final part of his training. Having put the Harvard through all its paces – during the day, at night and in formation – the students would complete the course by learning how to fly a jet aircraft.

The aircraft used by the RCAF was the T-33 Silver Star. Developed from the Lockheed T-33 Shooting Star, the Silver Star was built under licence by Canadair Limited and was powered by a single Rolls-Royce

Nene 10 turbojet rather than by the Allison J33s used by Lockheed. It had a maximum speed of 570 mph; well over twice the maximum speed of the Harvard.

The move to Gimli proved popular. Although the buildings there were older and a lot shabbier than those at Moose Jaw, in every other respect John preferred it. The food was much better, the atmosphere was friendly, the cadets were treated like officers and, during their free time, there were plenty of recreational facilities. The city of Winnipeg was only 60 miles away and Lake Winnipeg, so large it gave the impression of actually being the sea, was nearby and provided a beautiful beach where they could sunbathe and swim.

John's impression of his first jet flight was that it was:

> … like driving in a new Rolls after hacking around in an old, old Austin. The Harvard used to shake, rattle and roll its way through the sky. The engine would bounce around in its moorings, the nuts and bolts would work loose. But it's all different with the T-33. You can't even hear the engine from inside the cockpit. It doesn't even vibrate. When you open up the throttle, you get a really solid kick of power in your back. In the Harvard it used to take about 15 minutes to get to 10,000 feet. After take-off in the T-33 you hold it down to let the speed build up then, when you've got enough, you reef the stick back and you're at 15,000 feet before you have time to think about it.

After 12 hours with the instructor on the T-33 John made his first solo jet flight and enjoyed it. There was no hint of the reaction he had had after landing the Harvard and the only part of flying the jet that he didn't like was having to wear an oxygen mask which was such a tight fit that it was really uncomfortable and left a groove around his face when it was removed.

He wrote to his parents to tell them all about it and received a letter from his worried mother. He tried to reassure her:

> *I see in your letter that you say you are scared stiff about me. There is nothing at all to worry about. A jet is no more dangerous to fly than a Harvard. Besides, if I am not considered to be safe enough to fly a jet, they will cease to train me. There is absolutely nothing to worry about.*

John's time in Canada was rapidly coming to an end and although he had not enjoyed the 36 weeks spent at Moose Jaw, the 16 weeks in Gimli had more than made up for it. In August he took and passed his final exams with an average mark of 80 per cent. He told his parents not to be too impressed as some of his colleagues had much higher marks but he was pleased to have passed with such a comfortable margin. Life was beginning to look so much brighter and then one of his friends was killed:

*One of the best Turks on the course went into the ground from 20,000 feet with 500 gallons of fuel on board. It went up in quite a blaze. It took about 6 hours before it cooled down enough for anyone to take a close look at the wreckage. It's quite a shock when a good friend goes like that. One day you're eating a meal with him, the next day he's dead. It's a most unpleasant feeling. It's hard to believe that I'll never see him again.*

John also learnt that his Great Aunt Mary, who had looked after his mother and her sister Sybil when their mother died and their father returned to India, was ill. He wrote to his mother asking her to pass on his love to his aunt and hoped there was enough time for her to do so. Sadly there was not. Three days after he sent the letter his aunt died at the age of 86.

Having successfully completed his flying training and his final exams, the only thing left for John to do before leaving Canada was a three-week survival course.

This took place near Edmonton where the students were taught wood-craft, spent long days hiking – often getting lost – and nights sleeping in the open, in freezing temperatures. It was impossible to wash as, to get any water at all, they had to break the ice on the lakes. John's clearest memory of the course was that one of his colleagues, while chopping wood, managed to chop off one of his toes and had to be evacuated to a hospital immediately. At the time John thought that the course was a miserable experience but, once back in the RCAF base at Gimli with all its comforts, including hot baths, he felt that it had been quite enjoyable. Whether it had been any use to him was another matter. Obviously vital for Canadian pilots flying across the vast open spaces of their homeland, it would surely have been less important for a British pilot traversing the tiny, crowded islands of the United Kingdom.

By the beginning of November 1956 John had finished everything he had to do, including packing his trunks and sending them off to Montreal from where, he learnt, he would be sailing for home on 16 November. First class passages had been booked for the British trainees – all now qualified pilots – on the Cunard ship HMS *Saxonia* which was due to dock in Liverpool on 23 November.

While looking forward to going home, the news on the home front was depressing. The Suez crisis was coming to a head and, on 5 November, British and French forces had mounted an airborne invasion of Egypt. The USSR supported Egypt and John wrote to Sue telling her that he feared:

> I shall probably end up with fighting Russians in a couple of months. What a terrifying thought! I'd be scared stiff to suddenly find myself fighting in an aircraft. It's all very well to take-off and simply enjoy flying a plane. It would be a very different story to take-off with the intention of killing people and trying to keep alive myself.
>
> Especially trying to keep alive myself!

Happily the scenario that John envisaged did not happen. He enjoyed a wonderful voyage home although he said much later that he thought the luxury of a first class passage was probably wasted on a group of young men in their late teens.

When he eventually set foot in England after being away for over a year he was disappointed to find that the country in November presented a dismal, depressing picture. However, he was very happy to see his family again and anxious to meet Sue in London.

They arranged a time to meet and John arrived at the nurses' home by taxi. Sue's friends were curious about the young man who had been writing to her for such a long time and were anxious to see what he was like. Visitors to the nurses' home were monitored and John was shown into the sitting room where the visit was chaperoned. Sue was mortified to discover that while in Canada John had become a 'north American'. He had a crew cut and was wearing his red and white leather jacket, very tight trousers, a shirt with a string tie, white socks and crepe soled shoes. As a nurse at St Thomas's, Sue had become used to socializing with Guards officer types, who wore flannels and blazers and she was horribly embarrassed by the young man in flashy clothes who now smoked, took snuff and spoke with a pseudo Canadian accent. Although she had regarded him as just one of her boyfriends she was horrified at how much he seemed to have changed and decided to dump him forever. Her friends thought the whole situation was extremely funny. She, of course, changed her mind about dumping him when they had a date that evening and she realized that, despite his odd behaviour and strange appearance, John was still the same person he had always been.

John's leave, following his return from Canada, became a very rushed and busy time. He was anxious to see as much of Sue as possible but had to try and fit in their meetings between others arranged by both his immediate and his extended family. He bemoaned the fact that, 'I'm unlucky enough to be cursed with dozens of relatives, who all want to hear about "dear John's exploits in Canada".'

He had also been informed that his next posting would be to the No. 4 Flying Training School at RAF Worksop in Nottinghamshire where, he said, the RAF would again teach him to fly but this time they would be contrasting the differences between the crowded land and skies of the United Kingdom and the emptiness of the sky over the vast Canadian prairies.

By the middle of January 1957 flying had begun at Worksop. On the 14th John had his first solo flight in a de Havilland Vampire which he enjoyed. It was, however, very different from flying in Canada:

*I love flogging around at about 1,000 feet taking a look at all the local towns. The trouble with this country is that there are so many it tends to become a little confusing.*

The previous week there had a been a crash at Worksop. Sue wrote to John to tell him:

*I spent a very worried 24 hours last week on your account. I heard on the 7 o'clock news that a jet from Worksop had crashed, killing the pilot and a civilian. There was plenty about it in the papers but no name. You must admit it was rather a coincidence and I didn't really get much peace of mind 'till the next day it gave the pilot's name in a discreet paragraph in the Times.*

*This, by the way, is not meant to make you feel 'a great guy,*
*causing flutterings in a female heart'! But I was pretty worried.*

When John replied to this note he told Sue:

*The fellow who went in lived next door to me. A very nice chap he*
*was, too. He was engaged to be married in about a month's time.*
*Too bad. I was at his funeral on Saturday morning – he got a full*
*military do with last post being played etc.*

Flying, or the lack of it, was as difficult at Worksop as it had been at
Moose Jaw. The weather dictated when it would possible and when not
but, unlike the heavy snow falls in Canada, the conditions at Worksop
that most affected the airfield were rain, and the fog and smog that hung
over everything and was so prevalent in Britain in the 1950s. During some
weeks little or no flying was possible at all and John found the situation to
be very boring. It made him so lethargic that when there was something
for him to do he could hardly be bothered. He told Sue:

*I've been sitting around the flight rooms all week waiting for the*
*good weather which never comes to Worksop. I was lucky enough*
*to get in two flights this last week, but I literally spent the rest of*
*my time listlessly lying in an armchair.*
    *It's an incredible existence, when I stop to think about it. I get*
*£60 a month for sitting in an armchair! Quite fantastic. If the*
*great British public was to know that, the RAF would be wiped*
*out due to the public outcry! Still, I don't suppose the Army or the*
*Navy are much better.*

By March, John had managed to put in quite a few more hours' flying
and was hopeful of finishing the course within a week or two. Then he
had an accident.

He set out on a navigation trip and climbed to 30,000 feet. The pressure inside the cockpit was the equivalent of 16,000 feet above sea level
and John levelled out to have a look at his map. Suddenly there was a loud
bang and his map disappeared. The Vampire's canopy had burst and parted
company from the rest of the aircraft. He quickly lost height and made

an approach to the airfield. He landed safely, came to a halt and got out of the aircraft to examine the damage. He then discovered that not only had the canopy burst; as it came free of the aircraft it had hit the tail and punched a large hole in it. He was lucky not to have had more damage to his aircraft or a more serious ending to the accident.

With a posting due, John had been recommended for day fighters which meant that he would be flying the beautiful Hawker Hunter. He expected to be told that his conversion course would be held either in south Wales or in north Devon but, after several weeks, the posting had still not come through and he was told he would probably not leave Worksop for another two months. At the end of April, however, he received some very unwelcome news. He was being posted to Thorney Island to fly the Vickers Varsity, a twin-engined piston transport aircraft. He was bitterly disappointed but determined to see the positive side of this development and wrote to Sue to tell her:

> *… this posting has at least decided my career for me – I am definitely going into civil airlines. The great thing about this is that I shall be able to get myself all the necessary licences required for civil airlines while I'm still in the RAF, which means that when I get out of the Air Force in 1960 I'll be lined up for a job in an airline company. So, although I shall always regret not having flown Hunters, flying Varsities will be an extremely useful experience.*

Later that year the then Defence Secretary, Duncan Sandys, decided to end the use of fighter aircraft completely, believing that their role could be taken over by unmanned missiles. So even if John had converted to the Hunter he may still have ended up flying the Varsity. Duncan Sandys' decision was later overturned but not before untold damage had been done to the British aviation manufacturing industry.

Knowing that he would not be flying jets for much longer John made the most of the time he had left at Worksop. At the beginning of May 1957 he made what he described as:

> *… a little navigation trip to Harpenden. Unfortunately I missed Harpenden and found myself slap over London before I knew where I was. I didn't realize at first that it was London. I*

*thought that it was rather a large town … Then I saw a winding*
*river running through the middle of it. Then I saw the Houses of*
*Parliament. The horrible truth dawned on me. You've never seen*
*anybody leave London as fast as I did. I gave her all the throttle I*
*could and fled northwards.*

*By a stroke of luck, I was on a course which took me right over*
*Harpenden. So I found St Hilda's and did a few steep turns over*
*the old place. Unfortunately, I was getting a little short of fuel, so I*
*could only spend a couple of minutes over Harpenden. Still, I can*
*at least say that I've paid them a visit.*

Had they known that their son was overhead, Viola and Wynne would, no
doubt, have been pleased to see him. While John's career was progressing,
they too had been working very hard and St Hilda's School was flour-
ishing. Its reputation as a fine educational establishment was ensuring
that they were never short of new pupils and had allowed them to make
more investments in the fabric of the school including the building of
a swimming pool. Colonel and Mrs Hutchinson had also managed to
buy themselves a small car, an Austin A40, which made their busy lives
considerably easier.

John also acquired a car, having obtained his driving licence during
the Suez crisis when driving tests were suspended. At the end of 1957,
when conditions had returned to normal, John was notified that he would
have to take the test and, although he did pass it, he was rather nervous
beforehand as he thought that he was a better pilot than he was a driver.
Everyone who knew him felt that this opinion was entirely correct. Some of
Michael's most abiding memories of his elder brother were of the number
of car crashes that he had and of his parents' worries about John's driving:

*He used to drive around in a manic fashion and was forever*
*coming home having hit something. I remember clearly that he hit*
*everything from a milk float to an oil tanker.*

His sister Mary recalled:

*He had several car crashes, and we all have memories of him*
*coming home after a particularly bad one in Featherbed Lane,*

*making a very dramatic entrance into the house, carrying broken*
*glass from the picture frames he had in the car.*[1]

John first flew the Varsity in June 1957 and didn't enjoy the experience at
all, saying that it was not his sort of flying. He had more bad news when he
found that he was being posted to RAF Kinloss in Morayshire, Scotland,
the following month for a conversion course onto Avro Shackletons and
bemoaned the fact that he would never be able to see Sue. During the short
time that he was at Thorney Island they had managed to get together a few
times but with Sue still working hard at her training, while also coping
with the practical side of shift work at the hospital, and John being in
Scotland, their future didn't look bright. Sue had often warned John not
to get too serious about her. She said that she still had a lot of work to do
to ensure that she, too, would have a career and she didn't want him to
be hurt by expecting more of her than she was able to give at that time.
They had agreed to put any thoughts of marriage off for a further two
years during which time John thought he would sort out his finances so
as to be able to buy an engagement ring and warned Sue that by April or
May of 1959 he would be making a 'highly formal proposal'.

Apart from the dreadful weather John liked Kinloss. The people were
friendly, the beer was good and although flying a Shackleton was different
from any other aircraft he had flown, it was enjoyable. It carried a crew
of 10, although during the early stages of the conversion course was
flown with just four crew members, and was referred to by its crews as,
'50,000 rivets flying in loose formation'. The aircraft was based on the
Avro Lincoln design which, itself, was based on an Avro Lancaster bomber,
and had made its maiden flight in 1949. Known initially as the Avro 696,
it was designed by Roy Chadwick to fulfil a requirement for a long-range
maritime patrol aircraft and was powered by four Rolls-Royce 2,450 hp
Griffon engines, each with two three-bladed contra-rotating propellers. The
family of the designer's wife had a connection with Sir Ernest Shackleton
and Chadwick, himself, had re-designed the Avro Baby as a seaplane for
the Polar explorer to carry on board his ship, *Quest*. Chadwick is said to
have told his wife that the Avro 696 was, '… a kind of maritime exploring
aeroplane' that he wanted to name 'Shackleton' in memory of Sir Ernest
and the happy day that they had spent with him on the *Quest*.[2]

At first John had problems taxiing the aircraft, being unable to keep it in a straight line, but he soon mastered the correct technique. As well as the taxiing problem, he found it difficult to adjust to the amount of time spent in the air. The flights usually lasted for seven or eight hours and, on each flight, one of the crew was allocated the task of catering for the others. John thought that one of the advantages of this system was that he might also become a chef as well as a pilot but he did admit that there were difficulties in cooking and making drinks while in the air:

It's rather frustrating at times. You brew up four cups of tea and have them all nicely lined up on the galley. Then, just as you are about to take them up to the front, you hit an air pocket and all four cups are suddenly on the floor. It's a heartbreaking experience – especially as it takes hours to boil the water up.

He also found the night flying to be extremely tiring, being a creature who liked his bed. These flights usually began around 21.00 and didn't finish until 05.00 the next day. John recalled one night flight where he:

… scared the poor crew out of their lives. I scared myself, too. Some of those landings were nearer to controlled crashes than landings.

In addition to the long flights there were exams to take and, in September, an air display on Battle of Britain Day. Between all these activities John tried to arrange for Sue to make the 600 mile journey to Kinloss for a visit. She had a long weekend due to her but, although they explored all the travel possibilities, it proved impossible for her to get a direct train to Aberdeen or one via Glasgow that would give her a chance of a proper visit. John's car had a hole in its front, the result of another crash, and he was waiting for his insurance company to arrange its repair so would have been unable to fetch her from Aberdeen station anyway. Then St Thomas's Hospital changed the dates of Sue's free time, which meant that it coincided with the air display when John would not be free. He was despairing of them ever being able to get together and anxiously awaited his next posting. He was praying that it would be to St Mawgan, a Coastal Command station near Newquay in Cornwall which, although not close to either Sue or his family, would be more accessible than the north of Scotland.

Before the posting came through he managed a quick trip to Harpenden to see his family and was able to visit Sue as well. He found his family in fine form. His parents were well and cheerful, Michael had just received his GCE 'O' level results and had passed all eight exams, which John said 'put him to shame', and his sisters were:

> … bouncing along in the same old way, cheeky little things that they are. The first thing that Mary did was to present me with a 2/6 Pan book. I asked her what I'd done to deserve that honour and was told that it was a sort of consolation prize for not having been in the Isle of Wight with them!

At the beginning of October John was informed that he was no longer a pilot officer; he was now Flying Officer Hutchinson. In the same week he had bad news about Sue. She had collapsed at work with stomach pains which turned out to be appendicitis and had to have her appendix removed. She came through the operation with no problems and told John that a few days' convalescence in the north of Scotland might help to speed her recovery. While he was delighted at the thought of seeing her again, he cautioned her against making the trip if she had any doubts about coping with such a long journey so soon after her operation. She assured him that it would not be a problem and he wrote to tell her:

> *Darling, I feel like spending the rest of the evening leaping about in a moonstruck way but I've got another exam tomorrow, which rather foils my moonstruck leapings. Imagine having to work in my present state of exhilaration – it's terrible. I think I shall have to run around the airfield a couple of times; that should take some of the bounce out of me.*

While she was in Scotland John asked Sue to marry him but she thought it was a crazy idea, believing that they were too young to marry. She was just 21 and John was still 20. She reminded him of her intention to complete her nursing course before thinking about getting married, but she didn't say no either.

When she returned home to complete her convalescence they both looked forward to meeting again at Christmas by which time, John was sure, his posting would have come through. Several of his colleagues had already got theirs, some of which were overseas and so John was quite confident that all the overseas postings had already been allocated and that he would be spending the next two years in Great Britain, preferably at St Mawgan or at nearby St Eval.

Finally he received the news of where he would be going and he learnt that he was the only one of his course to get what was regarded as the very best posting of all in Coastal Command; he was going to Singapore for two and a half years. While he was the envy of every person in the Mess, John was absolutely horrified and dreaded the day that he would have to leave the United Kingdom, and Sue, once more.

# Chapter 6

# A Brilliant Achievement

*My most brilliant achievement was my ability to be able to persuade my wife to marry me.*

Sir Winston Churchill, 1874–1965, British statesman

Having dropped the bombshell of a posting to the Far East, the RAF then tried to spoil John's Christmas break by not allowing him to leave Kinloss until 23 December. With the prospect of a two and a half year separation while he was in Singapore, he again asked Sue to marry him. He told her that he would feel much better if they were engaged before he went as he was certain that if they did not get engaged, Sue would meet and marry a doctor from St Thomas's while he was away.

Although she had wanted to complete her nursing training before even considering marriage and there was still one year to go, this time Sue accepted John's proposal. Since she could not graduate and become a State Registered Nurse until February 1959, she and John made plans to marry on 14 February that year. It meant that Sue would not be able to start her nursing career, nor would she be able to become a stewardess on an aircraft or a ship's purser but she would, at least, have completed her course and would be qualified to be a nurse at some later stage, if she wanted to do so.

While they were at home visiting their respective families in Hertfordshire, John and Sue announced to their parents, on Christmas Day, their intention to marry. Viola was delighted as she was very fond of Sue and had already told John that she would like to have her as a daughter-in-law. Wynne was also fond of Sue but was concerned about whether or not they would be able to afford being married. At that time the Royal Air Force did not recognize marriages between people younger than 25 years old and so John would not receive any married pay until four years after their marriage.

The reaction of Sue's own father to the news was not what she had expected. Although she knew that he liked John, his main reason for approving of the match seemed to be that John had a promising singing voice. Sue wanted to know what on earth that had to do with their proposed marriage; her father, it seems, may have been thinking of a new recruit for the church choir.

On New Years Day 1958, after a very brief Christmas break, John caught a train back to Scotland while Sue returned to St Thomas's. At King's Cross station, while they were saying goodbye, someone stole their suitcases. John wasn't concerned about losing his clothes and other belongings which were insured, or his passport, even though he thought he might have difficulties in replacing it. What caused him so much distress was the loss of the letters that Sue had sent to him over the past three years while he had been in Canada and Scotland. He couldn't bear the thought of a stranger reading the words that were so precious to him. Sue was also very upset to have lost a lot of her photos and a diary. John's father was annoyed because he thought the young couple had been careless in not watching the cases while they said goodbye.

Back in Scotland John awaited the finer details of his posting to Singapore and, having obtained the approval of both families for their marriage plans, suggested to Sue that they formally announce their engagement on 21 January. Sue, although she had already had her 21st birthday, also had to ask permission from the matron of St Thomas's before she could officially become engaged. She was due to take her State exams that October but couldn't complete the practical part until the following February as she had not worked enough hours on a ward due to the sick leave she had taken while her appendix was removed. She was then supposed to nurse for a further year at St Thomas's. When she explained the situation to the matron and told her that she would be going out to Singapore as soon as she could after the wedding she was told that there were two sorts of nursing trainees at the hospital; those who were the true Nightingale types and those whose nursing training would enable them to become very good wives and mothers. The matron was of the opinion that Sue fell into the second category, adding, 'You certainly don't fall into the first!' She accepted the fact that Sue would not be doing the year as a qualified nurse but since she didn't regard her as a true Nightingale type felt able to waive the extra year and gave her permission for the engagement.

John had been told that he would be sailing to Singapore sometime in April. He then received news that, before going overseas, he was to be posted to Aldergrove in Northern Ireland, from where he and other members of a crew would be flying the first Shackleton into Singapore. The aircraft that they would be taking had been used for tests at Boscombe Down and had a total of only 126 flying hours.

At the beginning of April John said goodbye to his family as he prepared for the ferry trip to Northern Ireland. He was touched that his father wanted to come to London with him to see him onto the train to Liverpool where he was to take the ferry. He took his leave of his mother, brother and two sisters at St Hilda's School and described it as '… a very tragic sort of scene'. His mother, he said:

> … does so hate me going and she knows that I am not to be one of the family in quite the same capacity for very much longer. It must be dreadfully sad for a mother – even worse than it is for a father.

The reason for the temporary stay at Aldergrove was for special instruments to be fitted to the Shackletons that were going to be operating out of Singapore. The modifications for the aircraft on the first flight were going to take about six weeks to complete and, since the RAF was short of second pilots and John had time to kill, his stay at Aldergrove was spent flying a Handley Page Hastings with 202 Squadron. This aircraft, although primarily a transport aeroplane, was used in Coastal Command for meteorological reconnaissance where the crews observed weather patterns and noted down readings. The flights were long – usually around 10 hours – and the pilots each flew for two hours at a time spending the hours in between reading, or writing letters. John told Sue that he considered the Hastings flights as, '… a very lucky break, because it gives me experience on yet another aeroplane at yet another job'.

RAF Aldergrove was a pleasant station but the living accommodation was 'rather primitive', consisting of basic wooden huts raised slightly off the ground. The washing facilities were elsewhere.

When John wasn't flying he, along with other members of the squadron, took turns in digging and planting the station garden. He also had to act as orderly officer on one occasion; the day before his 21st birthday.

Because of the IRA threats which were common even in those days, orderly officers had to carry a .38 revolver and 12 rounds of ammunition. Since he had never had to do this before John found the task quite daunting. In a letter to Sue he told her:

*I only hope I don't run into any IRA characters, because I am not very hot on firing a revolver. Weapons like that scare me stiff. I can't bear the noise! I always think the bang of a revolver is quite unnerving and the last time I fired one the recoil almost jerked the infernal contraption out of my hands and the shot went whistling up into the air instead of at the target.*

Happily his shooting skills weren't put to the test. The following day, his birthday, John received cards and presents from family and friends at home, including two cards that his sisters Mary and Viola had made themselves. His parents sent him a lovely volume of Shelley's poems, chosen by his mother, and his sisters gave him a book token which he later exchanged for a similar book, this time the poems of Keats. Sue bought him a gold signet ring.

He had planned to celebrate his coming of age with his first trip in a helicopter but the weather was so bad – pouring rain and high winds – that the occasion passed without any festivities at all and he went to bed early in preparation for another 10 hour flight in the Hastings the following day. A few days after his birthday he met the pilot who would be the captain for the flight to Singapore and told Sue:

*I didn't care for him very much at first sight, but perhaps I'll get to change. He seemed the type who is always laying down the law and generally being aggressive. I'm not too keen on that sort. Still, he was drunk as a lord when I was introduced to him so perhaps that is the explanation! We shall see.*

On St George's Day John was part of a crew that brought 30 ATC cadets back to England after a camp in Ireland. He told Sue:

*I had an agonizing day today. We flew over to Aston Down as planned … and there below us was the River Severn … they [the cadets] were practically ALL catching trains to London. You can't imagine the torment I was suffering. It would have been so easy to step onto a London train (I had enough money, too) and I would have been with you within a few hours.*

*… By the time this gets to you, we will have been apart for 3 weeks. Oh, God, how slowly time can drag … If we marry on Feb. 14th, and count it from today, there are 297 days to go – 7,128 hours. May each of them flash by!*

The date of the departure to Singapore was finally set for 12 May and three days earlier the crew who would be taking the Shackleton to the Far East received news that the commanding officer of 205/209 Squadron, who had been in Singapore since the previous January, had flown back to England by Comet in order to be able to go straight back to Singapore on the Shackleton. As John noted:

*We can find only one explanation for this. Since this is the first Shack to be joining the squadron out there, we guess that he is simply coming out with us for the glory of it so that he can be photographed as he steps off the plane at Singapore! Why else should he have done such a thing? It's amazing, isn't it?*

On 11 May John and Sue spoke to each other by telephone for the last time before he left for Singapore. It was a difficult time for them both. John wrote to Sue after the call to say that he hoped she wasn't too upset although she had sounded 'utterly broken-hearted' as she rang off. He wrote again during the afternoon of the 12th to let her know that everything was ready for their departure, their kit was already on board the Shackleton and there was nothing left to do until they got on board themselves just before 22.00 hours to start the engines. He told her not to worry about him. The aircraft had four new engines and the flight would be no different from any that he had made so far except that he would actually be going somewhere this time.

As the time for the departure approached the crew was surprised to see a number of the most senior officers at Aldergrove come down to where the Shackleton was parked. They had come to bid farewell to the crew and send them on their way. It was an unexpected gesture that was much appreciated by the crew and, after saying goodbye, they boarded the Shackleton and prepared to take-off. The journey was made in several stages, the first stop being El Adem in Libya. It was stiflingly hot and John found it fascinating that even though the war had been over for 13 years, it was still possible to see tank tracks in the desert sand.

After an overnight stay they departed for the next stage of the journey, flying over Egypt, Sudan and the Red Sea before landing in Aden which proved to be even hotter and more humid than El Adem. Then it was on to Ceylon [Sri Lanka] and a long flight over the Indian Ocean. John wrote to Sue from each stop that they made and told her that Ceylon was:

*… magnificent. Utterly superb – especially after the dust and dirt of El Adem and Aden. It is the lushest countryside I have ever seen in my life. It is called the jewel of the East, and most certainly lives up to that title. There are palm trees all over the place. The exotic flowers have to be seen to be believed. There are some fabulous colours and shapes. And then there is that permanent jungle sound permeating thro'. You know the sounds you hear in films taken in jungle country – this is exactly the same noise. An incessant creaking sound from what I assume to be crickets, together with the periodic shriek of some bird and the squeaking call of the chipmunk. There are lots of miniature chipmunks here and they are quite tame. They will come and eat out of one's hand without a trace of fear. They are lovely little animals. They've got huge brown eyes and the body is a light brown colour with white markings, and they have a long thin tail used for balancing purposes. They would make marvellous pets – you'd adore them. The birds are just like the flowers – exotic and decorative in their colourings. You see a bird take off in an absolute blaze of emeralds, reds and blues. They make a wonderful spectacle.*

The final stage of the trip was across the Bay of Bengal and the Nicobar Islands then down the Strait of Malacca between Sumatra and Malaya, now Malaysia. Ten minutes before the expected arrival time in Singapore the Shackleton was joined by two Sunderland flying boats which flew out to meet it for a flypast over Singapore. The crew had not known that this would happen but were delighted to see the Sunderlands:

> *It was terrific! We went roaring around Singapore at 500 feet with a Sunderland on either side. Then we went roaring over Changi itself at a slightly lower height, after which the formation broke up and we landed.*
>
> *There were photographers at the end of the runway to photograph the landing (done of course, by the W/C) and we stepped out of the aeroplane to face a positive blaze of flashbulbs. There were pressmen, group captains etc. everywhere. It was most impressive.*

Following this magnificent welcome the crew were taken to a tent where a reception had been organized. Then they went to the Mess where they found their rooms, each with its own veranda. That evening, after dinner, some of the other members of the squadron arrived at the Mess with their wives and a party began which finally broke up at 04.00 the following morning.

Although very different from any experience John had had before in the RAF, he liked Singapore and settled down relatively quickly to life on 205 Squadron, especially enjoying the hot weather which was reminiscent of the days of his childhood in India. After he had been there for two or three months he discovered that he would be returning briefly to the United Kingdom to fetch the next Shackleton and fly it back to the Far East. On this bonus trip he managed to see his family and Sue while he was home and told them that he thought he would also be back at the end of October to fetch the third Shackleton for delivery to Singapore. He suggested to Sue that he should put in for a short leave while on that trip and that they should bring their wedding forward to October and get married while he was at home.

Sue agreed but had to speak to the matron at St Thomas's to check whether or not she would still be allowed to complete her course as a married woman. This was something that had not happened before – St Thomas's nurses were single girls – but the matron realized that things were changing and, although she didn't really approve, she decided to allow Sue to return to the hospital to finish her exams after the marriage.

John also had to apply for permission to marry from the Station

Commander of RAF Changi, Group Captain Swales. He did so on 13 September and received a positive reply from the Group Captain four days later.

The date chosen for the wedding was 25 October, coincidentally the date on which John had made his first RAF flight in a Harvard, three years earlier. With her fiancé on the other side of the world, Sue was left to make most of the arrangements for the wedding herself with the help of both families. Knowing how the RAF could suddenly change its mind and allocate the flight to another pilot, they were not sure whether the ceremony would actually take place and Sue joked that she had another groom standing by to act as a proxy should John be stuck in Singapore.

Eventually everything was ready. Sue wanted her father to give her away rather than conduct the marriage service and so that task fell to her Uncle Sidney, also a clergyman, from Templecombe in Somerset. Her sisters, Pippa and Carola, and John's sisters, Mary and Viola, were asked to be bridesmaids and their dresses of aquamarine shot silk were made. Sue's godfather had the invitations printed and some of the ladies from Wheathampstead arranged the food for the reception which was to be held at the rectory. Colonel Hutchinson paid for the hire of John's morning suit and Sue hired a car to take them to their honeymoon in Newton Ferrers, near Plymouth, where she had booked a room at the Beacon Hill Hotel. John's only tasks were to arrange for a best man, buy a wedding ring and try as much as possible, given the circumstances, to ensure that he was in England on the right day.

He asked his friend, Hans Bang, whom he had met at St George's School, to be best man; although Danish, Hans had been brought up in England where his father was the UK boss of the Danish Bacon Company. John decided to purchase the wedding ring in England – perhaps not the best decision in the circumstances – and had to leave the date and time of his arrival in the lap of the gods and the RAF.

Right up until the week of the wedding no one was sure that John would arrive; then the trip was confirmed and he left Singapore expecting to have a few days in England before the actual wedding day. During a transit stop in Aden the aircraft was found to have a technical problem and, while the engineers worked on it, John spent the time in the Mess at RAF Khormaksar where he met up with some Hunter pilots and several friends who also flew Shackletons and were stationed there. To pass the time until the aircraft was serviceable they had, in John's own words, 'a monumental piss-up'.

When the aircraft had been fixed he left Aden and arrived at RAF Bovingdon, south-west of Hemel Hempstead, just before midnight on 23 October. He was met by Sue and her father who drove him to St Hilda's. He was exhausted and had just one day to collect the hire car, make sure that his suit fitted him, buy a wedding ring for Sue, attend a rehearsal at St Helen's Church and spend some time with his parents, sisters and brother.

Despite the tense situation that week, everything worked out beautifully in the end and, on the morning of Saturday 25 October, the couple at last became Mr and Mrs Hutchinson. Miraculously everything fell into place; the bridesmaids looked delightful, the best man was charming, the food was wonderful and the reception enjoyable and then it was time for them to leave for their honeymoon in Devon, a journey of approximately 250 miles. Today, with the motorways and better roads that have been built since 1958, the journey would still take over 4½ hours. In the autumn of 1958, with a hired car and an exhausted driver, and the dense blanket of fog that descended just before they reached Taunton, it would have taken much longer. Quite how long they didn't discover as, despite their best efforts, they were unable to reach Newton Ferrers that day. John was very tired and, having eventually reached Taunton, he found a car park, apologized to Sue and promptly fell asleep.

Sue decided that she had better find a hotel in the town where they could spend that night and consulted the AA handbook that had been provided with the car, for the names and addresses of suitable places. She marched into the first place that she came to, still wearing her going-away outfit and dropping confetti as she walked and asked for a double room for one night. The man behind the desk told her that he was very sorry but they were fully booked. She then went to the next hotel in the book where she received the same reply. Eventually when she had exhausted all the addresses in the handbook she returned to the car. She had quite a difficult task to wake John but when she did manage it he just shrugged his shoulders and said, 'Oh well. We'll just have to sleep in the car'. Sue was horrified and told him that she hadn't waited for the whole of her 21 years only to spend her wedding night in a car. Apart from it being the least romantic idea anyone had ever had, the car in question was very small and didn't even have reclining seats. She decided to go back to the first hotel which was quite large, and see if they couldn't find her somewhere to sleep. She spoke to the same man as before. He seemed to be greatly amused by the situation and eventually admitted that he did have a twin bedded room free but that it was usually left empty on a Saturday night. Sue asked to see it and was taken to a pleasant room with beautiful peach coloured silk eiderdowns, a bedside cupboard between the two beds and a bathroom across the corridor which they would have to share with two other couples. She couldn't understand why this room had not been offered to her before but snapped it up immediately. The man told her that they would be serving dinner for only another 20 minutes so she hurried back to the car, shook John awake again and they made their way back to the hotel. It transpired that Taunton's hotels were all full with the parents of the boys at King's College. It was half term and the break was so short that the parents visited their sons rather than have them come home for just two days. Although this explained the lack of hotel accommodation it still didn't clarify the situation with regard to the room that Sue had just secured. The question of dinner was, however, of more importance at that point as they had eaten nothing since breakfast, having been too excited to eat at the reception.

They rushed up to their room threw down their bags and went directly to the almost empty dining room where they found that the only food left was what John described as 'rather institutionalized roast chicken'. It had to do as, although it was still quite early, the chef had gone home.

When they returned to their room they decided that the beds needed to be rearranged so moved the bedside cabinet out of the way, pushed the beds together and remade them. It was as close as they could get to a double bed and was certainly much better than spending their wedding night in a hire car. They could hear the sound of gentle music from some-where in the hotel but it was very quiet and didn't disturb the inaugural marital proceedings at all. Just as they were drifting off to sleep there was suddenly an ear-splitting noise from directly underneath their room. It was the hotel's band warming up for the last hour of the weekly dinner dance. They now understood why that room was usually vacant on a Saturday night. The noise was deafening and, unable to sleep, they began to make love again when suddenly, no doubt as a result of their activity, the two beds parted company and Sue fell through the gap onto the floor. Seconds later John landed on top of her. The earth really did seem to move but not in the way they had expected. Sue remembers hitting the floor with such a bang that she was surprised they hadn't ended up on the dance floor below. It rather spoilt the moment so they pushed the beds back together, intending to sleep. The room was sparsely furnished and very hot so they removed the peach silk eiderdowns from the beds and, with nowhere to store them, rolled them up and put them on the windowsill. They then opened the window for some welcome fresh air and went back to bed.

The next morning was grey and wet. They managed to get down to the dining room while breakfast was still being served and then returned to the room to collect their belongings and make their way to Newton Ferrers. Sue thought that they should put the room back to its original state and so they moved the bedside cabinet back between the two beds. Then she realized that the eiderdowns were nowhere to be found. Remembering that they had last seen them when they had put them on the window sill they went over to the window. The view was not pretty; the room was at the back of the hotel and looked out onto a small area which contained a large coal store. That was where they discovered the errant eiderdowns, elegantly draped across a coal bunker, soaking wet and covered in coal dust. They were horrified and, knowing that they could not afford to pay, either for them to be cleaned or for their replacement, hurriedly packed their bags, paid the bill and left for Newton Ferrers where they had a wonderful honeymoon.

As for Taunton and the eiderdowns, nothing more was heard about them. Both Sue and John felt very guilty about sneaking off, and have never dared to return to the hotel.

Thirty years later the town of Taunton again featured in another Hutchinson calamity – but that story must wait.

# Chapter 7

# Different Worlds

*There's so many different worlds*
*So many different suns*
*And we have just one world*
*But we live in different ones*

From Brothers in Arms by Mark Knopfler, British musician
and songwriter

After returning from his honeymoon, John was back at RAF Aldergrove
at the beginning of November 1958, waiting for the next Shackleton that
he would be taking to Singapore. Although now a married man he was
once again parted from Sue who would soon be returning to St Thomas's
Hospital to complete her State exams. John wrote to her there to tell her
how much he was missing her:

> … *as for being apart from you, that needs no words. I feel awful.*
> *I think I feel worse today than I have done after any of our*
> *previous partings. We've been so close together during the last nine*
> *or ten days and to be forced apart at this stage is too ruthless for*
> *any words of mine to convey …*
> *It seems so impossible to realize that I am apart from you*
> *yet again. Life for us seems to consist of agonizing partings and*
> *they don't become any less agonizing as they increase. In fact, I*
> *reckon this is one of the worst partings ever – it is as far as I'm*
> *concerned, anyway …*

*We are leaving at 4.0 a.m. tomorrow morning [5 November]*
*so I must get my early night's sleep. God bless you, my darling*
*Mrs Hutchinson.*

The departure went like clockwork and they had a fairly uneventful journey back to Singapore via El Adem, Aden and Ceylon before reaching Singapore late on 9 November. John was amazed at the reception the crew received and then realized that it was not for the entire crew but for just one member:

*I'd just stepped out of the aircraft to the sound of much clapping,*
*my feet had barely reached the ground, when I suddenly had a*
*pair of arms flung around me and kisses were being planted on my*
*cheeks. After I'd recovered from the initial shock, I discovered that*
*the enthusiastic woman was Mrs Swales, the station commander's*
*wife. Isn't that sweet? She was thrilled and delighted to hear*
*that all our plans had worked out so well and sends us her best*
*wishes and congratulations. G/C Swales was there, so was W/C*
*McCready; everybody seemed to be there to congratulate us! And*
*then when I got back to the mess … . It was incredible. Everyone*
*seemed to be sharing our joy. They all made me feel very, very*
*happy when I arrived back here, darling – it made such a differ-*
*ence. I expect you'll find exactly the same thing when you go back*
*to the hospital. It's really very wonderful, my darling, to realize*
*that so many people have thought about us and taken an interest*
*in us. I am quite overwhelmed by it.*

The day after his arrival in Singapore John sent a letter to his family at St Hilda's School. It was obviously still in his mind how difficult it must have been for his parents to say goodbye to him and he wanted them, and his brother and sisters, to know how much they meant to him. He wrote:

*Thank you all very, very much indeed for being such a help to me*
*when I was home. You gave me tremendous moral support both*
*before the wedding and before my return to Aldergrove.*
*It's rather strange to think of myself as a married man – in a*
*way I find it rather sad to think that I've now got a home of my*

*own to build up, instead of having St Hilda's as my one and only home. It's difficult to explain – I just know that it makes me feel rather sad. It's all making me feel awfully old all of a sudden! I hope you won't mind us visiting you as often as possible – I love coming home to see you all, I really do. Many thanks for all that you have done for me, Mummy and Daddy. You've given me a wonderful upbringing and a home that I could never, ever forget. I hope Sue and I will succeed in the same way with our children – I shall be very proud if we do. I only wish I could thank you in some more concrete way than just saying 'thank you'. It seems so inadequate. I shall always be very, very grateful for being a member of such a happy and wonderful family ...*

*God bless you all. Thank you, Mike, for being such an elegant usher and thank you, darling girls, for being such lovely brides-maids – you were all wonderful.*

The family was very touched to receive such a letter and Wynne and Viola kept it, along with the other letters that John had sent to them over the years. On the back of the last page, Viola had written, 'Very special'.

Three days later John received unwelcome news. He had been hoping to return to England and be part of the crew to fly the seventh and last Shackleton from Aldergrove to Singapore but at the last minute he was replaced by a colleague who had to get home urgently to see his father who was seriously ill. He tried to make the best of it and told Sue:

*It came as an awful and stunning shock to me when I first heard the news this morning – I nearly burst into tears on the spot, but felt that the squadron was hardly the place for such violent emotions. So I went straight back to my room and slowly tried to adjust myself to the situation there. I am now almost adjusted, but still very depressed. I am comforting myself with the thought that we have had a wonderful wedding, an absolutely beautiful honeymoon and that you'll be with me in March. That's a lot of things to be grateful for, my darling. So let's forget that there was ever a possibility of my coming home for the 7th aircraft, and concentrate on the planning of your journey out here. That's what REALLY matters most of all.*

Determined to be positive about the situation, John went to see the station commander, Group Captain Swales, to enquire if there was a possibility of arranging an 'indulgence passage' to get Sue out to Singapore without having to wipe out their entire savings to pay for a commercial fare. Indulgence passages could be granted if there was a spare seat available on an RAF aircraft whose destination was where the person in question needed to go. Even if permission was granted it could still be revoked if some crisis came about and, in any event, the actual seat was allocated at very short notice. It would be a stressful process for Sue to go through should a passage be granted but would save them a lot of money. Had John already reached the age of 25, Sue would have automatically received transport to join her husband but since the RAF regarded John as being old enough to fly its aircraft but not old enough to be married, it was likely that they would have to pay for Sue's fare and for all their belongings to be sent out to Singapore. They were also not eligible for married quarters which meant that they would have to find and rent their own accommodation.

Group Captain Swales was sympathetic to their situation and told John that he would give the application his wholehearted approval. It then had to be submitted to the Air Ministry and they knew that it could take some time before they found out if it had been approved. In the meantime they had to assume that the application would be unsuccessful and Sue had to try and arrange a passage herself although they both hoped that the Air Ministry would be as sympathetic as the station commander before the time came when she would have to part with the money for a ticket. This hope became more urgent when John's car, an MG that he had bought soon after arriving in Singapore in May, developed problems that proved to be very expensive to fix.

Despite the transport problems they were both encountering and the postal delays due to the start of the Christmas rush, John did succeed in remaining more upbeat than he had before the wedding. The marriage had given him a new purpose and, if he did sometimes sink into a depression while considering the large amount of time that he and Sue had had to spend apart, he didn't allow it to take over his life as it had sometimes done before. His letters were generally quite cheerful, although he did worry a lot about Sue. Her health was again giving her problems. She was having severe stomach pains which ultimately meant an operation and, in addition, she was working very hard at St Thomas's in order to pass her State exams so that she could get a nursing job at Changi Hospital when she eventually got to Singapore. John was very worried about the prospect of more surgery, coming as it did, just over a year after her appendectomy but, despite his worries about his new wife, he obviously enjoyed showing her off to his colleagues, if only in photos, and reported to her in one letter:

> *I showed a New Zealand friend of mine a few photos of you at teatime today. The only reaction I got out of him was 'I can't think how an awful person like you manages to marry such a beautiful doll'. So, my beautiful doll, yet another person has fallen at your feet! I can see that I shall have to be very selective about the people I introduce you to!*

All such thoughts were suddenly forgotten when 205 Squadron suffered a major tragedy. Shackleton VP254, the aircraft in which John had arrived in Singapore in May, had taken off early on the morning of Tuesday 9 December on a regular patrol with 10 crew members and one passenger. After it had been airborne for about 2 hours it received a report that 13 men had been sighted on an atoll by a United States Naval aeroplane and the Shackleton was directed to the atoll, over which it circled to guide a fishing boat that appeared to be making an attempt to rescue the men. Having radioed to base at around 12.00 to say that the men had been rescued, the Shackleton resumed its patrol. That message was the last that was heard from the aircraft.

It had been due to land back at Changi at 18.00 hours but it didn't arrive. That evening two aircraft took-off to search for it but found nothing and the next morning John was part of another crew sent up to see if any sign of the missing aircraft could be found. He was particularly shaken because the crew was the one with whom he had flown on the first delivery flight into Singapore. The pilot was the chap that John had not liked very much at their first meeting but he believed him to be a fine pilot and a very experienced one. He just couldn't believe that an aircraft as big as a Shackleton could disappear with no trace but two days after it had vanished it had still not been found.

On the third day of the search John's crew reported seeing a patch of what appeared to be fuel on the waters of the South China Sea and nearby the crew of another aircraft saw what was believed to be yellow lifejackets, but they were empty. The following day there was still no news of the aircraft but there were two more sightings of lifejackets. By now, most of the men conducting the search were of the opinion that none of the missing crew members would be found alive. In between his own search and rescue missions, John wrote to Sue to tell her what was happening. It made him think about how she might worry if she heard about any similar incidents and wanted her to know that she would never find out about any such thing that involved him by newspaper reports. The Royal Air Force never gave out any details until the families of those involved had been informed.

Like the other crew members, John also thought that the chances of finding alive any of the missing crew were slim. He told Sue that:

*The two pilots alone had a total of NINE children between them. There were only TWO single members in the crew – that means that 8 families are ruined. My God, it's awful to think of the poor wives involved. I feel so utterly sorry for them – what agony it must be. The only thing I can say is that if there are any survivors, they will be found. Virtually every aircraft at Changi is on the search and all available aircrew are being used.*

The next day John spoke to the wife of one of the crew who was missing and believed to be dead, and told Sue:

*She's being incredibly brave about it, but darling, I've never seen such a pathetic sight. The poor, poor woman. She looks really ill. I really feel like crying my heart out for her. Talking to her has suddenly brought home the whole extent of the tragedy. This woman has 5 children, one of them only 2 months old, and now they are all fatherless. Oh, God, why do things like this have to happen. To think that this tragedy is repeated 10 times thro' the various members of the crew. Ten families ruthlessly broken. It doesn't bear contemplating, it really doesn't. I don't think I've ever seen a more heartbreaking sight, tho' than this poor woman looked tonight.*

The commander of 205 Squadron, Wing Commander McCready, had gone to Labuan in North Borneo to conduct the search for the missing aircraft from there. While he was away his wife, who could not drive, asked John to drive her in their car so that she could visit the wives and families of the missing airmen. John was again amazed by the courage shown by the women:

*One or two of the wives do appear to be broken and have taken the news very hard. But some of them are absolutely magnificent. There is one in particular who is not only keeping up her own spirits, but is actually looking after one of the other wives as well. And she goes dashing around trying to cheer up all the others when she's got time. Honestly, darling, to see this courage is really one of the most inspiring things I've known. It makes you realize that human nature has a truly noble side to it. There is one wife who has no family of her own, her husband has no family either and she has 5 children. She has got NOWHERE to turn to. Her husband was all she had, apart from the children. It must be the most terrible blow to her and yet she is by no means broken. She is already picking up the threads of life again and facing this awful tragedy with sheer guts. I am lost in admiration for them and have the very deepest respect for the wonderful way in which they are behaving.*

John then told Sue about his own misfortune. While driving Mrs McCready around to the homes of the wives and families of those that had been lost so that she could give them her own words of comfort and offer them help, he had 'pranged' her husband's car. Contrary to his previous bad record where cars were concerned, this crash was not his fault. He had been overtaking another car along a main road when a man pulled out from a side turning and ran into him. The Wing Commander's car, a huge 1947 Chevrolet, was badly damaged. John's only comfort was that it was not his fault and when the squadron commander returned to Singapore and heard about the accident, he was very understanding. John was relieved that because it was not his fault the insurance would pay for the damage to be rectified. When he discovered that the insurance policy had expired and that his boss had forgotten to renew it he felt he had to offer to pay for the damage himself. He was very relieved when Wing Commander McCready declined the offer.

A week before Christmas part of the mystery of the missing aircraft was solved. The crew of a search aircraft, flying over a tiny island – Sin Cowe Island – spotted a grave, complete with a cross, and a sign, cut into the grass in large letters. The sign said 'B 205' which was the identification letter of the missing aircraft and the number of the squadron. Hope rose briefly that some of the crew had survived but it was to be quickly dashed as there was no sign of any of them on the island. The aircraft carrier HMS *Albion*[1] sailed at once for the island and, when it was as close as it was able to get, sent one of its helicopters with some seamen to land on the island, exhume the body and bring it back to Albion so that eventually it could be reburied in a British military cemetery. Expecting to find the body directly in the ground, the naval men were surprised to find that the airman had first been placed in a very solid wooden box which they put into the helicopter along with the cross that had been put at the site of the grave.

Once back on board HMS *Albion* the coffin and cross were transferred to a Skyraider and were flown to Labuan. There the body was identified as being that of Flight Sergeant Dancy, the Shackleton's engineer.

It was believed that it must have been the crew of a fishing vessel who had found and buried the body so HMS *Albion* undertook the search for the boat that had found Flight Sergeant Dancy. They stopped all the vessels they came across and soon discovered the one they were seeking. Fortunately one of the fishermen spoke English and explained that they had been fishing approximately 300 miles north of Labuan, very near to Sin Cowe island, when they witnessed the Shackleton plummeting into the sea close by. The captain of the boat memorized the B 205 he had seen on the side of the aircraft as it sunk into the water and when they found Flight Sergeant Dancy's body they brought it to the island and buried him in the coffin which they built themselves. They also marked the grave with the cross which had an RAF tricolour, the aircraft marking and an RAF roundel on one side, all painted in the correct colours. On the other side was the date, 9 Dec 1958, and 13h 55m TIME, which was the time they had seen the aircraft plunge into the South China Sea. They made the sign, B205, in letters 10 feet high to enable the search and rescue aircraft to see where the accident had taken place and where the body of the airman was to be found. The fishermen, although not Christians themselves, gave Flight Sergeant Dancy a decent Christian burial and then spent a lot of time leaving information for the search parties. As John said:

All this must have taken these fishermen a hell of a long time and must have been incredibly hard work. Yet they did it all very thoroughly and most meticulously. A really admirable effort on their part.

Sadly the wreckage of the Shackleton was not recovered and neither were the other bodies which also included that of the Acting Deputy Commissioner of Police in North Borneo, who had been a passenger on the Shackleton.

Flight Sergeant Dancy's body was reburied with full military honours in the Ulu Pandan Cemetery but was again exhumed when the Kranji Military Cemetery was built in 1975. This cemetery was to be his final resting place and his grave is now marked with a traditional Commonwealth War Graves stone.

The cross that the fishermen created so beautifully for the airman was brought to England in the early 1970s and now hangs in the church of St Uvelus at St Eval in Cornwall, which was once known as the RAF Church when there was an Royal Air Force station there. It is now the Church for the Coastal Command and Maritime Air Association and so is a fitting home for the cross.

Sometime later, long after the crash, when it would no longer have the power to upset her, John told Sue that he had been due to fly on that Shackleton but he and another pilot had swapped duties for that day because, being new to Shackletons, the other pilot wanted the flying experience.

After the funeral of Flight Sergeant Dancy and a memorial service for the rest of the crew, life began to get back to normal at RAF Changi. John spent Christmas with a married colleague and his family and was pleased to be away from the Mess as, despite the hot weather, it did seem more like Christmas with a home-cooked lunch and excited children playing with their new toys. He was pleased to be able to tell Sue that on Boxing Day he had mastered the art of 'hula-hooping' and said that he found it to be a fascinating occupation and one to which he might become addicted.

Sue had no time for such frivolity. As well as her health problems she had to try to get all their belongings packed and sent to Singapore, have the numerous inoculations that she needed for the move to the Far East and study for her State exams which would begin in February. Then her stomach problems became worse and she had to go back into hospital for a further operation. John wrote to tell her that when she was discharged she should get a company to do all the household packing and dispatch of their belongings as he didn't want her to tire herself. The hospital staff weren't so considerate; she was discharged two days after the operation and told she had to be back at work four days later.

Just before her exams began Sue received the news that she and John had been waiting for; she had been granted an indulgence passage to Singapore. She was told that she had been listed for a flight on 23 February which was a Comet and would arrive in Singapore two days later. After all the time they had spent apart everything seemed to be working out for them at last. John found a two bedroom semi-detached bungalow with a small garden that they could afford to rent and, by the time Sue arrived, he hoped to have their belongings unpacked and in place in their first home together. He had also had the car fixed so they would have no trouble in getting around when Sue arrived.

Ten days before the flight was due to leave Sue received the confirmation that she definitely had a seat on the Comet. She still had two more oral exams to take at St Thomas's but would be able to do both before she left. Then, just seven days before she was due to board the flight, John received a telegram to let him know that she would not be coming. She had contracted chicken pox and had been sent back to the rectory in Wheathampstead to recover.

John, meanwhile, had gone to Rangoon as part of the crew of a Shackleton which had been sent to accompany HRH The Duke of Edinburgh on a visit there. The crew were treated very well and, despite the two delays caused by technical problems with the aircraft, John enjoyed the trip and managed a visit to the Shwedagon pagoda, the top of which was made of solid gold encrusted with precious jewels. John thought it was beautiful but not as beautiful as the Taj Mahal and was of the opinion that its opulence was the reason Burma was such a poor country.

Despite the honour of being chosen to accompany His Royal Highness, John was anxious to get back to Changi as he was sure that there would be a telegram waiting for him to tell him that Sue had managed to get a seat on another aircraft. When he did reach Singapore there was neither telegram nor letter. He hadn't realized what a nasty illness chicken pox could be in an adult, and that Sue would have to wait some time before she was no longer regarded as infectious before being allowed to travel on an RAF aircraft.

Eventually, four and a half months after they were married, Sue arrived in Singapore on board an RAF Comet. John met her in the smart cream MG with red leather seats, as she stepped off the aircraft and, after settling in, she wrote to his family to tell them that he looked very fit and well. After all her health problems John was pleased to see that Sue looked fitter than he was expecting her to be. She had thoroughly enjoyed her trip on the Comet where she was one of only two wives to be travelling to Singapore. The crew treated the women like officers and their travelling companions were 50 soldiers, a colonel who was returning to Kuala Lumpur and made it his business to look after the two wives and eight very senior officers from the three services who were going to Singapore for a military conference at which the Duke would also be attending.

The first evening of the trip had been spent at Lyneham in Wiltshire where Sue had been surprised to bump into several of John's friends who were returning from Malta and had been diverted to Lyneham. Although she thought it a rather bleak camp she was very impressed by the electric blankets on the beds. The aircraft was due to take-off in the early afternoon of the following day but developed a technical problem which delayed the departure for three hours. In the end, after night stops in El Adem, Minwallah's Grand Hotel in Karachi and the Mount Lavinia Hotel in Ceylon they finally arrived at Changi and Sue and John's long separation was over.

A month after her arrival they acquired a puppy they named Pimms No. 1 because, as Sue said, he was a crazy, mixed up dog.

One night while John was on night flying duties, Sue was awoken by a peculiar noise and as her eyes adjusted to the darkness she saw a hand coming through an open window, trying to locate items to steal. She was unnerved by the experience and had been in Singapore too short a time to have made any friends in the immediate area. When John returned home they decided to look for another home and, two weeks later, found a flat built on top of a garage which would make it more difficult for thieves to break in. It was a very nice flat, both bigger and closer to Changi than the bungalow had been and the rent was $100 cheaper. The reason for the smaller rent was that the landlord was a self-confessed tax evader. His tenants were required to pay in cash and he refused to issue any receipts. John thought it to be 'an excellent scheme!!' despite the move having taken place while there was a big SEATO exercise going on. It proved to be a happy home for them and for Pimms for the rest of their stay in Singapore

For the SEATO exercise John and his crew flew two 15 hour trips and, during the first trip, managed to score two 'kills', both on the same submarine. It was declared to have been a 'most unusual feat' and one for which they were very proud especially as the submarine was American.

Although they were now paying less rent, money was still tight and Sue answered an advertisement for a position as a nurse receptionist at a private clinic. The doctor who owned the clinic was English and after he had spoken to her about her experience offered her another position, that of theatre sister at his private hospital. Sue was flabbergasted and although she pointed out to him that her theatre experience was almost non-existent he was not bothered. He was a charming man and very easy to work with but the matron was the exact opposite. She had a fiery temperament and was most unpleasant. Although Sue had to get up early to be at the hospital at 7.30 she only had to work until 12.30 so had plenty of free time during the afternoons, and the extra money helped them enormously.

Soon after Sue's arrival John began to have stomach problems which were, at first, thought to be dysentery. Tests in the hospital proved otherwise although an exact diagnosis was not made. This situation continued for some time and John began to lose a lot of weight. His doctors thought that if they could find no reason for his illness he might have to be sent back to England for further tests. He continued to fly, however, qualifying on both Percival Pembroke light transport aircraft and on Gloster Meteors. He also made several flights on two de Havilland aircraft, the Vampire and the Venom and this encouraged him to believe that he might be able to transfer to fighters and fly small jets after all.

Then, in July, Sue discovered that she was pregnant. Although they hadn't planned to have a baby quite so soon, she and John were thrilled with the prospect of becoming parents. Sue wanted to have the baby in England and John agreed, so the chance that he might be sent back there suddenly had its advantages. Later that month he was again admitted to the hospital and this time the doctors believed that they had found the cause of his stomach trouble. They thought that it was due to an inflammation of the intestines, possibly related to living in the tropics, which would likely disappear in the colder climes of England. They decided he would have to be sent home for good.

Thereafter events moved very quickly. John was told that he would be leaving during the second week of August which gave him very little time to settle his affairs, pack his belongings, sell the car, find a new home for Pimms and try to get a passage arranged for Sue, as she was still not officially entitled to a flight home. The officer commanding 205 Squadron noted in John's logbook that he was: 'A young pilot of promise whose premature repatriation through illness severely curtailed his Squadron experience.'

John had spent only 14 months of what was planned to be a 30 month posting, in Singapore. Eventually, on 14 August when almost everything was done, he left Changi on a special Comet used for transporting the sick. When he arrived at Lyneham he was immediately taken to the RAF hospital at Wroughton in Wiltshire. Sue was left behind in Singapore to stay with friends until a passage could be arranged for her.

It was rather ironic that after the months they had spent apart after their wedding, with John waiting in Singapore for his new wife to join him, it was he who was now back in England and Sue who was languishing in Singapore. She wrote John a sad little letter two days after he had left to tell him about the efforts that were being made on her behalf to get her home. There were aircraft leaving for England but they were all full; one was even carrying a polio victim. She hoped that she might be able to get a passage for home the following week but nothing was certain. She finished by telling him:

I'm afraid there isn't any news – but I thought I'd let you know I was still here! I do hope you are not too lonely – I'll be back soon.

# Chapter 8

# Golden Sunsets and Black Storms

*Living is strife and torment, disappointment and love and sacrifice,*
*golden sunsets and black storms.*

Sir Laurence Olivier, 1907–1989, British actor

Following John's discharge from the RAF hospital at Wroughton and
Sue's arrival from Singapore, the couple went to stay with John's parents
in Harpenden. John had been given one month's sick leave and, as the
doctors in Singapore had predicted, he completely recovered from his
stomach complaint in a very short time. Because he had been repatriated
on medical grounds he no longer had a medical flying category and in
September, following the sick leave, was posted to RAF Northwood, the
headquarters of RAF Coastal Command, where he worked for several
months in an underground office complex which had been built as a
nuclear bomb-proof bunker, until he regained his flying category. He and
Sue rented a one bedroom flat in nearby Chorleywood from a lady who
managed to consume a crate of gin on a weekly basis and who had Cavalier
King Charles spaniels. They weren't the only dogs on the premises as John
and Sue soon found a breeder of Rhodesian Ridgebacks and a puppy,
Grubbeshurst Nimbobo – Bobo for short – joined them in their small flat.

Life for John was very different from what he had been used to. Sue
recalled his horror when, one day, he discovered that his shirt drawer
was empty. He asked her if she knew where his clean shirts had been put
and she enquired if he meant the pile of dirty washing that he had been
depositing on the floor and that had been growing bigger all week. Having

spent his entire life with someone always there to wash his shirts, it hadn't occurred to him that life and domestic chores in England, away from an RAF station and a batman, would be very different.

In the meantime they awaited the birth of their first baby. Knowing that they would only be in Chorleywood for a short time Sue had not registered with a doctor there but had contacted one of her father's friends who was a doctor in Wheathampstead. He arranged for the birth to take place at the Red House Cottage Hospital in Harpenden. When John told the matron that he wanted to be at the birth she misunderstood what he meant and told him that there was a room in which fathers could wait while their wives were in labour. John told her that he meant he wanted to actually be present at the birth and she was horrified. In the late 1950s and early 1960s, when it was unusual for fathers to attend a baby's birth, the matron had no intentions of allowing a man into the delivery room. John had to resort to sending a strong letter of complaint to the hospital board but it was to no avail as the board supported the matron's views.

In January 1960 Sue and John took a train to Scotland to visit Wynne's brother George and his wife Betty. They might have driven up to Scotland had a John Lewis lorry not crashed into their car; a Sunbeam Talbot.

Although they only stayed in Scotland for a few days Uncle George was relieved when they boarded the train to return to Chorleywood telling them just before the train pulled out: 'Thank God you are on that train. I was sure that Sue was going to pop at any minute.' Sue was amused but absolutely certain that the baby would not arrive until the middle of February. She was so convinced of this that she and John went to visit 'Aunt' Norah and 'Uncle' Oliver in Crondall, near Farnham in Surrey, for a few days, at the beginning of February. The couple were not actual relatives but very close friends of Sue's parents and Oliver was Sue's godfather. Norah had a treasure cot and some other things for the baby which they wanted to collect as soon as possible. On the morning of 6 February John and Sue went for a long walk around Frensham Ponds with Norah. They came back for lunch after which Norah had to go to the Women's Institute Denman College in Marcham near Oxford where she was attending a course, leaving them to fend for themselves until Oliver returned from his job as MD of the *Farnham Herald* newspaper.

The baby was very active that afternoon and as a result Sue's back was aching so she went to bed with a hot water bottle and a copy of *Fanny Hill* to read. During the afternoon John brought her a cup of tea and asked if she thought the backache was because the baby was about to make an appearance. She told him that she had had no contractions at all and was definitely not in labour. By the time Oliver returned from work she felt no better and so he called the local GP. Crondall's Doctor Crawshaw was a no nonsense, ex-Japanese prisoner of war who took one look at Sue and said that it might just be possible to move her to a hospital in Aldershot but that he thought it might be safer if she had a home birth as the baby was well on its way. Frantic phone calls were made to Norah to get her back from Denman College while John and Oliver tried to calm their nerves with large quantities of Scotch.

Before Norah reached her home Sue and John were the proud parents of a son whose birth had been witnessed by his father after all. Timothy John Ekins Hutchinson arrived during the late evening of Saturday 6 February weighing a healthy 8 lbs. He had deep blue eyes and masses of brown hair and, as John told Viola and Wynne the next day:

The little devil – he really did catch us on the wrong foot! … He seems to be extremely fit and healthy and has a jolly lusty cry. In fact, I'm immensely proud of him!!

He explained that if Timothy didn't like his first name he had the choice of calling himself John and he hoped that no one would think his name was too much of a mouthful as they also wanted to give him the family name, Ekins. Timothy's paternal grandparents and aunts came to visit him a week after his birth, closely followed by Sue's father and step-mother, and both families fell for the little boy, and were of the opinion that he was a very good-looking baby.

His parents adored their son from the first moment they set eyes on him and he was no trouble to care for, being a very good baby with a placid temperament. Viola, and John's sisters doted on him and over the following years took great delight in spoiling him.

In April 1960 John regained his medical flying category and left Northwood for RAF Manby in Lincolnshire where he undertook a refresher flying course on a Hunting Percival Jet Provost before being posted to the Central Flying School at Little Rissington in Gloucestershire to take part in number

203 Course and learn to be a flying instructor. Little Rissington had the nickname of 'Hell on the Hill' which John thought was completely inappropriate as it was a wonderful station. The course, which began in May, lasted until September and John enjoyed it immensely, describing it as 'absolutely wonderful'. Although by this stage in his flying career he was not a novice, he learnt so much about flying that he had hitherto not known. Learning how to teach others taught him to analyse how he, himself, was flying and gave him a completely different outlook on the whole process.

Sue and Tim were able to join him at both Manby and Little Rissington and while at the latter the family met Patrick and Ruth Cliff who were to become lifelong friends. While the Hutchinsons lived a little way from the airfield, Patrick and Ruth lived close by and Patrick travelled from his home to the course on a bicycle, with a small engine on the back, once a week, leaving Ruth the use of their car. Sue did not have any transport herself and so Ruth was able to give her lifts when necessary and, since both women had small babies, they found they had much in common and spent a lot of time together.

The course students came from different flying backgrounds and all those who had not had the chance to fly on fighter aircraft were given the opportunity to make three flights on the beautiful Hawker Hunter that John had so wanted to fly before the government cuts had stopped him. Although this opportunity was optional he could hardly wait to get into the cockpit of the Hunter. Patrick, two years older than John, had been on a fighter squadron flying Hunters anyway and so knew what it was like but since it had been John's ambition to fly the Hunter, he went off for two days to nearby RAF Kemble where he made his three flights in a single-seater Hunter F4. He described the experience as 'fabulous and exhilarating' and although he admitted to being 'shit scared' he also said that 'wild horses couldn't have dragged me out of the aircraft'. It was during one of these three flights that he first went supersonic over the Bristol Channel and had a foretaste of what was to come later in his career. Patrick, the fighter pilot, couldn't resist teasing him about it since John was a 'ruddy Shackleton pilot'. The teasing, in which they both indulge, has been a hallmark of their friendship ever since.

At the end of the course in September John was delighted with his results:

I must have worked extremely hard because I achieved something that not many people do achieve, and I'm blowing my own trumpet here. You have various categories as a qualified flying instructor; you have A1 which is the absolute top and very few people get that; A2 which is above average; B1 which is average and B2 which is what you come out of Little Rissington with. And I managed to come out of Little Rissington – I think I was the only person on the course, who came out as a B1 so I was a real bloody pimply swot!

At the end of the course Sue and Ruth had to say goodbye to each other as their husbands were being posted to different stations. Although the two couples' friendship continued by means of letters and cards, it would be several years before they saw each other again.

John's success with aircraft was, sadly, not replicated with less exotic vehicles. He still had lots of problems with cars and these did not end when he and Sue bought a van. It had metal side panels rather than glass which made it cheaper to tax than a vehicle with windows. On the journey to their next posting – RAF Syerston in Nottinghamshire – the van was packed with their possessions; clothes, boxes, cases, baby paraphernalia, a fridge and Bobo who was becoming a rather large dog. Sue, in the passenger seat, was holding Tim. As they drove along John became aware of a weird noise coming from the van. He was concerned about it but relaxed when, as he began to pick up speed, the noise gradually vanished. Just outside the Buckinghamshire town of Aylesbury, while speeding down a dual carriageway, both John and Sue saw something come from behind and flash past them. It was the wheel of a vehicle and, while they speculated as to its origin, the rear nearside of their van hit the road and they suddenly realized that it belonged to them. Fortunately no one was hurt, either in the van or on the road, and they repaired to the Crown in Aylesbury to wait for Wynne to arrive from nearby Harpenden to rescue them all.

The posting to RAF Syerston lasted for three years during which time John taught many other RAF personnel to fly the Jet Provost. The students on his first course were 23 and 24 years old, much the same age as he was himself, but mostly came from some of the 14 University Air Squadrons. At least two of his students, Jerry Lee and John Widdall, became test pilots for British Aerospace. He also taught Angus Hamilton, Marquess of Douglas and Clydesdale, who was the son of the 14th Duke of Hamilton, the first man to fly over Mount Everest and also the person whom Rudolf Hess had tried to contact in 1941, when he unexpectedly arrived in Scotland on his one-man mission to end the Second World War. Angus, who became the 15th Duke in 1973 on the death of his father, remained in the Royal Air Force until he was invalided out in 1967 but he retained his love of flying for most of his life until, in 2001, he was diagnosed with dementia to which he eventually succumbed at the age of 71 in June 2010.

While at Syerston John not only taught others to fly but also improved his own flying category when he was graded as an A2 – above average. In 1962 he met fellow instructor, Derek Bell, and he and Sue became very friendly with Derek and his wife Sheila.

As instructors, John and Derek worked well together. The students had one main instructor and one who acted as a standby. Some students were perfectly capable of flying but when it came to examinations were so nervous that they couldn't properly perform the tests they were set. In order to help them John and Derek, who acted as either main or standby instructors for some of the students they had in common, would take the nervous student on a test when he was just expecting instruction. Not feeling the pressure of an examination the student would perform to the best of his ability and would often pass the test without realizing until afterwards that one had been set.

The Hutchinsons spent Christmas 1961 with their families in Harpenden and Wheathampstead before returning to the cottage they had rented in the village of Car Colston at the beginning of the New Year. With them went Sue's sister Carola and John's friend and fellow pilot, Dick Foster. The weather in Nottinghamshire had been very cold over the Christmas period and there was a lot of snow along the lane in which their home stood. Having been empty for several days the cottage was cold and damp and, while John unloaded their bags from the van, Sue took Tim inside and Carola set about lighting a fire. Bobo, the dog, went into the living room to secure his favourite place on the hearth rug. Someone decided to make some tea but they found that there was no running water as the pipes had frozen. They also discovered that there had been a power cut. Dick went out to collect some snow which he planned to melt and boil in a saucepan over the fire so that they could, at least, have a hot drink. Carola eventually managed to get the fire to light but, after a few minutes, there was a terrific explosion, which blasted burning coals onto the carpet setting it on fire. Carola was knocked off her feet by the explosion and landed on the hot coals on all fours. She was not critically hurt but had many pieces of coal and other debris from the fire embedded in her hands and knees. She could smell burning and found that Bobo was smouldering, sparks from the fire having set his coat alight. He had a light coloured coat but after the blast he was black from the soot and, terrified, he ran outside. The only parts of him that were visible were the whites of his eyes. He disappeared for some time but eventually returned home, none the worse for his ordeal.

Sue had taken the baby up to his bedroom just before the explosion and Dick had gone upstairs to help her assemble Tim's cot. John was just coming through the back door with their baggage when he was hit by the blast. Recovering his composure he was confronted by a scene of absolute chaos. He quickly established that Sue and Tim were safe upstairs, and that Carola and Dick were still alive. The explosion had blown out the chimney breast and the adjacent wall and there was a gaping hole through which the garden was visible. Sue dialled 999 and, when she was asked which service she wanted, said that she needed all three, justifying her request by telling the operator that Carola needed an ambulance to take her to hospital because she had been injured; the fire brigade was necessary because there had been an explosion in the fireplace and the police should also attend the scene because one wall of their house had been destroyed and the hole was a security risk. The operator said she could only call one of the emergency services and the fire brigade arrived after a difficult journey along the narrow snow covered lanes. The explosion was found to have been caused by the back-boiler in the fireplace exploding. Although John knew that there was a back boiler, he never dreamt that lighting a small fire to boil the water would have had such a devastating effect.

With the fire having been extinguished by the fire brigade, an ambulance arrived to attend to the occupants of the cottage. Tim had not been at all affected by the drama and was taken into the village of Car Colston where he was looked after by friends. Sue, Carola, Dick and John were then taken to hospital in Nottingham. John and Carola were both treated for shock and Carola also had her burns dressed. They were then discharged on the understanding that Carola would return the next day to have the pieces of embedded coal and other debris removed from her hands and knees. Having left the hospital they had to find somewhere to sleep that night as they obviously couldn't return to the cottage. Since John and Sue had some good friends stationed in married quarters at RAF Newton, the four disaster victims, still soot-blackened from the ordeal, piled into a taxi and arrived on the friends' doorstep at 23.00 to ask if they could stay. They were given beds for the night.

The next day, after John had explained the situation, his CO told him that he could move into the Mess. John then had to tell him that not only was he temporarily homeless, so was his wife, and his baby son and his rather large dog. The CO decided that the best plan would be to house them in an apartment at the Mess, usually reserved for visiting dignitaries and where, for some weeks until the cottage had been repaired, they were looked after in the style of visiting VIPs themselves.

John and Sue were expecting their second baby in June and this time all went as planned. Sue had opted for a home birth and John again intended to be there. The midwife had been informed and, unlike the matron at the hospital in Harpenden, raised no objections to this. When Sue's labour began the midwife was called and, seeing that the birth was not imminent, went downstairs with John to watch an episode of *Steptoe and Son* on the television. They were both so engrossed in the programme that Sue had to yell loudly from her bedroom to tell them that things were on the move and they really ought to get upstairs as soon as possible. Christopher James Colvin Hutchinson was born on Friday, 22 June without any of the drama that had accompanied his brother's arrival. He, too, was a handsome baby and was much admired by family and friends. John's friend and colleague Derek Bell was asked if he would be Christopher's godfather, a request to which he readily agreed.

John's commission in the Royal Air Force was for 12 years but he had an option to leave after eight years and decided that he would do so in April 1963. Before leaving he and Sue planned to make one final trip to Switzerland for a skiing holiday. Every year since they had returned to England, they had been to Zermatt in Switzerland with the RAF Ski Association, membership of which gave them subsidized rates at the top class resort. They both loved skiing and saved all their spare money for the yearly jaunt. Towards the end of February 1963, John, – now a flight lieutenant – and Sue arrived in Zermatt with the Ski Association. Skiing conditions that year were particularly good and the town's hotel and restaurant proprietors were confident of a profitable season. The ski resort was said to make around $10 million each year from visitors, tourism being the town's main source of income and employment.

In January a doctor in Zurich had diagnosed a case of typhoid; a mainly water-borne disease. The person suffering from the illness had been to Zermatt, which lies within the canton of Valais, but no officials in the canton had done anything about discovering for certain whether or not the typhoid originated in that area. Doctors in Valais believed that no action was taken because officials of the Zermatt municipality actively wanted to hide the fact that a serious health risk might have been identified as coming from the area, in case it affected the tourist industry. The doctors also believed that the population, and visitors to the region, had a right to know about the dangers to which they were being subjected. The Zermatt Tourist Office, however, announced that Zermatt's water was 99.93 per cent pure, allaying visitors' fears and ensuring that many more flocked to the area to enjoy skiing holidays.

The Hutchinsons, along with others from the RAF Ski Association, had their usual enjoyable winter break before returning home at the beginning of March to be reunited with Tim and Chris and to visit other members of their family, including John's parents, with whom they stayed for a few days at St Hilda's School.

Soon after their return John began to feel extremely unwell, with a very high temperature. By now living in married quarters at Syerston, with Tim and Chris, Sue:

> … watched in horror as John's symptoms grew worse. At first the RAF doctor diagnosed measles, but it soon became clear that it was much more serious.
>
> After two days in bed with a high fever I rang the medical centre as I was now really concerned and John was delirious. A young RAF doctor, just returned from Aden, examined John and asked me where we had been. He said he was pretty sure that it was typhoid as he had seen many cases in Aden. He took samples and blood tests and arranged for John to be admitted immediately to the RAF Hospital at Nocton Hall, Lincolnshire.

As soon as he knew the reason he was feeling so ill John had written to his parents to apologise for any trouble his visit may have caused them. He felt very bad that his presence at St Hilda's might have created problems as he knew what an impact his illness may have had on the school. It was, of course highly unlikely that any of the girls would have caught typhoid as, unlike Zermatt's facilities in 1963, those of the school were immaculate. John, however, told his parents:

> I've really done it, haven't I? I do hope life hasn't been terribly over-complicated for you. As soon as I knew I had typhoid, I thought immediately of the fact that I had been staying at the school. I am awfully sorry for any trouble or inconvenience I may have caused you.
>
> I'm feeling a good deal better now that my treatment is underway, but I'm pretty weak and very switched-off at times. My main problem is going to be that I may well be here for 6 weeks … And the final straw is going to be if Sue goes down with it. It's the end, isn't it? You go on holiday to make yourself fit and this happens. It's caused quite a stir in the medical world, apparently.

When John had been taken into hospital Sue was also feeling quite ill but the doctor told her that she would have to pull herself together and stop thinking of herself, as she had a sick husband to worry about and her children to look after. In the third week of March, a few days after John was admitted to Nocton Hall, she was feeling much worse and, despite the doctor's offhand dismissal of her growing symptoms, she too was diagnosed as having typhoid.

She was admitted to the City Isolation Hospital in Lincoln, with the children in an adjoining cubicle. Two days later John was transferred to the same small glass-walled cubicle which contained two beds and a washbasin. He was not pleased as he had been far more comfortable at Nocton Hall.

Although the children had not been to Zermatt with their parents they were put into isolation as a precaution but, being so young – Tim was just 3 years old and Chris was only 9 months – neither knew what was happening to them. Tim especially couldn't understand why he wasn't allowed to be with his Mummy and Daddy. When it was found that, as expected, the children were not suffering from the disease, they were released into the care of family members and friends to be looked after until their parents were well. Tim went to stay with Sue's Aunt Kath in Bedford, with whom he had stayed when Chris was born and Derek and Sheila Bell looked after Chris for two weeks. Then he went to stay with Sue's sister and brother-in-law, Pippa and Roger Noyes, and their little boy, David, who was the same age as Chris.

At one stage in the illness it seemed as if John might not survive. The doctors were very concerned about his condition and were by no means sure that he would recover. Although he had told his parents that he was feeling better he certainly wasn't out of danger and he remembers having an out of body experience where he seemed to be floating above the bed, looking down on his own fever-racked body. He says, perhaps not entirely seriously, that he thinks he managed to return to his body and eventually get better, because he heard Sue shouting at him, 'You will not die'.

Sue was also very ill and the doctors were worried that neither she, nor John, was responding to the drug, Chloromycetin, that they were administering. Sue's blood count became dangerous and they both still returned positive specimens. After a conference between several doctors it was decided to use Penbritten, a new and untried drug. As Sue says:

It was a gamble but after two weeks the gamble paid off and we were on the road to a full recovery.

After six weeks in hospital John spent a further two weeks at RAF Hedley Court to regain his fitness. I returned to our fumigated married quarter where I was reunited with the children.

John and Sue were not the only ones from the RAF to have the disease; at least seven people from the RAF Ski Association party were known to have contracted typhoid while in Zermatt, including a flight lieutenant from the headquarters of No. 1 Group, Bomber Command at Bawtry who had also been taken into the RAF Hospital at Nocton Hall where he shared an isolation ward with John. Both officers had been treated as VIP patients.

It soon became clear, even to Zermatt's officials, that the reputation of the town was rapidly deteriorating. Had they acted promptly when it was first established that there was a typhoid risk in the area it might have been possible to limit the damage to the tourism industry. However, since there had been visitors from across the world who had been infected before they returned to their homes, the story was being reported internationally.

On 24 March the newspapers gave the news of the first death due to the typhoid outbreak. The victim was a 62 year old Swiss woman and her death forced the Swiss authorities to act to contain the disease. By this time, however, there were already 300 people suffering from typhoid and the Swiss Army quickly evacuated 35 more suspected cases from Zermatt. *The Times*[1] reported that:

> The authorities at Zermatt are being accused of having known about the outbreak in February. The communal administration is reported to have sent out then a circular to householders telling them to boil water before drinking it. The contention that it would have been 'unfair' to have cancelled the Gornergrat ski contests earlier this month, and that this might have resulted in a panic exodus, has been angrily brushed aside.

When asked why the ski race was not cancelled, the head of the Zermatt tourist office explained:

> There were entries from Britain, France, Germany, Italy, Finland, America, Austria and Switzerland. Zermatt was fully booked. There was no sense in cancelling, since everybody was already here.[2]

However they tried to excuse it, the authorities were undoubtedly guilty of a shameful attempt to hoodwink the public into believing that everything was as it should be, when they clearly knew that this was a lie. When further investigations were made it was discovered that the disease had spread because raw sewage had been seeping into broken water pipes. The deplorable state of the town's water and sewage system had been known for a long time but it had been judged better to hope that nothing untoward would happen rather than spend money to make the structures safe. The newspaper, *La Tribune de Genève* stated:

> Sanitary installations at Zermatt were notoriously inadequate and needed a complete transformation, but this had been precluded as the local populace had voted against the project.

As the number of typhoid sufferers rapidly mounted, the officials and the population engaged in the tourist industry, were largely unrepentant. They seemed to be more concerned about their pockets than the sickness and deaths for which their greed had been responsible. Eventually all the hotels and restaurants in the town were forced to close until it was certain that there would be no more cases of typhoid. It was estimated that these closures would be for between six to eight weeks during which time, it was reported, Zermatt would lose revenue of approximately £20,000 per day. It must have made the townspeople regret not allowing the municipal authorities to go ahead with their proposed project to upgrade the provision of water to the town. That project would have cost Zermatt just £65,000.[3]

The final toll of the Zermatt typhoid scandal was 389 people regarded as having been dangerously ill, and three deaths; two Swiss women and an English man.

Knowing that he was going to leave the Royal Air Force in 1963, John had been studying for his civil licences so that he could get a job as an airline pilot. His research had shown that there were many opportunities in civil aviation at that time. The prolonged stay in hospital, however, meant that his course had been disrupted and he was concerned that he would not be able to take his civil exams, although during the last four weeks in hospital he worked very hard on his correspondence papers. He admitted to his parents that, 'It worries me sick at times'.

When he left both the hospital and the RAF and returned to civilian life in April, he discovered that it would not be as easy to find a position with an airline as he had been led to believe.

# Chapter 9

# Hitting the Ground

*Trouble in the air is very rare. It is hitting the ground that causes it.*

Amelia Earhart, 1897–1937, American aviatrix

After leaving the Royal Air Force John applied to several airlines but discovered that there had been a general downturn in employment and no one was being hired at that time. It was a dreadful shock to him to suddenly find himself unemployed – something he had not experienced before. Now with a wife and two small children to support, he knew he would have to find a job very soon and chased every vacancy he could find. Eventually he was offered a position and, in the summer of 1963, joined McAlpine Aviation at Luton Airport. For the early part of his time with the company John was the only pilot but, during the three years he was with McAlpine, it expanded and others joined, with John becoming the chief pilot.

The civil engineering company had purchased their aircraft to enable directors to visit various construction sites around the United Kingdom and Europe, but then made the aircraft available for transporting jockeys, race horse owners and trainers to racecourses around the country and on the Continent. They also expanded into the engineering side of aviation, offering maintenance facilities to owners of small aircraft. John was involved with this part of the business as well, as it was he who did the air tests after the work had been completed by the company's engineers.

During his eight years with the RAF John had amassed a total of around 2,000 flying hours; his three years with McAlpine added another 2,000 hours to the total. He was kept very busy and was on call all the time. Sue also played her part by keeping track of John's flights, ensuring that his timetable was always up-to-date and answering the numerous phone calls that he received to book new trips. If he was called out at short notice it was Sue who contacted the meteorological office to get the weather reports while John got ready to leave.

The aircraft he flew were small executive, single or twin-engined aeroplanes like the Piaggio 166 which had a passenger capacity of between six and eight, the faster Cessna 310 which had room for four passengers and the Helio Courier which seated five passengers and was a short take-off and landing aircraft, particularly useful when landing at racecourses and on building sites.

Because of the nature of the operations, John had to do everything himself. There was only ever one pilot per flight and he had to make all the arrangements such as contacting the met. office, completing customs and immigration documentation, supervising the fuelling of the aircraft, loading baggage and looking after the passengers. The flights were a bit like 'bush flying'. The aircraft had no auto pilots and he often had to find the destinations using one inch to one mile Ordnance Survey maps. It was very hard work but John says of his time with the company: 'I owe McAlpine a huge debt of gratitude. They gave me a massive start in civil aviation and a huge wealth of experience. I was very lucky.'

John's first task after joining McAlpine was to take an aircraft out to Athens. The Helio Courier had been flown into the UK from America in five sections, onboard a Pan American Airways freighter. It was assembled by McAlpine engineers at Luton Airport before being flown by John to Athens over a two and a half day period. The aircraft was needed by a construction company 200 miles north-west of the Greek capital where a dam across the River Acheloos was being built. John remained in Greece for a few days, handing over the aircraft to the pilots who would be using it, before returning to the UK as a passenger.

While the trips to construction sites were usually straightforward and uneventful, the transportation of people from the racing fraternity was much more interesting. He met many jockeys and trainers and particularly liked owner and horse breeder John Osmael Scott-Ellis, the 9th Baron Howard de Walden, whom he described as a 'wonderful gentleman'. As a young man, Howard de Walden had been driving a car in the southern

German city of Munich when a man, deep in thought and not taking care of where he was going, walked in front of his car and was knocked down. He was unhurt but had Howard de Walden killed him, the course of modern history would have been changed forever as the man was none other than Adolf Hitler.

Another of John's favourite passengers was owner and breeder Stanhope Joel, a larger than life, incredibly generous man who came over to the United Kingdom from his home on Perot's Island in the Southampton parish of Bermuda. When John flew these men he was well looked after as he would be invited to join them at the races rather than wait for them with the aeroplane and the invitations included lunch where the champagne flowed for all except the pilot. If they knew in advance that there would be spare seats on the aeroplane Sue would sometimes be invited to the races as well.

On one occasion John and Sue were invited by Bernard van Cutsem, another favourite trainer, and father of Hugh van Cutsem who would, one day, become a close friend of Prince Charles, to watch his horses being trained at Newmarket. They arrived early one misty morning and watched the beautiful creatures being put through their paces. Their host then took them back to his house in the village of Exning, Suffolk, two miles south-east of Newmarket, for breakfast. The visit was an eye-opener. A full English breakfast had been prepared for them, served by a butler, and a large number of the day's newspapers were laid out for them to read should they so wish, all of which had been freshly ironed.

As well as trainers, John also flew a number of jockeys during his time with McAlpine. Australian Scobie Breasley was one of his passengers and, although he hadn't known it at the time, the jockey's daughter Loretta and her husband, jockey Brian Swift, had been in Zermatt at the beginning of 1963 where they too had contracted, and survived, typhoid. Other jockeys who became regular passengers were Ron Hutchinson, Jimmy Lindley, Greville Starkey, brothers Doug and Eph Smith and Lester Piggott. John recalls how most of the jockeys would read the *Sporting Life* during the flights while Lester Piggott would always have his head in a copy of the *Financial Times*. Piggott, unlike the trainers, was not a generous passenger and when it was impossible to land at a racecourse and a taxi had to be taken from the airfield, would tell the taxi driver to find his pilot who would pay for his fare. Although John regarded him as a superb jockey he was not a charismatic man.

One day while on an air test of a Piper Comanche belonging to Lotus car boss, Colin Chapman, John had a nasty experience. Having completed the test he was approaching Luton Airport when he discovered that the undercarriage was stuck and he was unable to lower it for the landing. He went around and made several attempts to get the wheels down, to no avail. Eventually he decided that he would have to make a wheels-up landing on the grass alongside the runway. He spoke to the McAlpine engineers on the ground by radio and they also concluded that there was nothing else he could do. The emergency services were alerted and were in place as he came in to make his landing on the grass strip. Thinking of how annoyed Colin Chapman would be if he wrecked his aeroplane, he made one final attempt to lower the undercarriage and, as if by magic, the wheels came down. But because there was only one light to show that the undercarriage was in place, he was worried that the mechanism still might be malfunctioning and so flew over the control tower from where the controllers were able to tell him that all wheels were down. He then elected to touch down on the runway rather than the grass and made a perfect landing with no further problems, much to his relief. Some time later he was not so lucky.

McAlpine had been considering purchasing a helicopter and sent John to a company called Management Aviation which was based in Bourn, Cambridgeshire, to learn to fly one. He was taught on a Hiller 12b, a basic helicopter that was often used for crop spraying. John passed the course and obtained his helicopter private pilot's licence. Having got his licence he was doing some practice flying and, as he came in to land in a field, the helicopter suddenly started spinning around violently. John tried everything he knew to stop its wild gyrations but nothing worked and he became more a passenger than a pilot, unable to do anything to control it. Eventually it hit the ground and proceeded to bounce around the field until it turned over and crashed onto the main rotor, leaving John hanging upside down in his safety belt. He could smell the fuel that was dripping out of the tank and knew that he had to get away fast in case it exploded. Fortunately the crash had made a hole in the Plexiglas bubble canopy and John quickly unstrapped his seat belt, put his hand through the broken canopy and managed to pull himself out of the helicopter. In doing so he cut the back of his hand which began to bleed but, although very shaken, he was able to get away from the aircraft and ran to a point 50 or 60 yards away and sat down.

Across the field was a farmer in a tractor and soon John could see him stop whatever it was that he was doing and begin to make his way to where he was sitting. He was very relieved that help was arriving so soon after the crash. The farmer climbed out of the cab and came across to John to ask him if he was all right. John told him that he had cut his hand and that he was feeling a bit shaken but that otherwise, he seemed to be fine. The farmer looked at him and said, 'That's good' then returned to his tractor cab. Instead of fetching medical supplies he got into the tractor and drove off, without offering any assistance whatsoever, leaving John, bleeding and stranded in the field. The shaken pilot concluded that the old farmer must have witnessed lots of helicopter crashes in his fields and thought that what had happened was all quite normal. Happily for him another helicopter belonging to Management Aviation flew across the field a few minutes later and, seeing what had taken place, radioed to their base to report the crash.

Soon a car arrived to take John back to the company headquarters in Bourn. He immediately went to see his boss to apologize for what had happened. The boss told him not to worry about it and, instead of the flowers and grapes that are usually given to aid recovery from an illness or accident, John received something much more to his liking from the company – a crate of Scotch. When the wreckage was examined it was found that the driveshaft to the tail rotor had broken.

Having lost the concessions they had had with the RAF Ski Association, holidays for John and Sue were a thing of the past, especially as they had taken out their first mortgage to buy a bungalow in Hitchin. They were therefore delighted when John had to go to Athens to pick up the Helio Courier that he had flown to Greece on his first assignment with McAlpine, and his boss suggested that he might like to take Sue with him. She jumped at the chance and went along to help with the navigation and, at the same time, have a short break.

They flew to Athens by BEA, both smartly dressed because they were representing McAlpine. When they reached Athens they found that their bags were missing. Not only were they without clothes and toiletries, the weather was extremely hot, it was a holiday weekend in Greece and all the shops, except those in the hotel were closed. BEA gave them £25 to buy a few necessary items which they managed to get from the hotel that McAlpine had booked them into, the Athens Hilton, and for the remainder of the weekend Sue swapped her smart silk suit for a swimsuit that she bought from a stall on the beach.

Despite their lack of suitable clothing they did manage to do a small amount of sightseeing before they had to leave for the UK. There was a lot of political unrest in Greece at that time and, one evening while sitting in Constitution Square, they were approached by a Greek man who spoke good English. He could see that they were visitors and that they had no idea about the mood of the growing crowd. He told them that they were in danger as there was likely to be a riot and that if they didn't leave immediately they would be caught up in the demonstration. His information was accurate. Soon tanks appeared on the streets, along with armed soldiers and police, and their new Greek friend hustled them into his car and drove off at speed. He took them to his parents' house where they were invited to have dinner before he decided it was safe enough to venture out again and drove them back to their hotel. They were extremely grateful to the young man as they had had no idea that they were at risk and would have been unable to escape from the square had they not been taken away so promptly by car.

When, on the Wednesday following the public holiday, it was time to leave for the return trip to England, they went to the McAlpine office at the airport where they had to wait while a minor problem with the aircraft was fixed. While John completed all the paperwork for the flight, Sue chatted to the manager and mentioned that they had spent their entire time in Athens without their luggage. He excused himself for a moment and went into another of the company's offices, returning with the missing bags which, he said, had been delivered there before the weekend, presumably because they were labelled with McAlpine tags. None of his staff had any idea what they were supposed to do with them and so had just stored them while waiting for them to be claimed.

With the technical problem fixed and the paperwork completed they put their newly found bags into the Helio Courier, climbed aboard themselves and took-off on the first leg of their return journey. This took them from Athens to Corfu where they landed to refuel. They made similar stops at Brindisi, Naples, Nice, and Dijon where they stayed overnight. Between

Nice and Dijon John had got lost, having followed a river valley which proved to be the wrong one and which meant he had to make a 180 degree turn and retrace his route until he found the valley that led them in the right direction. They landed safely in Dijon where they had time to buy some wine and cheese to take home with them, before having dinner in the company of a delightful old American couple staying in the same hotel.

They left Dijon the next day and headed for England. During this stage of the journey Sue felt sick and, for the first and only time in her life, actually was airsick. She had managed to grab a bag put onto the aircraft specifically for this purpose but, having used it, had no idea what to do with it. John was dismayed, telling her there was no way he could carry on flying with the offending item so close to him and so he took the only course available to him – one that nearly 50 years later he still feels guilty about – he opened the window and dropped the bag out, hoping fervently that it would land in a remote spot and not hit some poor French man or woman on the head.

Having landed at Luton the airport Customs' officials came out to the aircraft to check their papers and clear them through Customs. They had to deal with more stinking items as the cheese they had bought in Dijon was so ripe it was about to run off the aircraft unaided. Opening the hatch where the wine and cheese had been stored, the Customs' officer reeled back in horror at the smell that assailed his nostrils. Customs' formalities were expedited, the officers left without checking what was behind the foul smelling cheese and John and Sue were spared the expense of having to pay duty on the wine which was in excess of the amount that they were allowed to import into the United Kingdom at that time.

In the summer of 1966 the major airlines were again hiring pilots so John applied to BEA, BOAC and Qantas and was offered positions with all three companies. He had enjoyed his time with McAlpine very much but it was not the sort of flying that he wanted to do for the rest of his career. He was more interested in flying big jets and travelling across the world. He rejected the idea of working for BEA, as its routes would have only taken him to Europe and although he would have loved to pursue the job with Qantas and move the family to Australia, his mother was not well and he didn't want to leave England while her health was in question. So he happily accepted the offer made to him by BOAC and said goodbye to McAlpine in September 1966. His decision to leave the company meant that he had to take a cut in his pay but he realized that his long term prospects were much better served by joining the UK's only state-owned long haul airline.

That summer was memorable for John not only because of the change in his career; it was also the last summer he was to spend with his mother. Viola had been having health problems for some time. When Sue was doing her nursing training at St Thomas's Viola had been admitted to the Grosvenor Hospital for Women, part of the St Thomas's group, where she had had a hysterectomy. Sue had visited her several times and the family was heartened with her reports and the fact that Viola seemed to have recovered completely.

In the intervening years she had, however, had more periods of ill health. She had problems with her breathing and was susceptible to colds and flu. In 1966 she had had flu like symptoms that had prevented her from presiding over the sports day at St Hilda's but as she began to feel a little better, John suggested that he take her, as he had done before, to Northamptonshire, home of the Ekins family of which she was a part. He was delighted that he was able to do this for his mother as they had a very enjoyable time finding references to the Ekins family in churches and on memorials throughout the county and visiting the places where her paternal ancestors had lived and worked. While Viola explored, with John sometimes helping her, he also made trips to his car to listen to the football results on the radio. He remembers hearing, on Saturday 30 July, that England had finally beaten Germany 4-2 after an exciting match that had gone to extra time, and were the new holders of the Jules Rimet trophy and winners of the World Cup tournament for the first time.

They returned from their family history tour and Viola soon had more problems with her breathing. She was referred by her doctor to the Luton & Dunstable Hospital where doctors found that she had fluid on her lungs. The fluid was drained and she was advised to take a complete rest, which she did until the start of the autumn term at St Hilda's. Although she intended to continue teaching she found that unless she rested during the afternoon she simply didn't have the strength to take any classes at all.

The family was very worried about her condition and John and his father decided that the time had come to get some proper information about why she was feeling so ill. Without telling her, they made an appointment to see her consultant at the hospital. He extracted a promise from them that they would not disclose to Viola the details he was about to give them. He then told them that she was suffering from lung cancer, that it was advanced and that she didn't have long to live. Completely stunned by what they had been told, Wynne and John returned to their homes to digest the awful news. It seemed wrong to them that this should have happened with no warning and they began to wonder if the cancer had been present when Viola had had the hysterectomy. They thought that it might have been developing during the times she had felt unwell since the operation and that no one who had treated her since then had noticed, until it had spread through her body and reached her lungs. It also seemed very unfair that Viola was dying, but had not been told. She was, after all, a highly intelligent, calm, practical woman and deserved to be treated as such, not dealt with as if she were a child and that the truth of her situation was none of her concern. They sought Sue's advice, both as her daughter-in-law and as a nurse, and she agreed that it was wrong to keep it from Viola and so she was told. It was the right decision. Viola was grateful to know while she still had time to put her affairs in order, and her unshakeable religious belief helped her through the difficult times that followed. She didn't complain about what was happening to her. She knew that she was in God's hands and that she would soon be in His presence.

Viola was 58 on 11 December, by which time she was becoming very frail. She spent Christmas at St Hilda's although she was too weak to leave her bed and couldn't face any food. Her family was also there, although none felt that it was a time for celebration. On New Year's Eve 1966, while John and his father were at Viola's bedside, she took her last breath. Her end was quite peaceful and John remembers that the very last word she uttered was 'Jesus'.

Viola's death, at such an early age, was a terrible blow for the entire family. John, who had been devoted to his mother, felt her loss very much. It was she who had passed on her love of God, of poetry and literature, and of flowers, birds and animals to her sensitive, firstborn son and although John knew that his father loved him, it was Michael who was close to Wynne and who enjoyed the more practical things in life that he could share with his father. For John it had been his mother who had given his life stability, writing him numerous letters both while he was at school and when he joined the RAF. It was she who kept him in touch with the family and what was happening at home. And it was she who, despite her own fears for his safety, had encouraged him in his ambition to fly and had paid for his first flight even though times were hard and money in short supply.

After he became a pilot John took his mother flying and she had a wonderful time, delighting in swooping and diving through the vast blue sky. She showed no signs of fear; she was, as John described her 'an intrepid lady'. She lived her life in the same courageous manner and, when she knew the end was near, faced her untimely death with dignity and an unswerving faith in the Almighty.

# Chapter 10

# Skilful Pilots

*The greater the difficulty the more glory in surmounting it. Skilful pilots gain their reputation from storms and tempests.*

Epicurus, 341–270 BC, Greek philosopher

When John joined BOAC in September 1966 he was sent on a conversion course to fly the Boeing 707. Having successfully completed the course he was surprised to learn that his next task would be to attend a navigation course. In the mid-1960s BOAC still employed navigators as neither their Boeing 707s nor Vickers VC10s had inertial navigation systems. When the Boeing 747 which did have INS, came into service these were retro-fitted to the 707s and VC10s. In the meantime pilots had to attend navigation training classes. One of John's regular instructors was Norman Tebbit who, after his airline career, became a successful politician, serving as Secretary of State for Employment, Secretary of State for Trade and Industry and Chancellor of the Duchy of Lancaster. In 1985 he was appointed Chairman of the Conservative Party and, in 1992, was given a life peerage, becoming Lord Tebbit of Chingford.

The route that was flown for navigation training purposes was between London and Bermuda, the logic being that if a pilot could find the tiny territory of Bermuda, whose total area is no more than 22.7 square miles, and which is surrounded by the waters of the North Atlantic Ocean, several hundred miles from the nearest landfall in the United States, then he could find anything. While John did not particularly enjoy navigation – he said it unnerved him – he has always managed to find Bermuda.

Having completed these requisite courses, John was finally able to become part of a BOAC operational crew when, as Second Officer Hutchinson, he began his commercial flying with the airline. At last he had achieved his ambition to be part of a crew flying large jet aircraft to exotic places throughout the world, and he loved it.

Depending upon where he was sent, the trips could last for two weeks or more but the children were used to their father being away and compared with the times that John and Sue had spent apart both before and during the early part of their marriage, a two-week separation for them was not difficult.

When they knew that John would be based at Heathrow, the couple had discussed the possibility of moving nearer to the airport. It may have been more convenient to live closer to John's workplace but they both rather liked the idea of distancing themselves from it so that their entire lives didn't revolve around the day-to-day proceedings at BOAC. Sue was a Hertfordshire girl, having lived there for most of her life and John's main family home in England had been St Hilda's, also in Hertfordshire. While many aircrew opted to live close to what would become the M4 corridor, they chose instead to remain in Hertfordshire but decided to look for a country cottage rather than their modern bungalow. Every week Sue scoured the local papers to try to find their perfect country retreat but hadn't managed to discover anything that was just right, was for sale at the right price and had good schools nearby.

Then, while John was away on another long trip, Sue came across a house that she thought would be perfect for them. It was an old house, complete with beamed ceilings, which had been restored in 1936. It also had a beautiful garden and a small orchard. The house, which was in the hamlet of Cromer, north-east of Stevenage, was being sold privately. Sue immediately telephoned the vendor and asked if she could come and see it that afternoon. She took the boys with her when she went to view it and, convinced that John would love it as much as she did and knowing that by the time he returned from his long trip it might have been sold, she decided to conduct the negotiations with the owner herself. She asked if he would accept her offer of the full asking price. He refused, saying that he couldn't possibly do business with a woman and would have to talk to her husband. She really wanted the house so ignored the old man's sexist attitude and explained that her husband was a pilot and would be away for nearly two more weeks. She told him that she didn't want to wait until his return as she was sure the house would have been sold by then. The old chap was unmoved by her pleas but said he would be happy to discuss the matter with her husband when he returned. For the remainder of John's trip Sue was on tenterhooks and kept going back to see if the house was still unsold. She found that not only was Cromer a delightful little place and the house beautiful, the hamlet possessed a windmill, the only surviving one in Hertfordshire, and there was a good school in the village of Ardeley, a mile and a half away.

On the day of John's return Sue drove to Heathrow to fetch him and could talk of nothing but the house on the way back to Hitchin. She told him that they had to go straight to Cromer to talk to the owner. John was tired after his long trip and wanted to go straight to bed when he got home so wouldn't be moved by Sue's entreaties. When he found where the house was, he told her that it would be too far away for him to reach Heathrow when he was on standby anyway. He then went to bed. When he awoke and Sue was still begging him to go and look at the house, he reluctantly agreed and was as enchanted with it as she had been. The owner told them that although he had had many viewings and some offers since Sue's first visit, the house wasn't yet sold and invited John to go outside with him where they could discuss the sale in private. When they returned the deal was done with a handshake. They later discovered that he had had several offers, some significantly higher than the asking price, but because Sue had been the first to view the house and make an offer, these had been put on hold until he could discuss the sale with her husband. Having found that John also loved the house and wanted to buy it, he agreed to sell it to them for the amount Sue had offered. He and his wife were moving to a smaller bungalow and asked if John and Sue would be interested in buying some of their furniture and Indian rugs as well. Since they had very little furniture anyway and certainly not enough to furnish the house, which was much larger than their bungalow in Hitchin, they were delighted and still have some of the pieces they bought from the old couple.

In April 1968 John was rostered to take a flight to Sydney. He was due to be away for at least two weeks which took up all of the boys' Easter holidays. Although they were disappointed that John wouldn't be there they had become used to the fact that he was often absent and knew that their mother would find something with which to entertain them during the school holidays.

On 8 April, John said goodbye to Sue and the boys and, since they had become a two car family, drove himself to Heathrow where he parked in the staff car park, on the north side of the airport. He caught the staff bus into the centre where the crew reporting office was located and, while on the bus, chatted very briefly to one of the BOAC stewardesses, Jane Harrison, who was also taking the same flight to Sydney. By this stage in his airline career John was an acting first officer although on the first leg of this flight to Zurich, he had no real function as the flight deck would be full, with a check pilot, Geoff Moss, monitoring the performance of the operating captain, New Zealander Cliff Taylor. Once Geoff Moss left the aircraft in Zurich, John would be able to take his normal seat which was behind that of the captain on the left side of the flight deck. The aircraft, known as Whisky Echo because of its registration, G-ARWE,[1] was operating as flight BA712 and was carrying 115 passengers, many of whom were emigrating to Australia, and 11 crew, five on the flight deck and six in the cabin.

The aircraft took-off at 16.27 from runway 28L and, as it left the ground, it shuddered and a loud bang was heard on the flight deck. As it climbed away from the airport, air traffic controller John Davis, who had given clearance for the departure, noticed through the control tower window that there were flames coming from the number 2 engine, closest to the fuselage on the port side.

John, hidden at the back of the flight deck behind the check captain, could see nothing of what was happening, either at the front of the aircraft or outside, but Geoff Moss, sitting alongside the window turned in his seat to look back towards the wing and engines on the port side. Seeing the flames he yelled out, 'Bloody hell! The wing's on fire'. By then the air traffic controller had called the pilot to tell him what he had seen and Cliff Taylor prepared to make an emergency landing at Heathrow. He was offered the same runway, 28L, from which he had left moments before and intended to use it. However the flames were getting so bad that Geoff Moss suggested that he ask for clearance for another runway as he felt that they would not be able to make the wide turn over nearby Hounslow that would be necessary to line up for the landing on 28L, before the fire was completely out of control. The captain was reluctant to do so but

Geoff Moss was adamant that they would not make it if they had to use 28L and insisted that they should land as soon as possible. Taylor finally agreed and was given clearance for a little used runway, 5R, on which he made a perfect landing 3 minutes and 32 seconds after taking-off. What no one on the flight deck realized until after their return to Heathrow was that the burning engine had fallen off and had miraculously landed in a water-filled gravel pit some miles from the airport in the village of Thorpe, where it sank to the bottom, presenting no further danger to anyone.

The cabin crew meanwhile, had prepared the passengers for an emergency landing and an evacuation which they began as soon as the aircraft came to a stop on the runway. Despite the flames rapidly spreading to the starboard side of the 707 and the cabin filling with acrid black smoke, there was very little panic. Although the emergency chutes were deployed, two of them twisted and burst after they were showered with sparks from the growing fire, and most of the passengers escaped through the forward starboard door whose chute was still in working order. They were assisted by a steward and stewardess. John, having no real function on the first stage of the flight to Australia, had left the flight deck and come into the cabin to see if he could help with the evacuation.

Those of us who have never experienced the possibility of being burnt alive can't possibly imagine what it would be like to be in that position but the crew of that 707, possibly because of their training or perhaps their own bravery, stayed at their posts, getting the passengers out of the burning wreck as fast as they possibly could. At the back of the aircraft stewardess Jane Harrison with whom John had had the brief conversation while on the bus, had resorted to pushing people through the open doorway as the chute at that exit had burst and the area near the tail was cut off from the rest of the aircraft by the fierce blaze. John, at the front, was nearly pulled through the open door on the port side, when he tried, unsuccessfully, to stop a passenger – one of the very few who did panic – from leaping onto the runway below rather than using the chute at the starboard door.

In less than half the time that the flight had lasted, the crew had managed to get the passengers off the burning wreckage and then made their own escape. At the back of the aircraft Jane Harrison had been about to jump when she realized that there were still some people onboard. She went back to fetch them but was overcome by the smoke and she, three women and a small girl, all died.

Cliff Taylor and John were the last crew members to leave, spending their final few seconds onboard shouting for anyone else who might be trapped. Hearing nothing and being unable to see or breathe properly they found that the remaining chute, which most of the passengers and crew had used to escape, was now hanging limply in the open doorway, so they went back into the cockpit and slid down a rope hanging from the window. Cliff Taylor went first and, when John attempted to get out, the ring that Sue had bought him for his 21st birthday caught in the rope and, for a few moments, he was unable to move. He eventually managed to free his finger and slid to safety.

Back at their home in Cromer, Sue was doing some gardening while the boys watched *Blue Peter* on the television. Suddenly Chris came rushing out to tell his mother that, 'Dad's plane is on fire'. *Blue Peter* had been stopped for a news bulletin about a BOAC aircraft that had caught fire on take-off and, having returned to Heathrow, was still burning on a runway there. Sue managed to reassure her sons that Daddy was quite safe as he had left for his flight much earlier in the day. However, moments later she did begin to worry when she received a phone call from someone at BOAC asking if her husband was at home. When she replied that he was taking a flight to Australia, the caller thanked her and hung up. Some time later that evening she received another call, this time from John telling her that there had been an incident at Heathrow and that because of it, his flight had been delayed but he would not be coming home. Relieved, and not yet realizing the horror that John had just been through, she again told the boys that there was nothing to worry about and started doing some ironing while she waited for more news.

The surviving crew from flight BA712 were all given a check-up by doctors at the airline's medical centre. John was examined by a very popular doctor, Alan Sibbald. He could see that John had no real physical injuries apart from some rope burns to his hands, sustained when he slid down the rope from the cockpit window, but he was obviously badly shocked and suffering from smoke inhalation and the doctor told him that he could not drive himself home. He asked where John lived and when he told him, said that he himself lived in Hertfordshire and that he would take him home. He drove him back to Cromer and, although he had not lied when he said he lived in Hertfordshire, he had omitted to tell John that his home was actually in Rickmansworth, in the southern part of the county, and over 40 miles away from Cromer in the north. Not only did he take the time and trouble to ensure that the young pilot arrived home safely, he also took him for a drink at the local pub before reaching John's house. Unconcerned that he was accompanying a man smelling of smoke and burnt aircraft fuel, in a filthy uniform, his face covered with black smudges from the fire, and who was attracting curious stares from other customers, Dr Sibbald marched up to the bar, ordered two large glasses of Scotch and brought them back to John with instructions to drink both. John gratefully accepted the drinks which, he said, 'Didn't touch the sides!' and, when he had finished, the doctor took him home. He told John to go and have a wash which he did, having first made the doctor promise that he wouldn't leave until he came back. While John was upstairs, Dr Sibbald spoke briefly to Sue, relieved to learn that she had trained as a nurse and would know how to care for her husband. He gave her some pills that he said would calm John who was still in shock and needed as much rest as he could get, before quietly leaving the house to drive himself home.

Despite the danger in which he had been, and the terrifying accident that he had survived that day, John's lasting memory of 8 April 1968 was of the care taken by Alan Sibbald. As he says:

I was a very junior chap at that stage. I was a second officer on board the aircraft and I had only been with the airline for about 18 months. Dr Sibbald was a very senior medical officer. He was just the kindest man; he took so much care and trouble over me.

He was a man I admired hugely. He was a great friend to all the BOAC pilots and he really understood what being an airline pilot was all about. He was also great fun socially and one of his party tricks was to stand on his head and drink a pint of beer; he never spilt a drop! He was a wonderful man.

John is also of the opinion that it was check captain Geoff Moss who saved his life. Had it not been for his observations of the burning wing and engine, and the fact that he managed to persuade Cliff Taylor not to waste time by insisting on a landing on runway 28L, he thinks that they may all have perished that day; perhaps along with many more people on the ground.

BOAC held its own enquiry into what had gone wrong with its aircraft and there was a major investigation conducted by the Board of Trade, both of which took several months to complete. When their findings were made public, it was disclosed that the accident had occurred because the 5th stage low pressure compressor wheel of the number 2 engine had failed due to metal fatigue. BOAC's emergency procedures in cases of fire were found to be inadequate and confusing, and the airport's fire services were heavily criticized, both of which were changed as a result of the accident.

On 24 May 1968, six weeks after the fire, all of the surviving crew, except the flight engineer, whose part in the incident was still being investigated, were invited to a reception where they were presented with certificates of commendation by the airline and told that they would each receive extra leave to take a holiday for two at a destination of their choice, with all expenses being paid by BOAC. Not having had a proper holiday as a couple since the disastrous trip to Zermatt in 1963, John and Sue were delighted to be able to go away again and chose to spend their holiday in Trinidad and Tobago, where some of John's distant relations lived and whom they were able to visit while they were there.

The day that BOAC chose for the reception to present the certificates to the crew would have been Jane Harrison's 23rd birthday. The following year she was posthumously awarded the George Cross, one of only four such medals to have been directly awarded to women and the only one in peacetime.

Having survived what was a major accident it would have been easy to think that fate would now be kind to the young pilot but, two months after the Whisky Echo tragedy, John's life was again in danger.

At midnight on 15 June 1968, BOAC pilots went on strike. Their contract of service had expired nine months before and although negotiations about pay and conditions had been taking place, the matter had not been satisfactorily resolved. There were many people who had sympathy for the pilots, since their new contract was so much overdue. The British Airline Pilots' Association (BALPA) had instructed its members to restrict cooperation with the airline in the four weeks before the strike began but, although progress had been made in the discussions, it was unlikely that a settlement would be made within the timeframe demanded by BALPA and so the strike was called and went ahead.

With time on his hands, and in an attempt to keep himself employed while the matter was being resolved, John accepted an assignment to fly a BBC film crew to France in a twin engined Piper Aztec, which had seating for five people. The weather was bad and John was flying on instruments through torrential rain when, while making his approach to a small French airfield, the Aztec crashed into the ground. John was wearing his seat belt but it did not include any shoulder straps and as the aircraft hit the ground he was thrown forward onto the instrument panel. His face was badly cut, he broke some of his teeth and split his lip, before managing to get his passengers and himself out of the wreckage. Then he collapsed. He remembers waking up in a French hospital bed and seeing several pairs of eyes staring at him – they belonged to the BBC crew whose injuries were far less serious than his own. He said later that his face must have looked like a Frankenstein horror movie production, covered in cuts and very bruised.

John couldn't understand how he had hit the ground as his altimeter had shown that he was still flying at 300 feet when the crash occurred. The French authorities were not interested in finding out the cause of the accident as it was a private aeroplane and no one had been killed. They simply recorded it as pilot error. This was, of course, a disaster for John as it would ruin his reputation as a pilot and would certainly cost him his job at BOAC. The owner of the Aztec, a man called Richard Holbrook, flew out to France and spoke to the authorities about the lack of an investigation. He obviously wanted to know if something had been wrong with his aircraft but he also stressed the fact that John's career would be ruined if they refused to conduct an enquiry and just put it down to pilot error. His words eventually persuaded them and they agreed to begin an investigation.

When the pilots' strike was over, John was still not well enough to return to work and had to explain to BOAC what had happened and how he had been injured. He was immediately suspended, pending the results of the French enquiry. It was a very worrying time for him as he knew that if they could find no other reason for the accident, he would be blamed and his days as a commercial pilot would be over. The fact that the French had only started an investigation under pressure from the aircraft's owner did not bode well for a successful outcome for John.

He was forced to wait for several weeks before the result of the enquiry was made known but when it was, he was completely exonerated. The key to what had happened was that much of the flight had been undertaken in very heavy rain. It transpired that the Piper Aztec was known to have had some problems in these weather conditions before. When the aeroplane that John had been flying was examined, the altimeter was found to have been full of water, which had fed its way up the static line and got into the altimeter case. Because of this it was showing an error of 300-400 feet and when John thought he was still at a height of 300 feet he was actually just about to smash into the ground.

When BOAC learnt the results of the enquiry John's suspension was immediately lifted and he was able to return to work. This was the third time that his safety had been put at risk in aviation accidents, none of which was his fault and, as he says, three times is more than enough for one lifetime.

# Chapter 11

# The Keen Sense of Living

*Life consists less in length of days than in the keen sense of living.*

Jean-Jacques Rousseau, 1712–1778, French essayist, novelist
and philosopher

Despite the satisfactory outcome of the French enquiry into the crash of
the Piper Aztec, and the lifting of the BOAC suspension, it had been a
very worrying time. Not only had John's entire career been at stake, his
life, and that of Sue, Tim and Chris, would have been changed completely
had the French authorities insisted on laying the blame for the accident
at his feet. With a verdict of pilot error he would have found it very hard
to get another position as a pilot and, with a mortgage and school fees to
pay, life would have become extremely stressful and difficult.

The last thing that John and Sue wanted was to lose their home which
had become a very happy place for them. They loved the old cottage, and
the peaceful village of Cromer where they had good neighbours; it was
the perfect place to bring up the boys, who were also happy there. Chris
recalled that it was, '… a very happy household, where we had lots of
fun, laughter and friends'.

Prior to the move to Cromer, Tim had been at several nursery schools
and his parents had looked at St Andrew's Church of England Primary
School in Hitchin. A very quiet child, Tim was not happy at his nursery
school; he was painfully shy and didn't speak. His parents were not unduly
worried as they were aware that children develop at different rates but,
by the time he went to the primary school, Tim was still not doing as

well as they would have expected and they began to be very concerned about him. When Sue met his teachers they could offer no reasons for his inability to communicate but she sensed that they thought he had a specific problem and was not just a slow starter. She had taken him to a doctor who tested his hearing and eyesight and found that both were perfectly normal. He was also of the opinion that the little boy was not suffering from any mental problems. His lack of progress remained a mystery to everyone.

When he was 5½ years old John and Sue decided to send Tim to a different school where they hoped he would be happier and would begin to learn. They had heard good reports of St Christopher in Letchworth; a private, progressive co-educational school, one of whose buildings had been the childhood home of actor Sir Laurence Olivier, and whose primary school was run using the methods pioneered by Dr Maria Montessori which were to:

> … [give] the world a scientific method, practical and tested, for bringing forth the very best in young human beings. She taught adults how to respect individual differences, and to emphasize social interaction and the education of the whole personality rather than the teaching of a specific body of knowledge …
>
> The high level of academic achievement so common in Montessori schools is a natural outcome of experience in such a supportive environment. The Montessori method of education is a model which serves the needs of children of all levels of mental and physical ability as they live and learn in a natural, mixed-age group which is very much like the society they will live in as adults.[1]

At first Tim found it hard to make friends and still had problems communicating but he began to learn a little and started to enjoy school a lot more than he had done previously. The headmaster was very supportive and told Sue and John that their son could remain in the junior part of the school until he, himself, was ready to move on to the senior section.

In the meantime Sue took him for yearly check ups. It was not a pleasant experience as these were done by doctors who often had no experience of children with learning problems and had no suitable advice to give. It wasn't until the late 1970s that educational psychologists took over from medical doctors, the task of assessing children's educational needs. During the 1960s, when Tim was being examined annually, the experience was, at best, unproductive and at worst, depressing and sometimes offensive. Sue recalled one doctor accusing her of trying to make out that her son had a problem when, in reality, the problem was in her mind and there was nothing wrong with him.

When Tim was 8 years old however, he was examined by an Indian doctor who did have some relevant experience and told Sue that he believed Tim was dyslexic. Dyslexia was then not as well known as it is today. Nevertheless, the condition had been recognized, albeit by other names, since the nineteenth century when it was referred to as word blindness and, at the start of the twentieth century as strephosymbolia. The doctor assured Sue that it did not mean that Tim was backward or unintelligent – quite the opposite. Many people suffering from the condition have above average intelligence. It was simply that his brain handled information about letters and sounds in a different manner from the way other children's brains did. He told Sue that there were ways to deal with it and ensure that Tim could learn. He cited two famous examples of people with dyslexia – Sir Winston Churchill and actress Susan Hampshire. He might also have mentioned the equally famous physicist and Nobel Prize winner, Albert Einstein, and the author Hans Christian Andersen.

At last there seemed to be a real way forward for Tim. He was introduced to Rosemary, a teacher of dyslexic children, who began to teach him using a keyboard. Dyslexic children often cannot hold pens or pencils in such a way as to allow them to write, but the keyboard was something with which Tim could cope and he started to learn and to enjoy doing so. After his difficult early years when he was unable to articulate the problems he was having and could not understand the reasons why letters and numbers appeared in such a jumbled mess, the little boy began to blossom.

Chris did not attend a primary school until after the move to Cromer when he was enrolled at St Lawrence C of E Primary School, in Ardeley, where he did very well. He was a very bright little boy and, although dyslexia often affects more than one member in a family, he did not suffer from it himself. He and Tim had a good rapport and Chris often helped his elder brother by speaking for him when Tim was unable to do so for himself. Tim was able to remain at St Christopher after the move to Cromer although this did involve a journey of around eight miles each way and it was in the opposite direction to Chris's school. It was, however, a small price to pay for his parents when compared with the vast improvement in Tim's life.

Although John was away a lot during the boys' early years, when he did get home he liked to play with them. Chris remembers that he was a very 'hands on' father in that respect. He would sometimes bring them small presents from wherever he had been and Chris enjoyed the cricket and other outdoor pursuits, usually of a sporting nature, that he played with his father. Unlike his younger brother, Tim was not good at ball games – dyslexic children often have problems with these types of skills – but he did enjoy walking and climbing and learnt to ride a bicycle. He also started to draw rather good pictures, especially of animals which, unlike many children's artistic efforts, did look like the little creatures he was intending to portray. Having begun to lose the incapacitating shyness that had marred his earlier years, he decided that he would like to join the Cub Scouts in the nearby village of Walkern. It was a decision that brought him much happiness and camaraderie, and from which he gained an enormous amount of self-confidence over the years that followed.

When he was 10 years old Chris was entered for exams to gain a scholarship to Eton. The education department of Hertfordshire County Council had offered four scholarships to the public school but, although Chris could have had one of them, he really didn't want to go to Eton. He did, however, want to go to a boarding school – just not to Eton – so his parents enrolled him at Oakham School in Rutland. Founded in 1584 as a school for boys, it admitted girls for the first time in 1971, the year before Chris went there, and latterly has been described in the Good Schools Guide as '… a privileged but unpretentious and non-spoiling start in life for the lucky. All-rounders who also like work will get the best out of it but most will love every minute here.'

Chris did enjoy being at Oakham. He was particularly good at sport and became a keen rugby and squash player. He also enjoyed his visits home and recalled an occasion when his father took him back to Oakham after one such visit. John had bought a Citroën GS which, according to Chris, his father considered to be '… the best car ever'. The car was parked in the garage while John loaded Chris's bags into the boot. Having completed the task John then got into the driving seat and began to reverse the car out of the garage. A very loud crunch alerted him to the fact that the boot door, which he had forgotten to close before beginning to move, had collided with the top of the garage door frame and had parted company with the rest of the car.

Whether this was simply bad luck, or the result of having too many other things on his mind at the time, is difficult to judge but, over the years, John has acquired a reputation for being rather accident and disaster prone. His close friend, Patrick Cliff, laughingly advises everyone not to take holidays with John as he regards it as being a 'dangerous occupation'. As an example he cites a holiday in Mauritius during which John and Sue spent one week with him and his wife, Ruth. The weather had been perfectly calm but as soon as John and Sue arrived, the island was battered by a cyclone. Sometime later the two couples spent another holiday together on the island of Lamu in Kenya and Patrick swears that John and Sue nearly drowned him while trying to teach him to snorkel. When one also considers what happened in Zermatt, perhaps Patrick's advice is appropriate.

Tim had also been given the opportunity to become a boarder at St Christopher but had decided that he would rather stay at home and travel to school each day. He had remained in the junior part of the school for only one year longer than his peers and learnt to read and write, although his spelling was not always correct and his handwriting, over which he had to take such trouble, would have been regarded, by those who did not know what he had been through, as untidy. It didn't matter. He had been freed from the prison in which his mind had held him and his life changed completely. He made friends and became a popular class member. He discovered that he was good at maths and when he went into the senior school studied for his GCE exams. He was given extra time for these exams and took subjects such as English, maths, geography and biology. Instead of leaving at the earliest possible time, Tim remained at school and, as he enjoyed cooking, decided he would like to become a chef. He obtained a place at Westminster College which he intended to take up after the summer break of 1977.

As the children grew up and became settled and happy at their respective schools, Sue thought that she would like to return to work. She didn't want to go back to nursing and decided instead to train as a teacher. When her training was complete she obtained a position at Little Munden C of E Primary School where she taught for two years before moving to Walkern C of E Primary School.

John, having narrowly escaped the destruction of his own career in 1968, remained a first officer flying on the Boeing 707 for a further 2½ years. He recalls that the 707 was:

> … a tricky aeroplane to fly. It didn't have absolutely benign handling characteristics. It was very prone to a thing called Dutch rolling – a sort of roll-yaw coupling – and it was a difficult aeroplane to land very smoothly. It was quite a demanding aeroplane so it was rewarding in a sense. But it was the first aeroplane I went on to in BOAC so it was an important stage in my transition from a military pilot to my commercial airline career.
>
> It came as a great shock to do this navigation stuff. I can't say I enjoyed it. My attempts at navigating and plotting on a plotting chart were something akin to a spider crawling around all over the place, having first dipped its feet into red ink. But I never got lost.
>
> Then I went onto the 747 and – hallelujah, praise be! – it had inertial navigation. That's when I first came across INS and suddenly navigation became redundant and there were no more requirements for flight navigators.

John was posted to the Boeing 747 fleet in March 1971 and was sent on one of the first courses that the airline held for this aircraft. His particular course was conducted in Shannon and Sue went with him. He enjoyed it enormously: 'We had a very good time over there. It was fascinating. Being on a brand new aeroplane with new navigation systems and new avionics was really very interesting.'

In March 1974, while John was still a first officer on the Boeing 747, BOAC and BEA merged and the new company became British Airways. For John the time he spent on the 747 fleet was enjoyable and he thought the 747 to be:

> … a lovely aeroplane to fly despite of what it looks like. It doesn't look exactly aerodynamic – a great big bulbous aeroplane – but it flies absolutely beautifully. It really was a delightful aeroplane to handle both on the ground and in the air.

Happily for John, and for Sue and the boys, the time spent flying 747s was peaceful and didn't include any dangerous situations such as those with the 707 Whisky Echo, or the Piper Aztec. The camaraderie that existed between crew members did provide a lot of fun however, especially during the overseas stopovers, as one incident illustrates.

John arrived in Singapore with a flight engineer called David Wales and a captain to whom neither he nor David related on a personal level. John described the flight engineer as being, 'a very colourful character, red-haired, married and divorced more than once and a great puller of crumpet' and, having checked in to their hotel, the pair arranged to meet that evening and go out rather than have to spend the evening making polite conversation with the captain. When John turned up, David's suggestion for how they might spend the evening was not what he had expected. Climbing into a taxi, David said to the driver, 'Take us to the very best brothel in Singapore, my good man'. Soon they arrived at an establishment called the Sun Moon Lake Health Centre, a name that John says will be forever embedded in his brain. Since David had not told John what he intended to do, the latter was surprised when he marched up to a Chinese man sitting at the reception desk in the foyer. The ensuing conversation went something like this:

> Good evening. My name is David Wales and this is my associate John Hutchinson. We'd like to speak to the owner of this brothel please.

The man wanted to know why they needed to speak to the owner. It was a question about which John also wondered and when the answer came he found it difficult to stop himself laughing. David, with a perfectly straight face, told the man:

> We own a brothel in Teddington, Middlesex, England and we want to set up an exchange deal.

The receptionist left his desk and showed John and David into the office of the owner, a man named William Wong. Having again explained the reason for their visit, they were invited to take a seat while Mr Wong arranged for several crates of Tiger beer to be fetched so that he could properly entertain his important guests while they negotiated a deal for an exchange visit between the ladies of Teddington, Middlesex, England

and those from Singapore. After a lot of discussion and the consumption of a large amount of beer, during which time John was becoming more and more agitated, imagining himself face down in a monsoon drain with a knife in his back when Mr Wong realized that the whole thing was an elaborate joke, David suddenly declared:

Well, William, old boy, we're getting on fine here. I think we've got the makings of a deal but we really need to have a look at some of your ladies.

Several ladies were summoned and David looked at them before turning to the owner and saying:

I'm sorry, William. You haven't got the picture at all. At our brothel in Teddington, Middlesex, England, we cater for the absolute cream of British society. Our clientele are bishops, high court judges, peers of the realm. They're the absolute top flight of British society and they are used to the best that life has to offer. I'm afraid that the ladies that you are showing us are not really up to scratch at all.

By this time more beer had been offered and consumed and John and David were given the tour of the premises that they requested. David was again forthright in his opinions of what was on offer:

Bloody hell! Look at that bed; the springs are falling out of the bottom of it. The wallpaper is peeling off the walls and plaster is falling from the ceiling. You haven't got bidet or shower facilities. No, no, no, William. I'm sorry. The whole thing has been a terrible mistake.

Mistake or not, William himself was now extremely anxious to complete the deal with the owners of the brothel from Teddington, Middlesex, England. As David and John headed towards the door William galloped after them and once more they were ushered into his office where he promised to redecorate and re-equip the whole building so that the deal could go ahead. David pretended to consider the situation and then said:

Well, William. Tomorrow we leave for Sydney because we are internationalizing our brothel business and we want to have a look at the Australian scene. We will be back in Singapore in five days time and if you have managed to redecorate and re-equip the entire place then I think we will be able to sign a deal.

Mr Wong heaved a sigh of relief, offered another Tiger beer and then called a taxi for which he paid, to return his guests to their hotel.

Needless to say, on their return to Singapore they did not go anywhere near to the Sun Moon Lake Health Centre and John often wonders whether or not the owner had managed to completely refurbish the premises during the five days that he and David were supposed to have been 'having a look at the Australian scene'. For a long time afterwards, whenever he was in Singapore John wore dark glasses and kept a very low profile. As he said afterwards:

> To con a Chinaman I thought was a sort of pinnacle of con artistry; to con a Chinese brothel owner was, I think, the absolute ultimate. It was definitely one of the more memorable incidents in my flying career with British Airways. David was a brilliant flight engineer but an absolute nutcase!

After four years on the 747 John was offered a change by British Airways:

> I loved the 747 – it was a terrific aeroplane – and I stayed on it until 1975 when I got the chance of a command course. I could either go onto the VC10 or the 707, either fleet had command vacancies and I thought, 'Oh, well, I'll go for the VC10; I might as well get another aeroplane on my licence'.

The VC10 course began in October 1975 in Prestwick and this aircraft also became a favourite for John. As well as being a lovely aircraft to fly it also gave him the opportunity to visit places he had not flown to before such as the Gulf states in the Middle East and several cities on the continent of Africa.

Designed for BOAC to operate on their Far Eastern and African routes, the VC10 had made its maiden flight in 1962. The airline had always favoured American aircraft and would have been happy to rely on the Boeing 707 but the government wanted to support the British aviation industry and, since it financed the airline, the VC10 went into service with BOAC in April 1964, its first flight being between London and Lagos. It was joined a year later by the larger Super VC10.

The aircraft did have some advantages over the Boeing 707 – its rear-mounted engines, which left its wings clear of any obstructions, allowed it to generate more lift than the American aircraft, enabling it to use shorter runways than the 707. Although at first very useful in allowing it to operate to cities that could not be reached by a 707, that advantage was eventually lost when the Boeing 747 was introduced and many international airports extended their runways to cope with the much larger, wide-bodied jet. The engine location of the VC10 did ensure a much reduced noise inside the cabin which proved to be very popular with passengers, as did the specially designed undercarriage which guaranteed a much more comfortable landing. The VC10 had, as John recalled, 'a lot of passenger appeal'.

While he was on the VC10 course John met another pilot called Jock Lowe and the two men became friends. Jock described John as 'a great airman who knew how to get on with everyone'. Some years later their paths would cross again but, by April 1976, John had completed his VC10 course and finally became a British Airways captain, in command of one of the most beautiful British airliners ever to grace the skies.

During that year, 1976, Tim had the opportunity to go on a trip to the foothills of the Himalayas that had been organized by his Scout group. He was very keen to go and so John arranged a British Airways ticket for him to Delhi. He had never flown by himself before but he arrived safely in the Indian capital to be met by the Scout group. Because it was known that he wanted to become a chef, Tim was appointed quartermaster for the trip. Although he had been abroad before with his family, this was his first overseas visit without his parents and brother and he coped very well. He wrote a letter to them from India. While he was away, they had all gone to France for a short holiday and, although Tim's letter was brief, it did let them know that he was having a very good time. When he came back he was able to tell his grandfather, Wynne, all about the visit he had made to Kashmir and Wynne was pleased to be able to discuss this with his grandson, as it was a place he also knew. It brought the two closer together, as Wynne – having been the headmaster at St Hilda's for many years – had far more experience of talking to girls than boys. As a result of his Indian adventure Tim became a Queen's Scout and his family were justifiably very proud of him and his great achievement. He received the prestigious award at a ceremony held at the headquarters of the Scout movement in Buckingham Palace Road in London.

Tim found a Saturday job with the local butcher, delivering the customers' orders on his bike. He was a favourite with the ladies of the village who thought him to be a very polite young man. He also decided that he would cycle to school, which his parents allowed him to do but bought him a bike with a little motor on the back to make his journey easier.

Tim, with his new found independence, threw himself enthusiastically into all kinds of activities. He became involved in the plays that the school produced. He didn't want to act in them but enjoyed helping with the scenery and other tasks behind the scenes. One of his fellow students at St Christopher was a girl called Sally Pearson. She remembered Tim as a tall, good-looking boy – he was 6 feet 1 inch – who had been through a lot of problems because of his dyslexia but had triumphed over his difficulties. They both had a love of drama and Sally went on to be an actress when her school days were over.

Tim had celebrated his 17th birthday in February 1977 and he had made up his mind that for the remainder of his time at school, before leaving to take up his place at Westminster College, he would like to be a boarder. John and Sue had agreed that he could do so and he was planning to move away from home for the first time after the Easter break.

Wynne's 67th birthday was on 5 March – a Saturday – and the whole family planned to go to St Hilda's to see him that day. Chris was home from school and John did not have any flights that might make him miss the visit. When the time came for them all to leave for Harpenden Tim asked if they thought that his grandfather would mind very much if he didn't go. He asked them to explain to Wynne that he would visit the next weekend but that he wanted to go to school that day as there was scenery to paint for the latest school production. His parents promised to pass on his message and he set off for school on his motorized bike.

On the way back from St Hilda's just before 6 p.m. John wondered if it would be a good idea to drive via Letchworth to see if Tim would like a lift home. While he and Sue were trying to decide, Chris pointed out that his brother had gone to school on his bike and that if they called for him he would have to leave it at school and that they would have to take him back to collect it later. They all agreed that it would be best to leave things as they were and so they drove home. They were not worried about Tim as he was very reliable and they knew he would come home as soon as he had finished the painting he had gone to do.

By 9 p.m. Tim had not arrived and they had begun to worry. Then there was a knock at the door. In relief Sue thought that Tim must have forgotten his key but, when she opened the door, she found her neighbour, accompanied by two young policemen. The policemen had been told that John was a pilot and was often away from home, so they had been to the neighbour to enquire if she knew whether John was at home at that time, as they had some news that they didn't want to give Sue if she was alone. They asked the neighbour if she would come with them to the house. Hearing this and seeing their neighbour's ashen face, John and Sue knew that something terrible had happened.

The policemen came in and asked if they had a son called Tim who had a motorized bike, although they obviously knew the answer, having spoken to the neighbour. Dreading what they might be about to hear, John and Sue confirmed that they did have a son called Tim and that he had been expected home earlier in the evening but had still not arrived. One of the young men then told them that Tim had been involved in an accident. They immediately asked where he had been taken so that they could go and visit him but were gently told that Tim had not survived the accident. He had been hit, head-on, by a car and had been taken to Lister Hospital in Stevenage. In a daze they both listened while the young policeman explained that there had been a group of young people creating a fuss at a bus stop. Tim had glanced at the scene as he went past, veering slightly towards the centre of the road as he did so, and the driver of a car coming from the opposite direction had done the same. The man was in a hurry to get home with the fish and chips that he had just bought and didn't realize that he had swerved into the centre of the road at speed until he hit Tim's bike. Tim's neck was broken and he died instantly. That it had happened so quickly and that he therefore couldn't have suffered, was his parents' only consolation.

While one of the policemen remained at the house in case Chris, who had been tired and had gone to bed, awoke, John and Sue went with the other to the hospital where Tim had to be formally identified. At the hospital Sue was told that only John was needed to make the identification and although she wanted to accompany him she was stopped by hospital staff. No doubt they believed they were being kind to the young man's mother in insisting that his father make the identification but Sue will forever regret that she wasn't allowed the chance to say goodbye to her lovely son. It would have been kinder to both parents if they could have been together. Heartbroken by Tim's loss, they each needed the support that the other could have given them at that moment. John, however, bravely made the identification of his son alone and returned to Sue to tell her that Tim looked very peaceful and that there were no signs of any injury to him.

They asked if it would be possible for any of Tim's organs to be donated to help someone else but were told that because he had died earlier that evening, it was too late for that to happen. It was possible, however, to use Tim's corneas and so one of his lasting legacies was the gift of sight to an unknown person.

Sue and John were taken home by the policeman and were thankful to learn that Chris was still asleep. They left him sleeping, allowing him a few more hours of peace before his world was shattered, as theirs had been, by learning of the loss of his brother.

Early the next morning Chris was told and then Sue and John went to see the Revd Roe who, it being a Sunday, was taking an early church service. As he emerged from St Helen's Church at the end of the service they broke the news to him and he was, Sue recalled, 'wonderful' despite the pain of losing his eldest grandchild. They then went on to St Hilda's to tell Wynne, Michael, Mary and Viola who were also distraught. When they arrived home they found that their neighbour had told their friends in Cromer, sparing them that ordeal but there were so many other things to which they had to attend.

The following days were passed in a blur of misery during which time Sue and John were 'shell-shocked' but outwardly calm and were able to deal with the numerous practical arrangements that had to be made. Tim's friend, Sally Pearson who would, some years later, become Chris Hutchinson's wife, recalled that Sue had put on her 'public face' in order to be able to cope, while beneath the surface, John had just 'crumbled'.

Neither John nor Sue could sleep properly and were becoming exhausted. Sue went to see her doctor and was given some Valium to help her but, after taking the pills for only two days, threw them away as they were making her feel worse. She believes that it was the effort that they had to make, to ensure that all the arrangements were completed properly that kept them both going. Their friends and neighbours helped by making things as easy as possible for them – informing people, making tea, arranging flowers. They began to receive letters and cards; so many that the local postmen got together and decided, unofficially, to make two deliveries each day to their house. Everyone was incredibly kind to them in those first few days.

One of the activities that Tim had enjoyed was bell ringing at the fourteenth century church of St Mary in the village of Rushden, two miles to the north of Cromer. With that in mind, Sue and John decided that he should be buried in the churchyard there. They met with the Rector at Rushden and the service was organized.

On the day of the funeral the church was full to overflowing, both with mourners and with flowers. Tim's uncle, Roger Noyes, a newly ordained minister who was married to Sue's sister Pippa, had been asked to give the eulogy. Years later he remembered that:

> There was no one place to speak from, without scores of people at one's back. Many of Tim's school friends were packed into the Chancel beside the altar. Thus the directness of 'eye contact', to extend human sympathy, was not impossible but difficult. I seem to remember speaking from the Chancel steps but turning constantly to face everyone by turn.

Roger began, at the request of Sue, John and Chris, by thanking everyone for coming that afternoon and for their many kindnesses during the sad days since Tim's loss. He continued:

> That this is a terrible dark day there can be no doubt but you all, the young and those older alike, you all have lifted a corner of that darkness and let in a light, the light of human friendship and love, by your presence here today. Here, both to remember and honour Tim, and to care for his family. For that – thank you – you have begun to make the day more hopeful.

There is, perhaps, another reason why the sadness and darkness of Tim's death should not totally overcome us. For surely, no life that is given by God – no matter how long it is lived – can be without purpose. We need to be clear about the goodness God has been working in the years of Tim's young life. We need to recall the details of the goodness that was vibrant in the quality of Tim's life and achievements. And, in so remembering, then to use this occasion to make our own determination not to forget. Not to forget by taking that remembered goodness we met in Tim, into ourselves; into the heart of our daily lives and so, through us, offered on to others in our future. In that way nothing begun by God in Tim's life is lost; nothing can be said to have been wasted. The quiet goodness known and worked by Tim will go on and endure.

So, perhaps then, please do not be overwhelmed by tragedy and despair but have the courage to remember the quiet beginnings of a fine young man – a cheerful, willing and trusting, trustful friend – one who enjoyed the doing for others he learnt in the Scouts, one who loved laughter and gave loyalty and, as one of his school friends said to me yesterday, perhaps there is Tim's liking for cooking and different things to eat to fit in there somewhere.

But then it's not for me to remember what I knew and liked in a nephew, or as John and Sue's son and Chris's brother, it is what each one of you, please, remember with affection and kindness that is important now.

Together we all saw the goodness of God growing into life in Tim. Now is the time for being glad, together, to have known Tim and making that gladness and goodness real in the promises we make for our future life.

# Chapter 12

# Tragedy in Life

*There's no tragedy in life like the death of a child. Things never get back to the way they were.*

Dwight D. Eisenhower, 1890–1969, 34th President of the USA

Both John and Sue had been given compassionate leave when their respective employers had been told about Tim death but after the funeral John felt that he had to get back to flying as soon as possible. British Airways suggested to him that he might like to take Sue on the next flight that he made and gave him the choice of a trip to either Cairo or to Nairobi and the Seychelles. Grateful for the kindness that was being shown to them, they chose the latter. They flew off to Nairobi with John as the operating captain and then onwards to the Seychelles where Sue remained while John took the aircraft back to Nairobi before returning to join her in the Seychelles where they stayed for a two-week break. John had told the cockpit crew about Tim, and Sue told one of the stewardesses. All the crew members were very kind to the couple, listening to them when they wanted to talk but not forcing any conversation and, when it was time for them to return to England, both felt that they had benefitted from the trip: the two weeks in the sun had been good for Sue, and John had needed the therapy that flying provided.

For 14 year old Chris, Tim's funeral had passed in a blur. He was angry that he had lost his brother but didn't want the sympathy that friends and family tried to give him. He felt that, after everything his elder brother had been through in his early life, it should have been he who died, not

139

Tim, and he felt guilty that he was still alive. He wanted his life to get back to normal as soon as possible but, in the absence of the bereavement counselling that is available today, he didn't know how to cope with his loss.

The previous year he had been on an exchange visit to Germany where he stayed at the home of a pilot who flew for the German airline, Lufthansa, and whose son, Thomas, was a similar age to him. It had been arranged that the boy would visit Chris during his Easter holidays and, although John and Sue were willing for the visit to go ahead, believing that it might help Chris, they felt they had to tell the boy's parents about what had happened and leave it to them to decide whether or not their son should make the trip to England. Happily it was decided that Thomas should come and his visit did provide a welcome diversion for Chris.

While John went off on another flight Sue took both boys to stay with her 'Aunt' Norah, who had moved from the house in Crondall where Tim had been born, to Beominster in Dorset. On a visit to the beach at Charmouth one day, while Sue sat in a deckchair reading, Chris and Thomas searched for the fossils that are easy to find along this stretch of the Jurassic coast of Dorset. After a short while, when Sue looked for the two boys, she was unable to see them on the beach or in the water. Terrified that something had happened to them, she stood up and looked towards the land where she spotted two small figures three-quarters of the way up the cliff. Knowing how unstable the cliffs were and how dangerous it was to attempt to climb them, she began to fear that she might also lose her younger son and his German friend. A man on the beach saw her looking upwards and also spotted the two boys. He came across to her and told her that he would go and call his brother-in-law who lived nearby and ask him to drive to the top of the cliff. He then shouted to the boys to continue climbing and not try to come back to the beach. The man's relative had arrived at the cliff top before the boys reached it and was there to help them as they emerged from their climb and were reunited with Sue. Both boys said that they had had a terrific time and neither seemed to realize what danger they had been in nor the anxiety they had caused Sue. Afterwards, when he had had a chance to think about it, Chris apologized to his mother for having done something so stupid.

He was anxious to get back to school and, after Thomas returned to Germany, departed for Oakham quite cheerfully. John and Sue felt that he was beginning to come to terms with the loss of Tim and were confident that with the help of his housemaster and the headmaster, who Chris had described as being 'fantastic', he would be better able to get back to normal at school than if he had remained at home.

Chris, according to his own account, had 'charged around' trying to get his life back to normal again but, although he had wanted to return to school and the company of his friends, nothing was the same anymore. He gave up the sport that he loved and seemed to have lost his way. Just after the annual school fête which he had told his parents not to attend, Sue received a telephone call from his housemaster to tell her that Chris was in hospital. He had been taken there to have his stomach pumped after he had been found behind the gym with an empty bottle. It turned out to be a bottle of sherry that he had won at the school fête and which he had intended to give to his father.

In June, when Chris had his 15th birthday, he was going to be confirmed. His parents and godparents were due to attend the service but the day before it was to take place, John and Sue received another call from the school, from the chaplain this time, who told them that Chris had decided that he didn't want to be confirmed. Unlike the impromptu drinking session however, this decision was well thought out. He had simply told the chaplain that he didn't believe in it anymore and didn't want to take part in a ceremony that would mean nothing to him.

After the African holiday Sue returned to work. The staff at the school had been very understanding but the most surprising show of support came from a little boy who was in the class that Sue taught. He was usually a little tearaway but on the day that Sue came back to the classroom he came up to her, put his hand in hers and told her that he was very sorry to know that her little boy had died. It was a difficult moment for Sue but the child's touching gesture was one that she really appreciated and which she has never forgotten.

Soon after returning to the classroom Sue had to take time off again because she suddenly lost her voice. Investigations revealed that she had polyps on her vocal cords and she was told that she would have to have an operation to remove them. The operation was done but it took some time before she was able to speak again so she was unable to return to school.

Then, in July, John was given the opportunity to join the elite band of Concorde pilots whose total number, over the working life of the aircraft, was less than that of America's astronauts. He accepted eagerly and believes that:

... it was a wonderful healing aid after Tim's death – it made me focus on something else.

The great majority of the pilots who went on to Concorde did so because they loved flying and Concorde was the absolute ultimate thing that you could fly.

His posting to the Concorde fleet came through in August and he began the long period of training to convert from subsonic to supersonic passenger flight at Filton, north of Bristol where, eight years before, the first flight of Concorde from a British airfield had taken place. The move, coming as it did so soon after Tim's death was, perhaps, the one thing that helped John to survive the loss of his son. Sue went with him to Filton and, by resting her vocal cords for several weeks, recovered from her operation and regained her voice. She had began to think about her future. Teaching no longer seemed as important to her as it once had and her heart was no longer in it. By February 1978, the first anniversary of Tim's death, she had decided to give it up.

The time they spent away from the family home also gave them a chance to think about what they would do in the future. Although the house in Cromer had been a very happy family home over the years, the village was becoming busier and therefore not as peaceful as it had once been – they had lost two much loved cats to the increasing traffic flow and now that their son had gone they no longer felt the same about the house.

John wasn't able to talk about Tim and, over 30 years later, still finds it difficult, although he does say that he thinks of him every single day of his life. Sue wondered what they should do with Tim's room. They didn't want it to become an untouched shrine but it would have been hard to remove his belongings and use the room for any other purpose. They eventually came to the decision to sell the house, believing that it was the only way forward for them, as the house and the village where the boys had grown up now held too many sad memories.

While they were searching for a new house they were told about a row of four tiny cottages in a village a few miles to the north of Cromer. Hertfordshire Preservation Society had bought the cottages, which were believed to have been built largely in the fifteenth century but with later additions, and had put a preservation order in place. They had not had the funds available to restore the building which needed a lot of work and so the cottages were put up for sale again and were purchased by a local craftsman, Peter Hardy, who began the restoration, planning to turn them into one home. John and Sue went to look at the building but decided against buying. Although they could see its potential, it had very little ground belonging to it and Sue wasn't sure that she even liked the village itself as it had no traditional village facilities. There were plenty of amenities in the surrounding area but the village itself possessed only a church and a village hall.

The search continued until one day John came to meet Sue at school and told her they had to go to their solicitor to sign some papers. Sue wanted to know why she was being dragged off to a solicitor at short notice and in such a hurry. John told her that he had been thinking about the row of cottages and had decided that it would be a good investment to buy them and have the craftsman who was restoring them continue with his work but incorporate some of their own ideas about how the house should look. Sue was still not convinced but was swept along by John's enthusiasm. They bought the building and arranged for the conversion to continue, with Peter Hardy completing the work.

They then had to sell the house in Cromer. It was likely that it might take a little while for the sale to go through and they were hopeful that the conversion of the new house would be complete by the time they needed to move. Inconveniently the house at Cromer sold rather quickly and the new house was nowhere near finished so they had to find somewhere else to live temporarily until the building work was complete. Luckily they were offered the loan of a house for as long as they needed it by Sue's yoga teacher, Elke, and her husband, Friedel who lived in the village of Cottered close to Cromer in a house which had grounds of 6 acres. In the early part of the twentieth century it had belonged to a wealthy glass and china merchant, Herbert Goode who, after a visit to Japan, had returned, determined to build a Japanese garden in the grounds. It took him 32 years, during which time he had brought designer Sayamon Kusumato and 43 gardeners from Japan and had imported many Japanese garden features to enable him to complete the project. In the garden was a traditional Japanese residence and it was this that Elke and Friedel Englemann offered to lend to the Hutchinsons. The offer was readily accepted and the Japanese house became their home for the next six months until their own home was ready.

Eventually the four cottages were converted into a beautiful new home, The Maltings, with all the character of the past but with the benefit of modern heating, lighting and plumbing. John and Sue again packed their belongings and said goodbye to the Japanese house, moving into their new home in late 1978.

Despite their initial misgivings about the cottages and the lack of land and traditional village facilities, the move proved to be good for them both. They planted the ground around their new home and although it was not as big as they really wanted, it has matured into a pretty garden. They also managed, many years later, to buy a small field which adjoins the property and now let it to a local farmer who grazes sheep on it. It has become the perfect country retreat. They have many friends in the small community and, over 30 years later, are still happy to be in the same house. They are both glad that they decided to move there and have no intentions of going anywhere else. John has said many times that the next time he moves it will be in a wooden box!

# Chapter 13

# New York to Paris, or London

*No flying machine will ever fly from New York to Paris ... [because]
no known motor can run at the requisite speed for four days without
stopping.*

Orville Wright, 1871–1948, American inventor and aviator

Concorde took its first faltering steps towards reality when the British and
the French decided to cooperate in its design and manufacture.

On 29 November 1962 a draft treaty was signed by the British Minister
of Aviation, Julian Amery and the French Ambassador to London, Jouffroy
de Courcel, which provided for complete equality in all aspects of the
aircraft's construction. In fact it was the French company, Sud-Aviation,
later to become Aérospatiale, which made the larger part of the aircraft
structure – the wings, controls and the rear cabin – whilst the British
Aircraft Corporation, later British Aerospace, built the tail and the forward
fuselage. The engines were developed by both Rolls-Royce and SNECMA
(Société Nationale d'Étude et de Construction de Moteurs d'Aviation)
and were based on the British Bristol-Siddeley Olympus engine which
was built for the Avro Vulcan bomber and was later redeveloped for the
ill-fated British Aircraft Corporation's TSR2. Concorde was eventually
powered by four Olympus 593 Mk 610 turbojet engines, each producing
38,050 lbs of thrust.

Sud-Aviation had, at first, planned to call the new supersonic aeroplane
the Super Caravelle, but the treaty with Britain changed those plans. Then,
in a speech delivered on 13 January 1963, French President Charles de

Gaulle referred to the Anglo-French project as a 'concorde' between the two nations and the name stuck. Britain had initially used the French spelling of the name but it was changed by Prime Minister Harold Macmillan who insisted on calling it Concord, without the 'e'. In 1966, with the Labour Party in power, Tony Benn became Minister of Technology. He explained how he ensured that the name of the supersonic aircraft regained the 'e':

> The original plan was that both the French and English Concordes would be spelled thus, with an 'e'. But Macmillan had been insulted by de Gaulle on one visit; de Gaulle had said he had a cold and couldn't see him. So Macmillan came back and removed the 'e' from the end. When I went to Toulouse for the [French] roll-out in 1969 [sic 1967], I decided to put it back again. We had to have the same name for the same aircraft, and besides, it was reversing an insult to the French, which I wasn't in favour of.
>
> I didn't tell anybody I was planning to do it, but once I had announced it in Toulouse, they couldn't do anything about it. I said: 'E stands for excellence, for England, for Europe and for the entente cordiale.' I might have added 'E stands for escalation' because, of course, it was very expensive, but I didn't say that at the time.[1]

In the October 1964 general election the Labour party's tiny majority had brought an end to 13 years of Conservative rule. The following month, with the government being pressed from all sides to reduce spending, Prime Minister Harold Wilson announced that Concorde was to be scrapped. The development costs had initially been planned at around £140 million but that figure had risen steeply and, by the time Wilson moved into Number 10, was estimated to have doubled. What the Prime Minister hadn't appreciated, however, was that the Concorde agreement signed by Britain and France had contained a clause prohibiting cancellation by either country and so, a mere two months later, he had to reverse the decision.

In the meantime both the USA and the USSR had begun work on their own supersonic passenger aircraft. Just six months before he was assassinated, President John F. Kennedy had announced during a speech in Colorado Springs, that he would back the development of an American supersonic transport (SST). The Americans then declared that their aircraft would be better than Concorde and by the late spring of 1964 the US government had asked several companies to submit designs for both the airframe and engines, with contracts being awarded to Boeing and General Electric respectively, at the end of 1966. By then the Concorde engines were already being tested and just one year after the USA finally entered the supersonic race, the prototype Concorde, number 001, had been unveiled in Toulouse, with 002 being shown off at Filton not long afterwards. Three and a half years later, in May 1971, the American SST project was cancelled following spiralling costs and the axing of funds by the US Senate.

The building of the Soviet SST, the Tupolev Tu-144, began in 1963 and its design was so similar to Concorde that it was nicknamed 'Concordski' by the world's press. With no restrictions being made on its development costs, the Tu-144 forged ahead, making its maiden flight on 31 December 1968. Two months and two days later, on 2 March 1969, French Concorde number 001, piloted by André Turcat, took to the air for the first time, to be followed on 9 April by British Concorde 002 under the command of test pilot Brian Trubshaw.

On 13 September 1970 Concorde landed at Heathrow for the first time to a barrage of complaints from local residents about the noise of its Olympus engines. This was the earliest of many similar objections to the noise made by Concorde.

Although ahead in the race to be first into the skies, the Tu-144 had problems of its own and numerous changes had been made to its design, including the addition of mini wing-like structures called canards at the front of the aircraft. These changes were shown to the world when the aircraft was exhibited at the Paris Air Show of 1973. On 3 June, the final day of the show, Soviet pilot Mikhail Kuzlov, was putting the aircraft through its paces just after the Concorde had displayed. Having made a steep dive he brought the aircraft in low along the runway and then pulled up sharply, some say to avoid a French Mirage whose crew was attempting to photograph the aircraft. The violent manoeuvre subjected the Tupolev to unacceptable stresses and it broke up and crashed into the Paris suburb of Goussainville killing all six crew members, eight people on the ground and injuring 25. Several houses were also demolished by the burning wreckage.

The crash effectively brought to an end the Tu-144's role as a passenger aircraft and by the end of 1975 it was being used purely as a mail and cargo transporter, leaving Concorde as the only supersonic passenger airliner in the world.

Concorde had completed all its tests by 1976 and came into service with Air France and British Airways when, on 21 January, Air France flight AF085 took-off for Rio de Janeiro while British Airways BA300 carried its passengers to Bahrain in Concorde G-BOAA.

The following month, 14 days after the first commercial flights had taken to the air, the two airlines were given permission by US Secretary of Transportation, William T. Coleman, to fly to Washington and New York for a 16-month trial period. Plans were made for the Washington services to begin in May but, upon hearing the Transportation Secretary's decision to allow Concorde to fly into New York, the Port of New York and New Jersey Authority, which ran Kennedy Airport, banned it from landing there because of its noise levels. The Port Authority had the backing of a significant number of residents, primarily from the borough of Queens where the airport is situated, who complained vociferously about the supposed noise they would have to endure. Air France and British Airways immediately took action to have the ban lifted and the Port Authority countered this by demanding that a six-month study of noise levels be carried out before any final decision could be reached. As Concorde test pilot, Brian Trubshaw commented:

> Bearing in mind that actual results from trials at Casablanca had been in their hands for months, one did not have to be a rocket scientist to smell the political game that was being played.[2]

It was felt by many that, having failed to bring their own SST project to fruition, the delaying tactics in banning Concorde from operating to New York were just American sour grapes.

The stalemate continued all through 1976. Both airlines began flights to Washington DC's Dulles Airport, which was owned and operated by the Federal Aviation Administration (FAA), in May of that year but New York, the financial hub of the USA, remained an elusive destination for another year.

On 12 May 1977 in the Federal District Court in Manhattan, Judge Milton Pollack declared that the Port Authority's ban on Concorde was illegal and that it should be allowed to make test flights to Kennedy Airport. Campaigners against the aircraft had formed a group called Concorde Alert and immediately after the judgement issued a statement through their chairman, lawyer Bryan Levenson, who said:

> The attitude of the community is total outrage … I can tell you one thing, the people are not going to take this lying down. We cost Kennedy $3 million to $4 million every time we show up there. I can see it happening once or twice a week on a regular basis if need be.[3]

Levenson also asked the District Attorney of Queens, John J. Santucci, to arrest every pilot that flew an aircraft breaking the noise regulations into Kennedy Airport, while Councilman Walter Ward said:

> … it is inconceivable that a few wealthy people could save a few hours of time, and the brunt of the burden is upon the persons living near the airport.[4]

Despite the continuing ban and the anger of local residents, one flight was allowed to operate from New York to Paris on 21 May 1977. This was to commemorate the 50th anniversary of Charles Lindbergh's solo flight across the Atlantic in his Ryan NYP, *Spirit of St Louis*. The crossing took Lindbergh 33 hours and 30 minutes; Concorde flew the same route in just 3 hours and 44 minutes.[5]

The protests continued and an appeal began on 1 June 1977 in the US Court of Appeals for the Second Circuit, before Chief Judge Irving R. Kaufman and Circuit Judges Mansfield and Van Graafeiland. The verdict, upholding that of Judge Pollack, was delivered on 14 June but Chief Judge Kaufman also said that:

> We accordingly direct that the district court on remand proceed to conduct an evidentiary hearing on the reasonableness of the Port Authority's thirteen month ban on Concorde landings at JFK.

The noise trials, the ban on Concorde landing at Kennedy Airport, the protests and the further hearing on the legality of the PNYA's ban, therefore, continued until October when the Supreme Court also ruled that Concorde should be allowed to operate into New York. Protesters were furious but what they failed to acknowledge was that the level of noise generated by Concorde had been found to be slightly more than a Boeing 727 but slightly less than a Boeing 707.[6] They had not protested against the Boeing 707; neither had the Port Authority banned the aircraft from using Kennedy Airport. Carol Berman, one of the anti-Concorde campaigners, was even quoted as saying that test flights of Concorde were not needed as it had '... flunked tests at each airport it had flown into'.[7] It was obvious that a certain group of people would have demonstrated against the aircraft whatever the findings of the trials but, on 22 November 1977, two Concordes – one belonging to Air France and the other to British Airways – finally landed at Kennedy Airport, bringing to an end 19 months of litigation.

Having overcome the intransigence of the Port of New York and New Jersey Authority and the ire of the members of Concorde Alert and a number of other outspoken critics, Air France and British Airways were able to concentrate on the task of establishing what eventually became the main commercial route for Concorde.

The trial period which had begun in May 1976, allowing Concorde to operate to Washington's Dulles Airport, developed into a regular route which, between 1984 and 1991, was extended to include Miami three times a week. There was also a brief extension to Dallas, in conjunction with American company Braniff International, which began in January 1979 and ended 18 months later due to poor passenger loads. The service to Washington itself ended in November 1994. The first scheduled service to Barbados, a weekly flight during the winter months, which later also operated during some summer months, began in December 1987 and continued until July 2003.

As with any aircraft, there were still problems to overcome and during the Concorde's life there were disputes over noise and costs and one or two technical issues. For the most part the aircraft behaved beautifully and when its first 12,000 hours flying check was carried out, it passed with flying colours and was declared to be structurally sound and fit for service well into the twenty-first century.

The original group of pilots selected for the Concorde were, under-standably, senior members of British Airways who had learnt to fly in the Royal Air Force during their National Service. Whilst it was logical to leave the pride of the airline's fleet in the capable hands of pilots with many years' experience, this did not prove to be the ideal solution that had been envisaged. The Concorde was quite different from any of the other aircraft that these men had flown and some of them had difficulties in adjusting to its way of behaving. This led to the airline's crew selection process being changed and the chance to fly the supersonic aircraft was also offered to younger pilots. About half their number had been in the Royal Air Force while the remainder comprised pilots from the Fleet Air Arm, other aviation branches of the Services and civilian pilots.

John's first flight in Concorde was a circuit detail from RAF Brize Norton in Oxfordshire and he has never forgotten how it felt to sit in the pilot's seat for the first time, start the engines and take-off:

> An incredible feeling and it never, never dissipated over the entire 15 years I was flying on them. It was just as exciting every time; a huge rush of adrenaline and a great sense of privilege that you were in command of this wonderful piece of machinery – magical, iconic.

On 9 December 1977, 17 days after the New York service began and while John was still completing his conversion course, British Airways opened a supersonic route to Singapore via Bahrain. It was a joint service with Singapore Airlines and one of the aircraft, G-BOAD, had British Airways colours on its starboard side and Singapore Airlines colours on its port side. Four days later, after only three return flights, the service was suspended following objections from the Malaysian government about supersonic flights in the Strait of Malacca.[8]

When John had completed his Concorde course he began flying to New York and loved every minute of it. It was a completely different flying experience from anything he had encountered thus far in his career, as it was for the exclusive group of passengers who now regularly flew on the supersonic aircraft in preference to the more conventional subsonic airliners. As well as being able to fly faster than in any other aircraft, those who travelled onboard Concorde also received a level of service far superior to that of other flights. They were known as guests rather than passengers and the airline treated them as such. They had their own check-in desks, an exclusive lounge in which to wait until departure time, first class meals, with a choice of three main courses, and excellent wine and champagne. They were sometimes invited to visit the flight deck for a chat with the crew and for the unsurpassed view from the windows and when they left the aircraft at their destination were given gifts that have now become collectors' items.

A year or two before, when he was a VC10 captain, John had had a drink with a friend, Michael Jeffrey. Their conversation naturally turned to current aviation matters and Michael said that he believed John would be flying Concorde within 18 months. John told him he was talking rubbish but Michael was convinced and bet John 5p that he was right. After becoming a Concorde captain John tried to pay his 5p debt but his friend told him, 'I'm going to collect my dues in the only proper way – flying supersonic over the Atlantic'.

In October 1978 Michael Jeffery did make the trip in Concorde from London to New York and collected his 5p from John who was flying the aircraft that day. The details of the wager were reported in a local news-paper[9] by journalist, James Hogg, who said:

> *Despite such frivolities John Hutchinson is intensely serious about Concorde, and justifiably proud of being associated with it.*
>
> *'British Airways and Air France have got the whole supersonic field to themselves over the next ten to twelve years, and I just hope that British governments have the courage to invest in a second generation of supersonic aircraft before the Americans come along and poach all our expertise for their own programme,' he told me.*
>
> *'When you think of all the problems that the designers of Concorde had to overcome, you realise that as a piece of engineering it's almost as fantastic as getting to the moon.*
>
> *'One of the most striking things is the absence of jet lag. That's because the cabin altitude – the altitude conditions simulated inside the plane – is only 5,000 ft., whereas in a Jumbo it's 7,500 to 8,000, which is much more of a strain on the body. And, of course, you're in the air for a much shorter time.'*
>
> *Because of the difficulties of getting permission to overfly various countries, British Airways is using its Concordes well under capacity, and John is hoping that eventually arrangements for the Singapore run will be completed …*

*Still, I got the impression that John Hutchinson would go anywhere they asked him, just as long as he was at the controls of a British Airways Concorde.*

British Airways did resume its Concorde flights to Singapore in January 1979 but they were withdrawn in November the following year. In December 1979, John was posted to Singapore for three months, flying between there and Bahrain. After a short leave in London he returned for another three month stay. Sue joined him on both occasions and they enjoyed their time there, thankfully with none of the difficulties that they had encountered in 1959 during John's RAF posting to the island. Nor did they have problems with their accommodation as they were able to rent a two bedroom, two bathroom, apartment close to both the shopping paradise of Orchard Road and the Tanglin Club – much enjoyed by all the Concorde crews.

While most airline crew members don't fly as a regular team, those who flew Concorde between Singapore and Bahrain went there as a fixed crew and were all based in Singapore. John, as captain, was teamed up with first officer W.D. 'Jock' Lowe, whom he had met 2 years before. Jock had gained his nickname while at university as a result of several southern students mistaking his County Durham accent for that of a Scotsman.[10] He flew Concorde from 1975 to 2001 and was Chief Concorde pilot between 1989 and 1991, becoming Concorde Commercial Manager for three years from 1996. The flight engineer who made up the crew was Bill Brown, whose father had also worked for BOAC, in a senior engineering capacity on the ground. While in Singapore Bill shared the apartment with John and Sue and says that the short time he spent there was the best flying time of his entire career.[11] After the first Gulf War, Bill re-trained and became a pilot himself eventually flying for Open Skies, an all business-class subsidiary of British Airways which operates between Paris, New York and Washington.

The base captain in Singapore was Norman Britton and he and his crew named themselves the 'A' team after the television programme of the same name. John and his crew were known as the 'Z' team. This was not a reflection of their flying performance at all but was taken from John's nickname, Zebedee, after the Magic Roundabout character who finished each programme by saying, 'Time for bed'. The name had been given to John because of his propensity for falling asleep at social events.

John believed the Singapore posting to be one of the best times of his flying career also, attributing it to Concorde itself, the skill of both Jock and Bill, which he valued highly, and the fact that working with them was so easy:

> We got to the point of understanding each other; we almost didn't need to talk to each other. It was all done by a process of osmosis. We just had this sort of absolutely fine-tuned understanding between the three of us and it was the most closely knit flight operation I've ever been involved in, in my life. It was absolutely amazing. You get to know each other's eccentricities and everything else – it was just absolutely extraordinary.

The three men became great friends while on the posting and remain so to this day.

Although the two main routes undertaken by Concorde at that time were of a similar length – at 3,923 miles Singapore to Bahrain is approximately 500 miles longer than London to New York – the performance of the aircraft was very different. Upper level air temperatures over the Atlantic are typically around -55°C at 50,000-55,000 feet; those closer to the Equator are significantly colder – approximately -85°C at a comparable height. This difference in air temperature affects the performance, as the colder the air, the greater the mass going into the front of the engines which, in turn, produces more power. Across the Atlantic a height of 60,000 feet was hardly ever reached. Because the cruise climb was slower in the warmer air, by the time the aircraft had reached 58,000 or 59,000 feet it was time to throttle back for the approach into New York.

Between Singapore and Bahrain however, in the colder air, the Concorde would shoot up to 50,000 feet, rapidly reaching Mach 2, and then keep climbing at rates of up to 7,000 feet per minute. Since this was not desirable, a protocol was built into the autopilot system whereby if the Mach number could not be sensibly contained by pitching the aircraft up and climbing, the auto throttles would kick in and take some power off to contain the rate of climb.

On the Atlantic route on days when the air temperature was warmer than normal at, say, -45°C, the limiting temperature on the aircraft nose, which was 127°C, could easily be reached before Mach 2. In this case the autopilot would fly to the temperature limit rather than the Mach number but would revert to the latter should the air become colder. In these warmer temperatures the speed sometimes only reached a maximum of Mach 1.96. As John says:

> The autopilot system was just amazing when you look at it in terms of the era in which it was designed.
>
> My admiration for the designers and aerodynamicists knows no bounds. They were absolutely outstanding; brilliant people led by Sir George Edwards; people like Sir Archibald Russell and Sir Stanley Hooker who had a great role to play in the intake design. They were incredibly capable men.
>
> And, of course, I have to admit that the French had something to do with it too!

During one night flight from Bahrain to Singapore in 1980 John was asked by one of the cabin crew if it would be all right for a passenger to come up to the flight deck as he wanted to make a video of the sun rising over the Strait of Malacca. The stewardess explained that he didn't have much tape left and would appreciate being told when to start filming so that he didn't miss anything. John agreed to the visit and asked the name of the passenger. He was told that it was Elvis Costello, then in his mid-twenties and taking a short break in Singapore and Australia before going on to New Zealand to play at Sweetwaters Festival in Auckland.[12] John had never heard of him but the stewardess told him that he should have, as he was a very talented pop musician. When it was close to the time for him to begin filming he was brought up to the flight deck and John welcomed him, saying that it was nice to have him on board. Elvis shook John's hand and replied cheerfully, 'Hello, mate'. John remembers thinking that it was a novel way to greet him – passengers didn't usually call him 'mate' – but there were more surprises to come. The conversation continued:

> John: I gather that you write music. I'm afraid I'm not really into pop music. I've actually never heard of you but I'm sure my son has. He's going to be very excited to hear that I've flown you.

Elvis: Don't worry about that. I write music, yeah. It's absolute fucking rubbish but as long as people go on paying to hear it and buying the music I'll go on doing it.

John says that from that moment he felt himself warming considerably to the young man who was not in the least bit arrogant and he later discovered that his music was anything but rubbish.

Eventually the tinge of dawn began to appear in the distance and some thunderheads towered above the 60,000 feet at which they were flying. It was a beautiful sight; below them the sea; ahead Sumatra, the Strait of Malacca and the Malay Peninsula. John told Elvis when to start filming and he began, adding a commentary at the same time:

God, this is absolutely fucking incredible. We're flying at Mach fucking 2, 60 fucking thousand feet and I've never fucking well seen anything like it in all my fucking life.

As the tape ran out, John remarked that the commentary was rather interesting and Elvis explained why he had made the film:

It's like this, mate. I'm going on a long tour. I'm going to Singapore then on to Australia and New Zealand. My Mum lives in London and I'm no good at writing postcards so instead I do videos and then send them back home. When I get to Singapore I'll send her this. She'll be fascinated to see everything I've seen from the Concorde flight deck.

At this point John suddenly had a vision of Elvis's mother getting the latest instalment from him and inviting friends from the Women's Institute to her home to have tea and cucumber sandwiches and to watch the fascinating film that her son had made for her!

Although he only met Elvis Costello for a few minutes, the meeting made a lasting impression on John. He has since heard from friends who live near to Elvis and his Canadian wife, Diana Krall, that he is still just as unpretentious as he was then and John, himself, says:

He's just a totally straightforward chap. He talks to anybody and he's not at all pompous; completely down to earth; just a really nice man and he is incredibly talented.

Not all the incidents that happened during the flights to Singapore were pleasant. One in particular could have ended very badly.

The flight, under the command of Captain Monty Burton, began in London where a rather odd woman boarded the Concorde, wearing a strange combination of clothes and shoes; a mink coat, tartan skirt and trainers. After take-off for Bahrain she stood up and began marching up and down the aisle singing patriotic songs including *Land of Hope and Glory, Jerusalem* and the *National Anthem*. The cabin crew, who were Singapore Airlines staff, this being part of the arrangement they had with British Airways whereby crews from each airline operated sectors in turn, did not immediately do anything to stop the woman. Having been serenaded by her for a while the passengers were becoming rather irritated and one man, on his way to Singapore to conclude a deal with a local construction company, made the almost fatal mistake of looking up from his newspaper and catching the woman's eye as she passed by. She took offence at this, stopped abruptly, went back to her seat and rummaged through her bag. She then pulled out a Swiss Army knife, returned to where the businessman was seated and plunged the knife into his head with such force that the tip of the blade broke off, remaining embedded in his skull. He only remembered seeing her raise her arm and then there was a blinding flash as the knife was thrust into his head. He immediately lost consciousness.

The cabin crew did not know what to do and rushed up to the flight deck to inform Captain Burton what had happened. He asked the flight engineer to go and deal with the woman which he did, armed with the emergency fire axe from the flight deck. The woman was returned to her seat and strapped in with several seat belts so that she was unable to escape and when the aircraft landed in Bahrain was handed over to the police.

The businessman regained consciousness just before arriving in Bahrain but refused to be hospitalized there, saying he would rather wait until he got to Singapore. During the transit time in Bahrain his wound was dressed by the airport doctor and the crew who would be taking the aeroplane on to Singapore boarded. They took-off, this time with John in command and upon arrival in Singapore the passenger was taken to hospital and was operated on by a leading American brain surgeon who was at the hospital in a short-term teaching capacity. He was unable to remove the tip of the knife which had become stuck fast in the man's skull and so had to remove a section of the bone to free it and replaced it with a plate. The blade had come within a millimetre of penetrating the man's brain. British Airways, although not responsible for the man's injuries, made all the arrangements for the medical care and paid all the bills. John telephoned the man's wife in England to tell her what had happened and Sue went to the hospital to visit the patient. She then made several calls to his wife to keep her up to date with his progress. During the last phone call they had, the wife invited John and Sue to come and stay with her and her husband when he was back home, which they eventually did when they returned to England at the end of the Singapore posting. Thankfully the man had made a full recovery.

During the few months that John was based in Singapore his son Chris flew out to stay with him in Bahrain for a few days while he was on a layover there. One day they hired a dhow with a boatman and sailed in the Gulf of Bahrain. They decided to stop for a swim and so the anchor was dropped and they dived into the water. After a while Chris climbed back into the dhow and was watching his father swimming when he suddenly saw a black silhouette in the water. He shouted to John that there was a shark behind him but then thought that it was, perhaps, just a ray and told him not to worry. But as he peered at the black shadow again he realized that he had been right the first time – it really was a shark. He again yelled out to John to warn him and witnessed his father almost running on water, climbing the anchor chain and diving into the dhow to escape the clutches of the creature.

Chris believes that, after the suddenness of Tim's death, the fragility of life was really brought home to his parents and they both chose to throw themselves into living their lives to the full. They have not always chosen the easy route. Chris recalled that when they learnt to scuba dive they did so, not in the warm waters of the Caribbean, but at Stoney Cove, a cold former granite quarry in Leicestershire. But, as Sue has said many times, 'You are dead for a much longer time than you are alive' and they have grasped the opportunities as and when they have come their way. Although the philosophy has brought them into danger on several occasions it has also offered them an almost unique experience of what the world has to offer and has greatly enriched their lives.

When Chris left school he decided that he wanted to go into hotel management and, after his training at the Royal Lancaster Hotel, Westminster College and Oxford Brookes University, became night manager at the Sheraton, Belgravia. Then, at the age of 24, he realized that, although he was good at his job, it wasn't what he really wanted to do. He wanted to become a pilot so applied to the RAF and was accepted. Before he began his service career however, he received a letter telling him that a mistake had been made and that he was just over the maximum age limit to become a Royal Air Force officer. By now very disappointed but still anxious to fulfil his dream he applied to the Navy, whose age limits were not as strict, hoping to eventually become a pilot with the Fleet Air Arm. He was accepted and began his training at Britannia Royal Naval College in Dartmouth.

Despite being extremely busy, when John was asked by his old prep school, St Michael's in Otford, if he would present the prizes at the annual prize-giving ceremony, he agreed. The ceremony was, however, the day after Chris's passing out parade and the graduation ball in Dartmouth that John and Sue attended, which meant that they had to get up very early the next morning to drive to Kent.

They had already reached Somerset and were speeding along the almost deserted M5 when, out of nowhere, a police car emerged and John had to stop. The policemen walked up to the car and one asked John if he knew what speed he was doing. John realized that he had been exceeding the speed limit by a large amount – he thought he was doing about 121 mph but he had actually only been clocked doing 117 mph – and the policeman asked him, 'Who do you think you are? A Concorde pilot?' Rather sheepishly John said that that was exactly what he was; a fact backed up by Sue from the passenger seat. John explained the situation and said that he had to be in Kent by the middle of the morning to present the prizes and deliver a speech at his old school. The policemen were very understanding and pleasant but said that unfortunately they had already called in the incident and that they would now have to proceed further. They waved John and Sue off, advising John to stick to the speed limit for the remainder of the journey, and told him that he would be hearing more in due course. Their journey passed with no more problems and they arrived at St Michael's just in time for the prize giving.

Soon afterwards John received a summons to appear in court in Taunton. Realizing that he was likely to lose his licence, Bill Brown offered to go with him to court so that he could drive him home again. The case was heard and John was banned from driving for one month. So ended the second Hutchinson disaster in Taunton, more than 30 years after the eiderdown saga of their honeymoon.

Aside from the 'huge rush of adrenaline' and the 'great sense of privilege' that John has admitted to, in being the pilot of the iconic Concorde, there was another element to the trips that John also enjoyed. Before the flight began he would always scan the passenger manifest to see who he would be flying and who he could invite to the flight deck. Over the 15 years that he was a Concorde captain, he flew very many well known people including Her Majesty Queen Elizabeth II. Sir Frank Whittle, the inventor of the jet engine, flew with Lady Whittle in September 1983 from New York to London to attend a dinner celebrating the 40th anniversary of the Gloster Meteor, the first RAF single-seat jet fighter. And Rolling Stone, Mick Jagger, was pleased to be invited onto the flight deck while on a mercy dash to London to fix the roof of his mother's house after it had blown off during the hurricane that hit southern England in 1987.

While John was very happy to have been able to fly many well known people in Concorde, his favourite group were the classical musicians. He was always delighted to find that he had onboard people such as violinist Yehudi Menuhin, conductor Sir Georg Solti, violinist, violist and conductor Pinchas 'Pinky' Zuckerman, violinist Isaac Stern, violinist and conductor Itzhak Perlman and pianist and conductor Vladimir Ashkenazy whom he regarded as being:

> … fantastic. They were all down to earth and I got the feeling with them that they were geniuses and they lived on a different plane. They don't have to compete like ordinary mortals have to compete; they are just on another planet altogether.

It was clear that some of these virtuosi were equally appreciative of John's skills on the flight deck of his supersonic workplace. Shortly after inviting

Vladimir Ashkenazy to spend the entire flight on the flight deck, John was surprised, and delighted, to receive a parcel from him containing two of his long playing records. Ashkenazy had written on the cover of one of them: 'To John Hutchinson with many thanks for a memorable flight on Concorde.'

He was especially touched by the thoughtful gift when he noticed that the writing on the package was the same as on the LP sleeve and realized that Ashkenazy had packed up and addressed the parcel himself.

The late Isaac Stern had been instrumental in saving New York's Carnegie Hall from demolition in 1960 and was its President for over 30 years. Having flown on Concorde's flight deck he gave John the telephone number of his agent in New York and told him that whenever he was there and wanted to attend a concert at Carnegie Hall he should telephone the agent who would arrange for him to use his own private box. John was thrilled to be able to make use of this offer on several occasions.

Israeli-American violinist and conductor, Itzhak Perlman, contracted polio at the age of 4 years and is unable to walk without the assistance of crutches. When John discovered that he was onboard one of his flights he was determined to invite him onto the flight deck. Despite odd looks from his fellow crew members who were concerned about the safety of the conductor, John helped him to a seat and ensured that he was safely strapped in. Perlman stayed with the crew for the entire flight and thoroughly enjoyed the experience. Several years later, after John's retirement from British Airways, Sue managed to get tickets to see Perlman at the Festival Hall in London. He was undertaking a series of concerts in the United Kingdom to celebrate his 50th birthday and Sue was lucky enough to procure centre, front row seats in the stalls. The concert was wonderful and during the interval John wrote a note to Perlman saying that he was sure he wouldn't remember him but that he was a former Concorde pilot who had flown him some years before and that he just wanted to congratulate him on the wonderful concert that he and Sue were enjoying. Before the interval was over John received a reply from the great man which said, 'Under no circumstances leave the Festival Hall without coming to my dressing room to see me'. At the end of the concert John and Sue were escorted to the dressing room where Perlman was chatting to friends and family. He looked up as John walked through the door and said to him:

Hello. Wonderful to see you again. How on earth could you think I might not remember you? Of course I remember you. You're the only pilot I've ever flown with who has thought to invite me up to watch the take-off and landing. It was the most fantastic experience of my life. It's something I shall never forget; it's something I will always remember. It was just fascinating for me.

John was impressed that Perlman did remember him and confessed to being: '… quite blown away by the fact that this great hero of mine had found this simple gesture on my part to be such a significant thing for him.'

Not all the well known passengers were as pleasant as the classical musicians. Former Prime Minister Sir Edward Heath was not popular and was regarded as being a grumpy, embittered old man after being deposed by Margaret Thatcher, and media mogul and former Labour MP, Robert Maxwell, was not liked at all by the crews. He always had a mobile phone to his ear – in those days they were the size of bricks – and made a fuss when asked to turn it off prior to departure, usually only doing so when he could see that his continued refusal would lead to the crew asking for him to be offloaded.

One passenger did behave so badly before leaving Heathrow Airport that he was removed from the aeroplane. Just before the flight was due to leave the chief steward came to John and told him that there was a serious problem with one of the passengers who was sitting at the back of the cabin, smoking and refusing to fasten his seat belt. John decided to go back and talk to the man himself. He put on his jacket and hat, trying to make himself look as important as possible, and then marched down to the back of the cabin where the man was sitting, properly strapped in and not smoking. Thinking that he had had second thoughts about his behaviour John thanked him and said that they could now get on their way to New York. Immediately the passenger unfastened his seat belt, stood up, pulled a pack of cigarettes from his pocket and lit one. Blowing smoke directly into John's face he enquired what he was going to do about it. John replied, very politely, 'I'm sorry sir, I'm not going to take you on the flight'. He then turned around and went straight back to the flight deck from where he called the dispatcher, told him about the problem he was having and asked him to get the police to come out to the aeroplane. A police sergeant and two constables arrived and, with John leading the way, marched to the passenger's seat only to find that he was once more strapped in and that there was no sign of a cigarette. The sergeant told him that the captain was not going to take him on the flight and he immediately stood up and began discussing the situation with the policeman saying that he would fasten his belt and not smoke again. He was told that it was too late. The captain had said that he didn't want him on the flight and so he would have to leave. The sergeant asked one of the cabin staff to fetch the man's belongings and put his hand on his shoulder to assist him down the aisle. Suddenly the man erupted saying, 'Take your fucking hands off me or I'll punch your face in'. A contented smile came across the sergeant's face and he said, 'Oh dear, oh dear – threatening a policeman in the course of his duty. I'm terribly sorry, sir. You are under arrest'. The two constables immediately swung into action and, with each holding an arm, frogmarched the man down the aisle and off the aeroplane, all three policemen receiving a round of applause from the other passengers.

John heard later that the man had been heavily fined at Uxbridge magistrates court, but thought no more about it until one day, a few months later, a letter arrived addressed to 'The pilot of Speedbird 001' with the date that the incident had taken place. It was from the disruptive passenger, an American living in New York, who humbly apologized for making such a fool of himself. He explained that he was terrified of flying and had never flown on Concorde before. He was also taking medication that did not mix with alcohol but because of his fear of flying had taken a few drinks in the Concorde lounge before boarding the aeroplane. This was the reason for his unacceptable behaviour, for which he was extremely embarrassed.

In August 1988 John was the pilot of a Concorde on which 83 year old Joyce Burton was flying to New York on what was only her second flight ever. The first had been in a Blériot monoplane around Leeds Park in 1913 when, aged 7, she set the record for the youngest person to take to the air.

Mrs Burton had no fears about supersonic flight and said of her trip on Concorde: 'This has been the most marvellous experience of my life.'[13]

Sometimes an incident occurs on an aeroplane that is not the fault of a passenger but happens because of the aeroplane itself. One such incident took place on a flight from New York to London. The aeroplane was half empty; the flight was progressing normally when at Mach 2 an engine surge – the breakdown of the airflow through the engine – occurred. John described it as being like a train crash; the aeroplane shook violently. The drill to correct the problem involved closing all four throttles which won't shut down the engines but puts them into flight idle; the deceleration is enormous: 'It's like going into a brick wall and the cabin crew, the trolleys and the passengers all nearly join you on the flight deck!'

The flight engineer on this particular day was John's good friend, Bill Brown and he thought he knew what had happened. He had noticed that the No. 3 intake had spontaneously driven itself fully shut which was not the correct position for it to be in. Bill suggested that, rather than go through the lengthy checklist to discover the cause of the surge, he could hard select the standby controller for that intake to see if he could restore control of it. John had complete confidence in Bill's ability and told him to go ahead. He did so and everything returned to normal. John then, '… got my voice down from a high-pitched treble and made a suitably reassuring announcement to the passengers'. Feeling that after the experience they had just been through they deserved a bit more attention he left the flight deck and went back to the cabin to chat to them and reassure them that everything was now working correctly and there was nothing to worry about. One elderly lady told him that he shouldn't worry about them but should be worried about the cabin crew who, she said, were 'absolutely terrified'. John then held a brief counselling session for the cabin crew before returning to the flight deck for the remainder of the flight.

Once the aeroplane came to a halt on the stand at Heathrow John again left his seat to bid farewell to the passengers as they disembarked. The sight that confronted him will remain in his memory forever. Concorde always carried a large stock of alcohol and after the engine surge the passengers, who numbered approximately 50, had drunk the aeroplane dry. Every bottle of whisky, gin, vodka, champagne, red wine, white wine, port and cognac was empty. As John said goodbye: '… the passengers thanked me for a wonderful flight and staggered off the aeroplane, pissed out of their brains!' What had begun as a frightening experience, ended with monumental hangovers for many of those who had travelled to London that day.

From time to time there are incidents that are neither frightening nor dangerous but just funny. On one flight, again from New York to London, the chief steward came onto the flight deck to tell John that he had a problem, as there was a couple in the forward toilet doing what he described as 'thingy'. John asked what he meant by 'thingy' and was told that they were having sex. When he enquired how the chief steward knew, he was told that he could hear their cries of passion and the thrashing around and crashing against the door. Since the toilets on Concorde were extremely cramped, John was of the opinion that anyone having sex there deserved an Olympic gold medal for athletic endeavour. He asked the chief steward if this was creating a queue of people waiting to use the facilities and when he learned that it was not, told him to leave them where they were, as they were obviously enjoying themselves, and then present each of them with a bottle of champagne with his compliments, and those of British Airways, when they returned to their seats. He also asked him to invite the lady to watch the landing in London from the flight deck. She accepted and as she came through the door, John turned in his seat and said: 'Good evening, madam. I hope you're enjoying your flight in Concorde with us today.' The lady, an American with a broad grin on her face, replied: 'Gee, Captain. It's the greatest ride I've ever had!'

John looked at her and she returned the look and, as John said:

I knew that she knew that I knew everything that had befallen! We landed and off she went clutching her bottle of Dom Perignon.

The man also left with his bottle and the crew boarded the bus to go to the crew report building. John remarked to the chief steward that he had never had that happen on one of his flights before and the chief steward said it was his first experience of it too. Then he told John that he hadn't heard the best bit – the couple had never met before boarding the flight! Apparently the woman had checked in 2 hours before departure and had been sitting in the Concorde lounge at Kennedy Airport waiting to board the aeroplane. The man, on the other hand, had rushed up to the gate at the last minute, checked in there and had then galloped onto the aeroplane and looked for an empty seat, finding one next to the woman as the aircraft was about to be pushed back off the stand. After a few drinks they had begun to chat and had then proceeded up the aisle to find somewhere private to cement their new found friendship!

# Chapter 14

# Pirates of the Caribbean

*... the Caribbean Sea, one of the world's most alluring bodies of water, a rare gem among the oceans, defined by the islands that form a chain of lovely jewels to the north and east.*

James A. Michener, 1907–1997, American Pulitzer
prize-winning writer

In late 1983, after John and Sue's silver wedding anniversary, John discovered that a friend from British Airways, Patrick Tisdall, had taken early retirement from the company and had bought a yacht which, for obvious reasons, he called *Severance*. With his girlfriend, Susan Northcote, he sailed it to Nelson's Dockyard in English Harbour, Antigua, in the Caribbean Leeward Islands where he planned to use it as a charter boat. He and his girlfriend, both of whom were excellent sailors, would take visitors wherever they wanted to go in the Caribbean and ensure that they had the holiday of a lifetime.

Since both John and Sue enjoyed sailing, it seemed to be a perfect opportunity to belatedly celebrate their wedding anniversary and so John arranged with Patrick to take a trip after Christmas. It was Patrick's first booking for his new business.

Although they wanted to explore the waters around Antigua, John and Sue were also keen to sail to Barbuda where they hoped to meet up with some Canadian friends and spend a few days in their company. On 24 January 1984 they flew to Antigua and were met at the airport by Patrick, who took them by taxi to English Harbour where they boarded the yacht. *Severance* was a beautiful 39 foot ketch and the Hutchinsons had a double cabin with its own bathroom.

They spent the first evening settling in while *Severance* gently rocked on the tranquil waters of English Harbour. The following day they went ashore to visit Nelson's Dockyard. Originally called His Majesty's Antigua Naval Yard it was built in 1725 as the headquarters of the British Leeward Islands fleet. It was here that a young Horatio Nelson was captain of HMS *Boreas* and, in the 1950s when the dockyard was being restored, its name was changed to Nelson's Dockyard in his honour.

Later that day and now back onboard the *Severance*, they pored over charts and made plans, both for the visit to Barbuda and for the remainder of their holiday. The next morning the anchor was raised and they sailed to Falmouth Harbour to take on fresh water, food and fuel. Patrick was very safety conscious and wanted to make sure that they had plenty of fuel should the weather make sailing impossible.

Having taken their provisions onboard they sailed on to Deep Bay, where they found three or four other boats had moored, and dropped anchor close to the beach, spending the afternoon swimming in the calm blue waters. That evening they had drinks in the cockpit and later a barbeque supper, before retiring early to their cabin. The Caribbean was already working its magic and they were happy and relaxed and looking forward to the trip to Barbuda the following day. The combination of fresh air, swimming, and the leisurely supper and drinks had made them drowsy and they fell asleep almost immediately.

Sometime after midnight they awoke to the sound of a loud crash and the door to their cabin bursting open. They could hear men's voices and a lot of shouting; one voice yelled out, 'You are English spies'. In the light from a torch being shone at them Sue could see that there were two men in the cabin. Still coming out of a deep sleep and not really understanding what was happening, John at first thought that it was Patrick fooling around. He started to sit up but found that there was a large curved knife being held at his throat by the taller of the two men. The other was pointing a pump action shotgun at their heads. Sue whispered to John to keep calm as it was obvious that the men were in a very excitable state and their behaviour was extremely threatening. In the faint light of the torch it was impossible to see them clearly or to judge their ages but the shorter of the two seemed to Sue to be really evil and was clearly the most dangerous; the cabin smelt strongly of their body odour.

At first it looked as if they had come aboard to rob the occupants of *Severance* as they wanted to know where the money was kept. John tried to explain to them that he didn't have very much cash but that what he did have was in his wallet in a lock-up in the corner. One of the men started to look for it but couldn't find it and when John suggested that he could get it for them, they became very agitated. He again explained where they would find the wallet and this time they did locate it and removed the cash before asking where the cocaine and guns were. John told them that he didn't know what they were talking about. Then they spotted the signet ring that he wore on the little finger of his left hand. It was the same ring that had caught in the rope when he escaped from the flight deck of the burning Boeing 707, Whisky Echo, and had been given to him by Sue for his 21st birthday. One of the men said that he wanted the ring and told him to take it off and give it to him. John tried to remove it but it wouldn't budge and the man grabbed him and, waving the knife over his hand, said that if it couldn't be easily removed he would just chop off the finger. Sue screamed at him to fetch some soap and he calmed down and did as she asked. Having put a lot of soap onto the ring and his hand, John was able to get the ring off and gave it to the hijacker who put it in his pocket. Sue was furious and told him to make sure that he didn't lose it as, although it was not worth much in monetary terms, it had a great deal of sentimental value to them both.

Having got whatever valuables they could, the men then decided that they should tie up their victims. Sue had gone to bed wearing a cotton nightdress but the night had been too hot for John to wear anything and he was naked beneath a sheet. As one of the men pulled back the sheet so that they could bind their wrists and ankles, he saw that John was naked and yelled at him, 'Gee man! You should wear clothes. This is disgusting'. They then pulled him off the bed and one said, 'Get your pants on man; get your pants on. That's disgusting!' When they recalled this later, both Sue and John thought how peculiar it was that two armed criminals should be so offended by the sight of a naked man.

John pulled on a pair of shorts and one of the hijackers tied his hands together and then his ankles and pushed him back onto the bed. Sue was also tied up in much the same way and the couple were bound to each other. The men then left them and returned to Patrick and Susan in the main cabin. They had told Patrick that they were terrorists, trained in Cuba, and that if those on board did not do what they were told, they would kill them. Patrick shouted to John and Sue to let them know that he and Susan were safe, although they were bound together and helpless to do anything, and said that they should do whatever the men wanted.

While the Hutchinsons were trussed up and alone in their cabin they heard the yacht's engine being started and felt the movement as the anchor was lifted and the boat began to move out of the bay. They wondered if there was anyone still awake on any of the other boats at anchor in Deep Bay who might have noticed something and raised the alarm but no one seemed to have seen anything untoward and they headed out to sea unhindered. After a while, the engine was switched off and *Severance* began drifting on the open water.

Although they were tied tightly and completely unable to move, John and Sue had not been gagged and were able to talk to each other. They discussed what was happening to them and what they could do about it, if anything. They also tried to work out what it was that the men actually wanted. Whatever it was they decided that the only thing they could do to minimize the risk to themselves and their companions was to cooperate. They thought that it was unlikely that either they, or Patrick and Susan, were the main targets and that the yacht was what they were really after, probably for a drug run. The way that the men had been behaving suggested that they were already high on drugs or alcohol. However the fact that they had been robbed and that the hijackers were still in no hurry to dispose of them suggested that they had time to kill and may have wanted something more than the boat. It was, of course, possible that they might need some help in manoeuvring *Severance* or perhaps in navigating to wherever it was that they intended to sail but Sue also thought that because they seemed to be in no hurry to dispose of them, they might first rape her and Susan and wanted to tell John that if this did happen he must keep calm and not react at all. She told him that it would mean nothing to her and she would be able to get over it; the main thing was that they should come out of this horrible experience alive. She thought that they should remain as still as possible so as not to provoke either of the men into further violence. John was horrified by what Sue had said but agreed that she might be right and wanted her to know that nothing the men might do to her would change the way he felt about her. Having not had the chance to see or speak to Patrick and Susan they did not know that the hijackers had already told them that they did intend to have sex with both women. Nor did they know that Susan had told them that she was in the middle of a very heavy period and that while she would not put up a fight if they still intended to have sex with her, it would not be a very satisfactory experience for them. It was her quick thinking that sealed Sue's fate.

A short time later the door crashed open again and the shorter, man who, they discovered, was known as Cox untied the rope binding Sue and John together and, pushing the barrel of the shotgun into John's back, dragged him to his feet and began pulling him out of the cabin. The taller hijacker, who the other man had called Jack, said to Sue, 'Hey, honky. Have you ever had a black cock?' John heard this as he was being manhandled into the main cabin and asked if he might kiss Sue goodbye. Cox allowed him to do so and John kissed her and told her that he loved her. He told Jack that he and Sue had been married for a very long time and that he loved her very much. He begged him not to hurt her. As he was pulled out of the cabin where Sue was still lying on the bed, neither was sure if they would ever see the other alive again.

In the main cabin John had a rope put around his neck and, along with Susan and Patrick, was bound to the mast. Jack then went back into the cabin, where Sue was tied up on the bed, to carry out his threat. Although she had made up her mind that her life was more important than anything that might now happen to her, she was terrified when she saw Jack pull out the knife again and use it to rip off her nightdress. He then undressed himself and fell on her but had forgotten to untie her ankles. Although very frightened she thought it would be best to help him do what he was determined to do and get the ordeal over as soon as possible. She knew that it would be horrible but began to convince herself that it would be no worse than a visit to a gynaecologist and kept telling herself this while the young man was raping her. Before he finished Cox came into the cabin and told him to hurry up as it was now his turn. Sue's heart sank. He was different from Jack – really nasty – and she thought that she would have trouble with him. She decided to talk to him and told him that she hoped he would enjoy himself but that she was, after all, a middle-aged woman and that she thought he would have much more fun with a girl his own age. He didn't seem bothered about the age difference and began to suggest things that they could do which he found very exciting. Sue was horrified with what he was proposing and told him that she wouldn't do anything like that and that if he tried to force her she would bite him so hard that he would forever carry the scars. She then let her thoughts drift towards the doctor's surgery again and while he raped her tried to convince herself that she was just having an examination. She also kept talking to him, asking him questions about his girlfriend; his family; Antigua.

After he had finished he staggered off into the bathroom and Sue, with great difficulty, because her wrists were still tied, eventually managed to wrap a sheet around her and went towards the main cabin where she saw John, Susan and Patrick roped to the mast. They all looked terrible. Cox had told them that Sue was dead. John wouldn't believe him and was immensely relieved when he caught sight of her and knew that the hijacker had been lying.

The yacht was bobbing about on the waves and Jack, who had taken a beer and a whole pineapple from the galley and had consumed them both, started to feel ill and vomited into the sink. In the confines of the cabin the smell, coupled with that of their sweat, was very unpleasant so, in order to diffuse the situation and to lessen the effect on both her and her companions, Sue went into the cabin and told him that she would help him. She got Cox to untie her hands and fetched a wet cloth to wipe Jack's face. She cleaned up the mess in the sink and told them that she would dress and then make coffee for them all. She went back into her cabin where she put on a T-shirt and some shorts. She was desperate to have a bath or at least a wash, but knew that she had to preserve the evidence of the rapes and so tried to ignore the urge to clean herself and went back to the galley to make the coffee. She asked if Susan might also be untied so that she could help her. This was done and Susan fetched some sea sickness tablets and gave one to Jack.

They all drank lots of coffee and tried to have a conversation with the two men. They were still bobbing around in open water and it occurred to them all that, despite the hijackers having had exactly what they had demanded, they might still be killed and dumped overboard.

Patrick had been untied once or twice to allow him to go to the cockpit and check that the boat was all right but he was always accompanied by one of the men so could do nothing to alert anyone to their plight. At around 4 a.m. he was again accompanied to the cockpit by Jack who also allowed Susan, now re-tied, to join them, leaving John and Sue with Cox, who sat on the fridge playing with the shotgun. Then the others returned to the cabin and Sue decided to wash up the coffee cups and pots. As she did so she managed to get one of the kitchen knives from a magnetic rack in the galley and hide it under her T-shirt. Neither of the hijackers saw what she had done but she believed that both Patrick and John had seen the knife.

By now they had been told to stop talking and Jack and Cox were having a whispered conference. They then told their victims what their ultimate fate was to be. At first light they were going to return to the island to fetch the boss of their gang and would then be leaving again with a parcel of drugs which they were going to take to Florida. On the way there, when *Severance* was in very deep water, they planned to kill the two couples and dump their bodies over the side. They told them that they would become 'shark meat'.

A plan had to be made to ensure that this did not happen but while they were without weapons and were being watched by two madmen armed with a large knife and a pump-action shotgun, the outlook seemed very bleak.

John said he needed to go to the bathroom. It was a genuine need but gave him a moment to think and he decided that, on his return to the cabin, he would pretend to be ill. He came back and slumped onto one of the bunks, saying that he felt ill. His face was deathly pale and no one had any difficulty in believing that he was unwell. He started to hyperventilate and clutched at his chest. His acting was so good that Susan was completely taken in and thought he really was having a heart attack and was going to die. She screamed at Jack, telling him to untie her as she had heart pills in the first aid kit and needed to give one to John immediately. He allowed her to fetch one and she gave it to John, telling him to put it under his tongue. John was unable to let her know that he was just acting and had to take the tablet that she offered. As the powerful drug took effect he believed that he might really have a heart attack. Slowly he began to feel a little better but still continued to act as if he was very ill. He said that he needed to go to the bathroom again but this time Jack wouldn't allow him to move and Susan fetched a bucket for him to use. Sue went over to help him and under the pretence of holding up a blanket to protect his modesty, managed to take the knife from under her T-shirt and drop it into the bucket. John grabbed it and hid it on the bunk.

It was now getting light and the hijackers decided that the time had come for them to go back to fetch the boss. Patrick was untied and was told to start back to Antigua. He was directed towards Five Islands Harbour and as they passed Pelican Reef was told to head for the nearest beach where they anchored just offshore. Cox then told Jack to guard the captives and, leaving him with the knife and the shotgun, started the engine on the dinghy being towed behind the boat and headed for the shore.

The couples were now only guarded by one man but they knew that in the confines of the cabin if he used his shotgun, he would injure or perhaps even kill them all. They knew they had to be very careful but didn't know how much time they had before Cox, and his boss and maybe others, would be coming back to the yacht.

Lying on the bunk, half covered with a blanket that was concealing the kitchen knife, John knew that he only had one chance to give the acting performance of a lifetime. He began moaning and clutching his chest once more and Susan, still believing that his distress was genuine, went over to him to see what she could do for him. She shouted to Jack to come and look and told him that if John died he would be in very big trouble. As Jack bent towards him, John suddenly threw off the blanket and jabbed the knife at the hijacker's chest, touching him but not injuring him at all. To everyone's amazement, Jack was so startled that he fell back onto the floor whereupon Sue sat on his face. Patrick quickly tied Jack's feet together and then disappeared. When he returned he had a gun with him which had been in the engine compartment all along and about which the others had known nothing. He had been waiting for an opportunity to grab it but having been shadowed whenever he was allowed to move around had not had the chance to retrieve it before then. Sue continued to sit on Jack's head and he was panicking. He was thrashing around on the floor trying to breathe and Sue thought that he was beginning to suffocate. After what she had been through because of him she wasn't really bothered but it was clear to them all that they would have no more problems with him and so she got up and his hands were also tied.

While Susan rushed over to the radio and made a Mayday call, John and Patrick went to the doorway, taking the shotgun with them, to see if the others were on their way back to *Severance*. The dinghy was still on the shore where Cox had abandoned it but they could not see any movement on the beach and hoped that the police would arrive before the gang came back to carry out their death threats. While in the doorway they aimed the shotgun towards the sky and fired it to check whether or not it was actually loaded. It was and the terrific bang that resounded around the bay must have alerted the gang to the fact that something had happened on the boat. They obviously thought that Jack had fired the gun as a warning to them and did not make an attempt to reach the yacht. Despite using binoculars John and Patrick could not see anyone on or near the beach but they both felt that the boat was being watched and were careful to keep themselves hidden.

Having heard Susan's Mayday call, the armed police in the capital, St John's, boarded a motor boat and began to speed out across the water to look for the yacht that had made the distress call. When they were almost alongside they realized that, although they had their guns, they had left the ammunition behind and so returned to St John's to fetch it, leaving *Severance* and its occupants unguarded. Happily others had also heard the call and, within a few moments of it being made, a beautiful white motor launch came speeding towards the yacht and four armed men, in smart white uniforms, boarded her. They had come from a German millionaire's luxury yacht, *Carinthia VI*, and were part of his security team. When they saw that one of the hijackers had been caught and was tied up on the floor they began kicking the terrified man. John, however, stopped them saying that Jack was his prisoner and that he would hand him over when the police arrived. Other vessels also turned up including a diving boat and a tourist boat, the *Jolly Roger*. Eventually, after all the other would be rescuers, the police finally arrived and Jack was taken into custody.

Sue told the men from *Carinthia VI* that she had been raped and that she needed to get to a hospital as soon as possible so that medical evidence could be obtained. She was determined that, after everything they had put her through, the two hijackers should be prosecuted. Susan went with Sue to the hospital while John and Patrick remained onboard *Severance* to give the police a full account of what had happened to them all. Although it was still very early in the morning a lot of people had been listening to the shortwave radio broadcast and were waiting to see who came ashore.

The guards from *Carinthia VI* took both women directly to the hospital which they said, had been a gift from the Canadian Red Cross to the people of Antigua and so Sue was hopeful that it would have modern up-to-date facilities. When they arrived her heart sank. The hospital was a dreadful mess. The waiting room had only a few shabby wooden benches and although Sue was told that there was a female gynaecologist who could attend to her, she wasn't at the hospital at that moment and had to be fetched from St John's. She was told to take a seat and wait while they sent someone to get her. When Susan asked to be directed to the toilet facilities she found that the doors to all the cubicles had been broken and ripped off their hinges and the hospital buildings in general had been allowed to get into a deplorable state.

When the gynaecologist arrived at the hospital Sue was pleased to find a very smart Antiguan lady who had done her medical training in New York and had specialized in treating rape victims. She apologized for the terrible state of the hospital. She told Sue that she had only returned to her homeland the week before and was disgusted with the way they had allowed the hospital to deteriorate. Sue in turn told her that she had been raped by two men and that she had not showered as she wanted to preserve the evidence. The doctor told her to climb onto the examination table and she began her work to obtain the proof of Sue's ordeal. The light was too dim and she asked a nurse to fetch the lamp from her desk but when it arrived found that the bulb was broken so had to do the examination by the light of a torch. Part of the problem was that there was no glass in the window and so the venetian blind had been pulled down to cover the gaping hole. As Sue was being examined she turned her head and found to her horror that she was being watched by a man, seemingly with no connection to the hospital, who had reached through the window and lifted the blind so that he could see what was going on. Sue yelled at him to get lost and, as she did so, the examination table collapsed. One of the legs had broken – the result of woodworm – and the table had to be propped up on bricks so that the examination could be completed.

Sue was concerned that she might have caught a nasty disease from one or the other of the rapists and although there was not very much information about Aids at that time she had heard about it and was very worried. The doctor managed to reassure her about this saying that there were no cases of Aids at all in Antigua. She told Sue not to worry and said that she would give her a very large dose of penicillin and that she would then write a report which Sue should take to her doctor when she returned to England so that more antibiotics could be prescribed. She wrote a prescription for the initial penicillin dose and called a nurse to fetch it from the pharmacy. The nurse soon returned with the news that they didn't have any of this particular drug and she was told to go to St John's and get some. There was then an argument about who would pay but eventually Sue was told to wait and about an hour later the nurse returned with the drug. She began to look for a suitable syringe to administer the penicillin and found one in her desk drawer. She told Sue that she couldn't sterilize the needle as the sterilizer was broken so instead held it in the flame of a match before delivering an extremely painful dose of the drug which left Sue with a nasty boil where the needle had penetrated her flesh.

Then, having no money at all, she and Susan had to get the hospital to pay for a taxi to take them to the British High Commission where John and Patrick joined them.

The High Commissioner's secretary tried to stop them seeing him as she said he was too busy. A British man had died there a few days before and the High Commissioner had to contact the man's widow and arrange for the body to be taken back to the UK, so he was unwilling to involve himself in any other problems. John, however, insisted and pushed his way into the man's office where they found him shuffling papers around his desk. John told him that they had to have help as they had not eaten since the day before, had had a terrible, frightening experience at the hands of two armed criminals, had no money, no documents, his wife had been raped twice and the yacht on which they had been staying had been impounded by the Antiguan police. Despite their dreadful situation the High Commissioner was very unhelpful and they were assisted instead by the crew of a large British-owned yacht who had heard about their predicament on the radio and who contacted the owner of the yacht in England to ask his permission to take the four victims onboard. He immediately agreed, although Patrick and Susan did not take up the kind offer, going instead to stay with some friends who lived nearby so that they could keep an eye on what the police were doing with *Severance*. John and Sue, however, were delighted to accept the generous offer. They were taken onboard the yacht, *Five Angels*, where the crew looked after them while the police completed their enquiries; the hijackers, both of whom were now in custody, were charged and the preliminary court proceedings were undertaken. They stayed on the yacht, in the owner's suite, for several days and the crew were wonderful. Not only did they look after them exceptionally well – nothing was too much trouble for them – they also talked to them, and allowed Sue and John to talk about their experience, which helped them both enormously.

Every time the police needed to speak to the couple they sent a car with at least one motorbike outrider accompanying it and John and Sue had to make more statements, attend identity parades after the second man had been caught and then go to the magistrate's court for the preliminary hearing which decided whether or not the two men had a case to answer. Wherever they were taken there were crowds of people who all seemed to know who they were and it was always a relief to get back to the *Five Angels* where they could relax away from the public's gaze.

At first the police told them that nothing like this had ever happened before but they soon discovered that this was a lie and that it was happening on a fairly regular basis. They couldn't help but notice that a man in a red Lamborghini always seemed to be wherever they were and they thought that he must be watching them. The police said he wasn't; he was just a government official but, as the days passed and they got to know the police who were guarding them better, they discovered that the man referred to by Jack and Cox as the 'boss' was employed by a minor government official who was, himself, employed by a government minister who organized the drug running. The government at that time was in the hands of the Bird family who had dominated Antiguan politics since Vere C. Bird, after whom the country's international airport is now named, became Antigua's first Prime Minister in 1981. During that time there had been accusations of money laundering, drug trafficking and arms smuggling levelled at the family, including Vere Bird's second son Lester, who became the country's Prime Minister in 1994 following his father's retirement.[1] Despite the controversy Vere Bird was knighted in 1998.

The police escort that the Hutchinsons were given was, they later discovered, because the police feared that they might be harmed by thugs in the employ of those government officials involved in drug smuggling who wanted to keep the case out of court.

When the preliminary hearing began, it was presided over by a magistrate; a delightful old gentleman who was the uncle of West Indian cricketer,

Sir Garfield Sobers, and the small court room was crowded with local people. As the evidence was heard, the magistrate frequently became distressed by the events that were being described and, dabbing his eyes with a handkerchief, had to adjourn the case to allow him to recover his composure. Eventually, however, the hearing was complete and he ruled that there was a case for the two defendants to answer. John and Sue, along with Patrick and Susan, were told that they would have to return to Antigua in about two months time for the case to be heard in the High Court. Before leaving Antigua John and Patrick went to see Lester Bird, one of whose functions at that time was as Minister of Economic Development, Tourism and Energy, and he extracted a promise from them that they would not make any statements in the press about what had happened to them provided that justice was seen to be done and that the trial of the two men was conducted properly.

When they arrived home Sue and John decided that they would tell their friends what had happened to them and began to do so immediately. They spoke to their friends in the village and also went to see others who were farther afield, including Patrick and Ruth Cliff. Patrick had, by then, also left the Royal Air Force and the couple were running a hotel in Kent. Sue and John wanted to tell their friends the whole story of the appalling nightmare they had lived through, including Sue's double rape and they talked about it for some hours which Patrick believes helped them. Patrick and Ruth's second daughter Gilly, by then a young woman, was at home during the Hutchinsons' visit and was in tears, listening to the terrible things that they had suffered.

Sue's 76 year old father also had to be told but, understandably, she wanted to spare him the most upsetting details. Whilst it was relatively easy to disclose to their son Chris the bare facts of the actual hijack and how they had all managed to survive it, it was far more difficult to tell him about the physical abuse his mother had had to endure. While still in Antigua Sue wrote him a very long letter telling him everything that had happened to her, saying that he could ask her anything about it and that she would tell him whatever he wanted to know. Chris was horrified at what his mother had written but was grateful to have received her full account. Later Sue decided to speak publically about her ordeal and went on to counsel rape victims. Her cheerful and practical disposition, coupled with her great sense of humour, enabled her to put her own suffering behind her and give comfort and support to others who had had similar horrifying experiences.

Life for the couple started to get back to normal. John resumed his flying duties but while he was away from home Sue kept getting disturbing telephone calls. They were from someone with a West Indian accent who told her that if she and John returned to Antigua for the trial they would be murdered. They were obviously being watched in the tiny village where they lived and some of their friends reported seeing one or two West Indians prowling around the area. John even had a phone call from a senior official at the Antiguan High Commission in London who tried to persuade him not to return to Antigua to testify. John was furious and felt that he was then within his rights to renege on the undertaking made to Lester Bird and so contacted the *Daily Mail* to see if they were interested in the story. He felt that if everything was in the public domain it might reduce the risk that he and Sue were under since neither had any intention of allowing themselves to be intimidated. They were adamant that they would return to Antigua for the court case. The newspaper was very interested and sent a journalist, Brian Vine, to speak to them. He subsequently wrote three articles, detailing everything that had happened to them, which were run in the paper on consecutive days from 16–18 July 1984.[2]

Having discussed the situation with a friend, Roger Pinnington, who would later become Chris's father-in-law, John was advised to contact Roger's friend Douglas Leese, a businessman with lots of contacts in New York to where John made most of his flights. Douglas pointed out to John that there were a lot of Antiguans living in New York – Lester Bird, himself, had been born there – and that it would be easy for one of them to plant something in John's hotel room while he was on a stopover, and then contact the drug enforcement agency. John would be arrested and deported, ensuring that he would not be able to return to Antigua for the trial and losing his career into the bargain. John was sceptical but Douglas told him that was the sort of thing that drug dealers did. This was confirmed the next time that John went to New York and contacted Douglas's friend who was the head of the drug enforcement agency at Kennedy Airport. He was very interested in what John had to tell him and took a full statement which he said would be kept on record and used should anyone try to plant drugs in his hotel room.

At the beginning of August, John and Sue received a letter from the

Assistant Superintendent of Police in St John's, Antigua, written on behalf of the Director of Public Prosecution, informing them that they were required to return to Antigua to give evidence in the High Court in the case against Ian 'Jack' Benjamin and Lesroy 'Cox' Reviere, which was due to begin on 1 October. Although relieved that it was all finally coming to an end, Sue was understandably nervous about giving evidence. The prosecution counsel had told her that she was the key witness and that he was going for the death penalty. It seemed to her that such a sentence would be rather excessive but the prosecution wanted it to be a deterrent to other hijackers. Although both she and John were confident that she had been right not to struggle, as she had been in fear for her life and those of her companions, they were concerned that the defence might take her acquiescence as proof of her consent and that the rape charges might be dropped. John again contacted the *Daily Mail* and was told that he and Sue would be accompanied to Antigua by what he described as 'two of their heavies' and by journalist Ann Leslie, who had been commissioned by the paper to report on the court case. She later revealed that she was not willing to merely accept the Hutchinsons' version of the events and wanted to satisfy herself that Patrick had had no part in the drug dealing. After a couple of days of investigation she was quite clear that Patrick was just as much a victim as the others.

On 1 October all four of the hijackers' victims went to the High Court. As Ann Leslie wrote afterwards:

> *Initially, the two youths had intended to plead not guilty, hoping the four Britons would not return to Antigua to relive the ordeal by giving evidence, and at an earlier hearing had swaggered and laughed in the dock as though they saw themselves as local 'macho' heroes.*[3]

When John, Sue, Patrick and Susan came into the court the faces of the defendants fell and their lawyer spoke to them in hushed tones. He then told the court that his clients wished to change their plea of 'Not Guilty' to 'Guilty'.

Ann Leslie's account continued:

> *Sitting behind the four Britons was Ian Benjamin's mother, her*

*face set with resentment; she had paid for her son's defence but neither looked at nor talked to him.*

*She has apparently become obsessed with the idea that the case would not have been brought had it not been for the fact that the victims were 'rich white people'. When the judge pronounced the verdict she hissed and spat 'white people!'*[xi]

Both defendants went to prison. Jack was sentenced to 10 years and Cox received 12 years for the armed robbery and they were both sentenced to eight years for the rapes; the sentences to be served concurrently. The judge was known to usually impose light sentences and, although the prosecution had hoped for more, he had, in fact, given the toughest sentences of his career to date. While he was in the mood for punishment he also castigated the victims for having spoken to the press and for bringing representatives from the *Daily Mail* to Antigua with them. They were not concerned with his anger; it was such a relief to know that their ordeal was now over that John commented to Ann Leslie, after looking at Jack, 'What a waste. I almost feel sorry for him'. Patrick Tisdall felt no such sympathy. Because of the actions of these two arrogant young thugs his retirement business had been destroyed before it had really begun and he and Susan Northcote eventually sold *Severance* and left the Caribbean to start a new life elsewhere.

# Chapter 15

# The True Face of the Earth

*The aeroplane has unveiled for us the true face of the earth.*

Antoine de Saint-Exupery, 1900–1944, French aviator and writer

On 10 September 1983 John was asked by the BBC to broadcast a short message from the flight deck of Concorde while over RAF St Athan in Wales where a Battle of Britain air show was taking place. The main commentary for the show was being given by veteran commentator Raymond Baxter, a Spitfire pilot during the Second World War, who introduced John's section:

> Fifteen minutes ago a British Airways Concorde service to New York took-off from Heathrow which means he'll be overhead at any minute. Captain John Hutchinson, in command, has promised to give us a call just before he goes supersonic.

Raymond Baxter then called the aircraft and John replied:

> BBC St Athan from Speedbird Concorde 193. You should, in fact, see us fairly soon. We're 13 miles to the east of the field. In fact we can see you down there now.

The message was acknowledged and John continued:

> I think we're probably going to go into cloud at any minute so

we'll start climbing and accelerating anytime now if you've got me on the screen there.

I'd just like to say what a great privilege and honour it is to be invited to talk to you like this from our Concorde up here and I hope very much that the St Athan air display is a tremendous success. It is, of course, a Battle of Britain display and as such I think it would be most appropriate to just remember, during the course of the day, those pilots who gave their lives during that battle and contributed in no small measure, I think it's fair to say, towards the freedom that we enjoy in our country today and also, of course, the freedom of the skies that we enjoy today.

There was a brief pause and then:

We're now getting our climb clearance. We're climbing to 60,000 feet; ground speed at the moment is 500 mph and our Mach number is 0.7. We shall be continuing climbing and accelerating like this and we'll be ready to go through the sound barrier at about 25,000 feet. It's interesting to note, BBC St Athan from 193, that at the moment we're doing a rate of climb of 5,000 feet a minute which is a vertical rate of climb of about 60 mph and that's a pretty heavy load for a transatlantic crossing. When we do some of our charter flights with Concorde where the aircraft is, of course, much lighter because we are carrying much less fuel, we can achieve up to 150 – 180 mph vertical rate of climb which I think is a fairly dramatic performance. It would probably only be matched by the fighters that the Royal Air Force possesses.

Raymond, if I may just also conclude by saying that I hope this won't be the last time that Concorde is visible in the Cardiff area. I'm hoping very much that everybody there will be able to get a closer look at it sometime towards the end of May next year and we'll all look forward to that very much if it comes off.

With that John's first broadcast ended and Raymond Baxter thanked him and wished him 'Bon Voyage'.

John had made the broadcast completely unscripted and the BBC was so impressed with his performance that the following year, when producer and director, Rick Gardner, was looking for a new team of commentators for its coverage of air shows, John was asked to audition for the team.

> I was surprised to say the least. I was also flattered and excited. I've no idea why they picked me but I'm looking forward to it all very much.[1]

Rick wanted John because he was 'very knowledgeable, had a high profile as a Concorde pilot and was a nice guy'.[2] Having completed his audition Rick told John that his voice was rather too posh and that his voice went up at the end of each sentence. John was keen to learn all he could and took Rick's remarks in good part. It was to be the start of a long broadcasting career for John and an equally long friendship between the two men.

John's new role, while remaining a Concorde pilot, relied heavily on the cooperation of British Airways since many of the shows on which he would be reporting were held at times when he would otherwise have been flying. Happily the airline seemed to be just as pleased by the situation as John himself and arranged roster changes to ensure he would be available during the days on which the air shows were being held.

For his first assignment John flew Concorde to the USAF base at Mildenhall in Suffolk and began his commentary from the flight deck before landing. Later he interviewed the pilots and engineers at Mildenhall about their aircraft. Dave McDonald, the flight engineer onboard the Concorde recalled how:

> Having arrived in the holding area some 15 minutes ahead of show time, this was the opportunity for JCH to do his piece to camera, from the left hand seat, so he duly left the operation to the co-pilot and me. While John was filming we accepted an offer to beat-up an almost deserted airfield (RAF) that was providing radar coverage for us. With nose and visor up, we thundered across the airfield, quite low. At this point John, finished with camera, looked around, saw 500 feet, 300 knots across an empty airfield and, thinking we were displaying at the wrong airfield and his reputation would be shot, said '… what the *#@!£!! are you doing?'

Later that year he was one of the commentators at the Farnborough Air

Show along with Raymond Baxter. Since the show was held over several days, the broadcast team was given accommodation in an old pub nearby. Sue joined John there and discovered that although the pub had lots of character, the bathroom facilities left a lot to be desired. The hot water system was erratic and usually only produced enough water for one bath. Sue asked Raymond Baxter if he would mind sharing the bathwater with her and used the bath when he had finished. The system worked well for them both although what the others did has not been recorded.

The Farnborough broadcasts that year were produced by Rick's team and included presenter Chris Serle who said that Rick introduced a real sense of adventure and excitement to the programmes. Chris and John worked well together too, each appreciating the other's expertise.

Chris recalled that when John was asked by Rick to do a parachute jump as part of a later broadcast, he replied: 'As a pilot I have an absolute rule that I never step out of a serviceable aircraft.'

He did, however, relent, and eventually agreed to do an accelerated freefall jump using a ram air parachute. He was trained at RAF Weston on the Green, the home of the No. 1 Parachute Training School's training drop zone and made the jump on his birthday. Just before doing so Rick said to him, 'Oh, by the way, John, I also want you to commentate' knowing that if it didn't work out he could add the audio part afterwards. He didn't have to; John did a commentary all the way down, pointing out Oxford, Weston on the Green and the actual drop zone and also gave some information about the wind direction. Then he landed, on his feet and directly on the drop zone. His first words were, 'Well, I vowed never to jump out of a serviceable aircraft and my only regret is I wish I'd done it sooner'. As Rick says, 'it was great television', and John broke the world record for altitude on a first jump. Chris Serle described him as a 'proper trouper' and said that he entered into it with:

> … boyish enthusiasm. John is boyishly enthusiastic about everything.
> There is no side to him. He is modest, charming and a complete gentleman. He wants to succeed but he also enjoys the success of others.[3]

Over the years there were several occasions where a Concorde flew in a display with the world famous RAF display team, the Red Arrows. On 18 May 1985 John was involved in such a display when he flew on Concorde as co-pilot and commentator on what was a unique, three-way display. The Red Arrows in their Hawks took-off to join Concorde G-BOAG after it left Heathrow Airport. The difference in this display was that both the Hawks and Concorde flew down to the south coast where the Cunard liner *Queen Elizabeth 2* was sailing off Portland Bill. There were two chase planes accompanying the Red Arrows – one had their team manager onboard while in the other was aviation photographer Arthur Gibson who took still photos of the display. Rick Gardner was with the Red Arrows in Red 1, filming the event with a video camera. The Hawks were vectored on to Concorde where they took up their position in front of the supersonic airliner and at a higher altitude. They made several attempts to get to the correct position for filming over the *QE2* before settling on a height of around 1,500 feet by which time passengers onboard the liner were clearly visible on deck, looking up at what was happening in the skies above them. Rick had asked the Red Arrows to make one of their formations a T as a tribute to Concorde test pilot Brian Trubshaw, which they did. The *QE2* passengers witnessed a wonderful display, Rick made a memorable film and the famous photo that Arthur Gibson took was called both the shot of the year and the shot of the century and was sold as a print and as a postcard.

John also worked with Rick Gardner and Chris Serle at the Biggin Hill air show where Concorde flew with a Spitfire on one side and a Hurricane on the other. Rick wanted a shot of the three aircraft coming towards John who, as they came close, would turn to the camera and make a suitable comment for the viewers. The Concorde was flying at near to its stall speed with the Second World War veterans flat out trying to keep up, but they managed it perfectly. John stood watching them with his back to the camera but as he turned to speak, Rick could see there were tears streaming down his face. The magical sight of the three aircraft flying in perfect formation towards him was just too much for John who is, as Rick discovered, quite an emotional person, but he quickly managed to resume his role as commentator and, since he was not in a close up shot, Rick knew that the viewers would not see his tears and continued filming him.

John and Sue's neighbour, Sid Batterbury, recalled that John had not been flying Concorde for very long when they first met. The other inhabitants of the village quickly learnt that they had a Concorde pilot in their midst but found him to be modest about his achievements and ready to join in with village life whenever he was at home. Over 30 years after they first met, Sid says of his neighbour:

> John is trustworthy, honest and kind. He never brags about his achievements and you will never hear him boast. He is very relaxed about his fame and people enjoy being with him – he has friends all over the world. He never says bad things about people, he is just a lovely chap.
>
> When he was flying Concorde he had a medical check-up every six months. He never prepared for it; he doesn't exercise, do any gardening or DIY but he was always fine![4]

John's involvement with village life included the annual fete and after he began his broadcasting career he enlisted the help of Rick Gardner, Chris Serle and the Red Arrows for one of these occasions. John had undertaken to find someone to open the fete and asked Chris if he would do it. He was happy to and stayed for the whole event, later attending a party held by the Hutchinsons at their home. John also contacted the Red Arrows and asked if it would be possible for them to fly over the village while the fete was in progress. They duly appeared at a pre-arranged time, having diverted on their way to an air display, and flew in formation over the tiny village with red, white and blue smoke streaming out behind them and, at John's request, Rick gave the commentary to accompany the fly past.

Having become very friendly with John, when Rick Gardner asked him to be godfather to his daughter Sally, he agreed. He took this duty seriously and has always found time in his busy schedule to keep in touch with Sally. He and Sue have often taken her to the theatre and it was John who was piloting the aircraft when Sally made her first flight. John was flying an Auster but the little girl described it as a 'stunt plane' and was thrilled with the experience.[5]

One day when John was having a drink in a pub with Bill Brown and Jock Lowe, the trio were chatting about their work on Concorde and one of them brought up the subject of using the airliner for charter flights. The idea grew and they formed a company to operate the flights which offered trips over the Bay of Biscay and the North Sea and special flights for company promotions.

The flights over the Bay of Biscay began at Heathrow Airport and lasted approximately 2 hours. Passengers were flown at subsonic speeds until they reached the Bristol Channel where the aircraft turned towards the south to fly over the Bay of Biscay at Mach 2 before returning to Heathrow after the champagne trip of a lifetime. They were the ideal way to celebrate a special birthday or wedding anniversary and, in the early part of the 1980s cost just £285 for the two hour flight.

Two flights were also made to Newcastle and the *British Airways News*[6] reported that 20,000 people came to the airport to see Concorde land, the supersonic part of the flight having first taken place over the North Sea.

In October 1983, car manufacturer Vauxhall-Opel booked Concorde as a reward for 75 of their dealers who had sold the most number of Cavalier cars. The trip was called the Cavalier Concorde Challenge and took place over two days. On the evening before the flight a celebratory dinner was held at the Chiltern Hotel in Luton. John flew Concorde into Luton Airport that afternoon and he and the crew were driven to the hotel in special Cavaliers, bearing the words 'British Airways Concorde Crew' along their sides. It was the first time that a Concorde had ever landed at Luton and the crew had to have a police escort to get them through the large crowd, estimated to be 12,000 people, that had assembled around the airport to see the supersonic airliner arrive. They had brought a group of people described as 'unsung heroes' with them from Heathrow for the experience of flying in Concorde even though they didn't reach supersonic speeds. Had they done so it was reported that the flight to Luton would only have taken just over 60 seconds. It actually took approximately 35 minutes since the speed was restricted to 330 mph to ensure that the passengers did have an enjoyable, albeit short, trip.

The dinner that evening was hosted by Mike Tearle, Vauxhall Motors' Field Operations Manager and John and his crew were the guests of honour. The following morning they returned to the airport where the 75 most successful dealers were joined by 10 employees from the Vauxhall factory in Luton who had been chosen by ballot, the Mayor of Luton, the Chairman and Managing Director of Vauxhall Motors and several reporters from local newspapers and radio stations. After the take-off the aircraft flew down over the Bay of Biscay where it reached Mach 2 and then landed at Bordeaux for a tour of two special vineyards – Château Pavie and Château Beau-Séjour Becot. This was followed by a 'Vin d'Honneur' ceremony at the Great Hall of the Monastery of St Emilion and then a long lunch at L'Hostellerie de Plaisance where the dealers received thanks for their sales performances and John and his crew were praised for their friendliness and efficiency.

When the speeches and the lunch were over they returned to Bordeaux Airport where they boarded Concorde for the return to Luton. Although late in October the weather was good and they were able to spot several towns and witnessed a spectacular sunset before landing.

A reporter from the local newspaper, the *Luton News* said in the account of the trip: 'The only question Vauxhall chiefs are asking now is: What can we possibly do to top all that?'

The following day a radio announcer from Chiltern Radio said of the trip:

> The two o'clock news will just have to wait while I tell you how much I enjoyed the Cavalier Concorde Challenge event. I don't know about you but my feet haven't touched the ground since! Many thanks to all concerned in the organization of a very smooth operation.[7]

There were more special flights to come. One that John remembered well was from New York to Detroit. Two Concordes left New York together. John's aeroplane was supposed to leave the stand first but the other, piloted by Colin Morris, blocked him in and got away first, although they arrived in the Detroit area together. The airport had parallel runways and they had been cleared to first do an overshoot at around 200 feet and then come around for a synchronized landing, one on each runway. All went well and the two Concordes touched down together. Later that evening John watched the local television news in his hotel room and discovered that they had caused chaos in the Detroit Airport area. There were traffic jams everywhere and there had been several accidents caused by car drivers looking up at the aeroplanes rather than at where they were going. As John said, it wasn't such a good advert for British Airways but it did show that Concorde really was an aeroplane that captivated the imagination.

The most exotic charter flight that John was involved with took place in

1990. A Miami travel agent chartered Concorde for a round the world luxury trip with several stops at exotic locations. The passengers spent three nights at each stopover, staying in first class hotels. The travel agent had also arranged for astronaut Frank Borman, commander of the Apollo 8 lunar orbital mission in 1968, to act as host for the trip. John was asked to take the aeroplane from London to New York, where the passengers boarded, and then on to Sydney via Acapulco, Las Vegas, Honolulu, Tahiti and Christchurch. A new crew would take over in Sydney for the return trip to New York. The travel agent had asked John if the wives of the flight crew would like to go along too and at first John had refused; a decision that didn't make him popular with Sue. When he explained why he had refused she could see the logic of what he said but was still disappointed. John was concerned that the cabin staff would be upset if their spouses were not also invited. Sue wanted to know if he had asked them what they thought about the invitation and, when he did ask them, he found that none of the cabin crew's partners could have come on the trip anyway. He therefore contacted the travel agent and accepted the offer.

Most of the 80 passengers were wealthy, elderly Americans; some couples, several widowers and a few single ladies. They all had one thing in common – they were fascinated by the supersonic airliner. There were four flight crew, the extra person being what was called a PR captain. It was his job to give the passengers a commentary about what was happening during take-off and landing and to point out anything of interest over which they might be flying. The four wives assisted the cabin crew in looking after the passengers, especially those travelling alone. One of these was a widower whose daughter had asked that special care be taken of him as he was diabetic. He was so excited about being on the Concorde that he often forgot his injections and tablets and Sue and the other wives made it one of their daily tasks to ensure that he had had his proper medication. Another was an elderly gentleman who was married but whose wife had not accompanied him. He had a heart problem and had been advised by his doctor not to make the trip but he was determined to fly faster than the speed of sound and so had ignored the advice.

Having flown supersonic over the Gulf of Mexico, their first stop was Acapulco, the largest city in the state of Guerrero on the Pacific coast of Mexico, with its beautiful beaches, golf courses and nightclubs. It was here that the first and only major problem of the trip occurred. The old gentleman with the heart trouble died. Because it was at the beginning of the tour and he had been sitting at the back of the aeroplane, no one had got to know him at this point and so his absence was not noted by the other passengers. His wife back in the USA had to be notified and when a call was put through to her she wanted to know if he had achieved his ambition of flying supersonic. When she found that he had she was very relieved and said that it was what he wanted and she was so pleased that he had managed to do it. She then asked for arrangements to be made to fly his body back home. This was all attended to and the trip continued, heading north again to Las Vegas.

As they made their approach into McCarran International Airport, Las Vegas, Sue could see what looked like rows of ants on the ground. These turned out to be cars lining the runway. Having landed they discovered that when people knew that Concorde was about to land they had come to the airport to see it. The casinos emptied – an unheard of situation – and the gamblers rushed outside to watch it touch down. There was great excitement in the desert town as the supersonic airliner had not been there before. It was Sue's first visit too and she was amazed to find that even in the ladies' restroom at the airport there were slot machines. Some of the passengers were equally astonished to find that she had never used them before and insisted on giving her some coins with which to play. Before it was time to leave she had accumulated a small pile of winnings which she tried to give back to the gentlemen who had put up the stake in the first place. They wouldn't hear of it and so she was left with a bag full of coins to take with her onto the next stop – Honolulu.

Having stayed in Honolulu for three days they took-off for the beautiful French Polynesian island of Tahiti which John said was; '… one of the most wonderful places I have ever been to'. It was during their stay in Tahiti that the passengers realized that one of their number was missing. The diabetic passenger had a Polaroid camera and during the first leg of the journey had begun taking photos of his fellow travellers on which he drew speech bubbles with witty little comments. By the time they reached Tahiti he had completed his self-imposed task and set about distributing the pictures to the others. He handed out all but one but couldn't find the missing passenger and sought the help of the purser to find him. She immediately realized it was the old gentleman who had died in Acapulco and quickly informed him that the man in question had been unavoidably detained in Mexico and had had, therefore, to leave the tour!

The three day stay in Tahiti passed by in a flash and soon they were getting ready to leave. Before they departed from the Polynesian paradise, however, John gave the passengers a breathtaking flight at 1,000 feet across the other islands in the group, circling Bora Bora and then returning to do a flypast over Papeete, the capital city of Tahiti before heading out towards Christchurch on the south island of New Zealand.

For John and the other crew members this was the last three days they would spend with their passengers before they went on to Sydney where they handed them, and the aeroplane, over to the crew who would be taking them back to the USA via Bali, Singapore, Sri Lanka and South Africa. The highlight of the stopover in New Zealand was, for John, a visit to Milford Sound which boasts the tallest sea cliffs in the world, and is situated in the Fiordland National Park on the west coast of the island. He was delighted to get the chance to see the cliffs and described them as 'truly breathtaking'. Despite the sad demise of the old gentleman, the first half of the round the world tour had been a huge success and one which John said:

> … seemed to get better and better as it went on and wherever we went we received a fantastically warm welcome. All in all, it was a trip I will always remember.

The passengers agreed that the trip had been fantastic and when they said goodbye to John and the rest of the crew wanted to present them with a very large tip that they had collected. John thanked them but explained that they were not allowed to accept gratuities. Eventually after some discussion it was decided that the money should be donated for a charitable purpose. John suggested that it should go to help the daughter of a British Airways colleague in New York who needed a liver transplant and the passengers agreed that it was an excellent idea. The little girl, 7 year old Jessica Stramezzi, had her transplant a few weeks after the trip. The operation went well and within five weeks she was out of hospital and despite the surgery, was soon playing, swimming and cycling like any 7 year old, much to the relief of her grateful parents.

# Chapter 16

# Discover your World

*Your work is to discover your world and then with all your heart give yourself to it.*

Prince Gautama Siddharta, 563–483 BC,
the founder of Buddhism

Fourteen years after the death of John's mother Viola, his father Wynne retired, having remained at St Hilda's as headmaster of the school since the loss of his wife. The Colonel, as he was known, was very popular with the girls and despite Viola having been the driving force behind the school, it continued to flourish during his time as headmaster. His own health was, however, deteriorating and he was eventually forced to give up his position to his deputy. Sadly his retirement lasted for only two years and he died at the beginning of 1983 leaving the school, by then a limited company, to his four children. John's sister, Mary Piachaud took over as headmistress in 1986 and made many more improvements before her retirement in 2002. She is now the sole owner of St Hilda's but John retains a keen interest in the school to which his parents had devoted so many years, and is chairman of the board of directors. It is a very successful establishment, usually oversubscribed, and, as the current headmistress Mrs Carolyn Godlee, says:

St. Hilda's is special. You can sense it from the moment you enter the building – a happy and purposeful working environment with its own unique, caring atmosphere.[1]

As well as his flying and broadcasting, John took on even more tasks during the 1980s. British Airways and the Cunard Line had got together to offer a luxury package across the Atlantic and back, flying Concorde one way and sailing the other on the cruise line's flagship the *Queen Elizabeth 2*. It was extremely good value; the trip was sold at less than the cost of the Concorde fare and proved to be popular. To promote it further Cunard asked British Airways if some of its Concorde captains could travel on the *QE2* sector and entertain the passengers by speaking about the supersonic airliner. The airline agreed and John was one of the pilots chosen, extending his CV a little further by becoming a lecturer on the ship. He found that he enjoyed giving the lectures about Concorde and that they were very well received.

John also became involved with a charity called Operation Happy Child which was run by staff at Heathrow Airport and helped local handicapped children.[2] Just before John's retirement Sir Donald Gosling, Joint Chairman of National Car Parks and a very frequent flyer, wrote to British Airways to say how impressed he was with the standard of service he had received with the airline and offered to make a donation to its charity of choice. In particular he wanted to tell deputy chairman and chief executive of British Airways, Sir Colin Marshall, that:

> During the year I have made new friends among the crews, in particular Trevor Wright who flew me to the Gulf, Peter Horton and John Hutchinson who introduced me to some of the marvels of Concorde, and too many more to mention.

In his reply Sir Colin mentioned three charities all organized and run by airport staff, Dreamflight, the Cargo Kidney Fund and Operation Happy Child. Thanks to the efforts of the staff who had impressed Sir Donald, the three charities received cheques for £5,000 each.[3]

In August 1985 John and Sue attended a party to celebrate the 85th birthday of Her Majesty Queen Elizabeth the Queen Mother at her childhood home of St Paul's Waldenbury in Hertfordshire. They were among 400 people attending the party and John was surprised when one of Her Majesty's aides approached him and asked, 'Are you the Concorde pilot?' He confirmed that he was one of the Concorde pilots and was asked to stay where he was as Her Majesty wanted to speak to him. Lord King the then chairman of British Airways had invited the Queen Mother for a flight on Concorde to celebrate her birthday and when she came over to speak to John she told him all about it, declaring that it was absolutely wonderful. She then asked John if he realized that when he approached one of Heathrow's runways, he flew past her London home, Clarence House. John confirmed that he was aware of this and the Queen Mother then told him that if the weather was good she usually came to her window, with her first gin and tonic of the evening, and waved to Concorde as it passed. She explained that she loved looking at Concorde as it was the most beautiful aeroplane. John told her that now that he knew she would be looking out for the Concorde, whenever he came in to land on that runway he would waggle his wings as he passed Clarence House and flash his landing lights. The Queen Mother declared it to be a 'wonderful idea' and thereafter whenever John passed Clarence House in Concorde that is what he did, first making an announcement to his passengers to explain that the wings were being waggled 'by Royal Command'.

In early 2011 when John was telling his friend, British Airways pilot and Past Master of the Guild of Air Pilots and Air Navigators, David Mauleverer, about this book, David expressed the hope that his experience at a Buckingham Palace Garden Party would be included. John didn't know what he meant and so David explained that soon after the Queen Mother's party he had been invited to Buckingham Palace and had been presented to Her Majesty Queen Elizabeth. When she learned that he was a British Airways pilot she asked, 'How is that young Concorde captain, Hutchinson, doing?' The only conclusion that could be drawn from this was that Her Majesty had been told by her mother about the Concorde captain who waggled his wings at her as he passed Clarence House.

For some time John had been the captain of the British Airways' club for young flyers, the Junior Jet Club. Founded in 1957 as the BOAC Junior Jet Club, its first captain was the legendary Captain O. P. Jones who had begun his aviation career in the Royal Flying Corps in 1917. By the time he stopped flying to take up a position with BOAC as a lecturer and advisor, he had spent 21,600 hours in the air.[4] John took over as captain of the club from fellow Concorde pilot, Captain Leo Budd and, in March 1984, its format and name was changed and it became the Flightrider Club with John as its President. He was puzzled by the changes to the club, as were many former members, wondering why it was felt necessary to alter something that had worked so well in the past and had meant such a lot to the children, many of whom as adults still had their Junior Jet Club logbooks. He assumed that the airline's marketing department had felt that the change in name might attract more members who would be the customers of the future.

One of John's duties as President was to write a letter for each edition of the *Flightrider* magazine which, in addition to his contribution, contained articles about places around the world, exotic animals, pop stars, and aircraft. In his letters John always tried to include information about aviation and interesting places around the world which was what the Junior Jet Club had been about and what had made it special. One letter, for example, told readers about the Paris Air Show which John had visited. He wrote about the Eurofighter project and the demonstration given by the Airbus A320 and then went on to describe some work he had done for the BBC, commentating on a programme about the Schneider Trophy race in Bembridge on the Isle of Wight and giving a brief but fascinating history of the race itself. On another occasion he described flying with the Red Arrows in their famous Hawk aircraft while they were doing training flights and practising aerobatics:

> To say I enjoyed the flight would be an understatement. It was a fantastic experience. The Hawk is a beautiful aeroplane to fly, giving a smooth ride with excellent all-round visibility, even from the back seat where I was sitting.

As President of the Flightrider club John had been invited by John Burley, the British Airways Manager USSR, to visit the Anglo-American School in Moscow. John accepted the invitation and he and Sue made several trips to Moscow to speak to the children at the school who were very interested in aviation and had 'adopted' a Concorde. During the course of these visits John and Sue got to know John Burley and his wife Liz very well. Whenever they went to Moscow they were entertained by the Burleys, attending the Bolshoi ballet and ice hockey games, and were taken to the

British Airways dacha in the countryside approximately 100 kilometres from Moscow. The two couples became good friends during those visits and remain so to this day.

At John's suggestion, Chris Serle was asked to join the Flightrider team. His remit was to '… contribute a regular column on his hectic way of life and all things interesting' and he did just that. His articles in *Flightrider* magazine covered subjects as varied as flying in an unpressurized Hercules transport aircraft with no oxygen mask watching six soldiers make a parachute jump, to making a live television programme in a studio and to finding ways of stopping babies crying at night.

At the same time that he was writing for *Flightrider* magazine Chris was also working on a television programme called *In at the Deep End* in which he and fellow presenter, Paul Heiney, were trained to undertake a variety of occupations – hairdresser, auctioneer, bookmaker and romantic novelist, to name but a few. John wondered if Chris would like to become a Concorde pilot and do a take-off for the programme. Chris would have loved to and so John offered to arrange it all with British Airways. Ultimately the production team did not take up the offer but Chris thought it was fantastic that John would have been willing to arrange it all for him.

John also asked Sue if she would write something for *Flightrider* magazine about a holiday they had spent in the Antarctic the previous year. Over the years that John was President, Sue wrote several articles about the exotic places that she and John visited, her accounts being illustrated to a large extent with photos taken by John, especially those of birds for which he has a passion.

By the end of 1988 the Flightrider club had changed its name again, this time to Sky Flyers and the magazine seemed to be becoming more focused on pop music, television and fashion than aviation. It continued in this vein for some time but gradually became a much slimmer volume and in 1995 John wrote his final letter as the club's President when, although the club itself still existed, the publication of the magazine ceased.

While continuing to work as a commentator at various air shows, John was asked to take part in a documentary which was to be filmed onboard a Concorde being flown by him from London to Washington and Miami. The programme was entitled *The Noel Edmonds Concorde Special* and featured Noel Edmonds on the flight deck with John. It was shown on BBC 1 television and was a great success. The following year John made another programme with Noel Edmonds, *Air Show '89*. He was particularly impressed with a display by Soviet test pilot, Victor Pugachev, flying a Sukhoi Su 27 Flanker at the Paris Air Show and with the Diamond 9 Tiger Moth formation team which displayed at Biggin Hill, especially as one of the team was a fellow Concorde pilot, Steve Bohill Smith. He also worked with Noel Edmonds on the next show, *Air Show '90* and, later that year, appeared on the BBC 1 Christmas programme, *Noel's Christmas Presents* when, dressed in an eighteenth century costume, he flew two small girls, Helen and Sarah Oldreive and their father David to New York on Concorde as one of Noel's presents.

Although John's main love is for aeroplanes, he also enjoys sailing and, for many years, owned a third share of a 28-foot sailing sloop, the other owners being his friend Derek Bell, and David Hopkins, both airline pilots. When David wanted to sell his share John and Derek advertised for a new partner and found Michael Thompson. The three men and their wives had great fun with the boat which was kept on the River Orwell in Suffolk and the three-way partnership worked very well. None of them had it for more than a fortnight during the school holidays and there were never any arguments about money. They did the servicing during the winter; cold, dirty work done mostly by Derek who revealed that John was less than enthusiastic about this aspect of boat owning, one day telling the others, who were wet and covered in engine oil, 'I really think that it's important that one of us keeps our hands clean'!

John and Sue sailed to Holland a couple of times, but the trip that they remember most vividly was one taken on an October day with both partners and their wives, and a friend, George Wells, whose in-laws lived along the coast at Thorpeness. They sailed from Lowestoft and had arranged to be off the coast at Thorpeness at midday so that they could wave to George's in-laws. They arrived on time but there was no sign of the old couple in their garden so they sailed around in circles for a bit hoping that they would come out. John had recently bought a 20 million candle power lamp while in New York and had brought it with him on the boat. He fetched it and began flashing a signal at the house. Eventually the couple appeared and waved excitedly before returning to their house. Satisfied that they had accomplished what they had set out to do, the party continued sailing down the Suffolk coast towards Aldeburgh. Suddenly they were startled by a loud bang and the bright flash of a maroon rocket being fired, signalling the launch of the lifeboat. They looked around but couldn't see why the lifeboat was needed so continued on their way only to be called on the radio minutes later by the lifeboat crew asking if they were in distress. John answered the call and said that they were not in distress. The lifeboat radioed back that it had had reports of a yacht signalling an SOS and whose crew were frantically waving. Rather sheepishly John replied that they had been waving to friends on the shore but that they were most definitely not in distress. Since the lifeboat was now at sea its crew decided to continue to look for the yacht and asked John to maintain a listening watch. Eventually it radioed that it had found nothing and was returning to the lifeboat station. It was obvious to John and everyone else on board that the 'yacht in distress' had to have been theirs and that some overeager person on the shore had seen the flash of John's lamp, assumed it was an SOS and had called out the lifeboat. John felt so guilty about this that he decided he would have to do something to ease his conscience.

Having given lectures about Concorde on the *QE2* he wondered if it might be possible to give talks to local organizations to raise money for the Royal National Lifeboat Institution (RNLI). He contacted several groups who were pleased to have him as a speaker at their events and paid him for the lectures. He gave all the money he received to the RNLI who were most grateful for his efforts and made him an honorary life governor.

Later he became President of the Royston branch of the RNLI which was so successful at fundraising that they raised enough money to help purchase a wartime lifeboat, the *Jesse Lumb*, for the Imperial War Museum, where it now resides in Hangar 3 at Duxford in Cambridgeshire as part of the museum's maritime collection. Although John now feels that his conscience is clear, the charity has become dear to his heart and he still donates money from his lectures to the RNLI.

The three partners no longer own the boat but they have all remained friends and regularly have what they refer to as their 'AGM' over a pub lunch, enjoyed by them all.

Having graduated from the Royal Naval College in Dartmouth Chris Hutchinson went to Linton-on-Ouse for training on fixed wing aircraft and then to RNAS Culdrose to learn to fly helicopters. By then, however, the Navy was cutting back on its pilots and, before he had completed his training, Chris found himself unemployed. John and Sue decided to give him a helping hand and paid for him to go to Perth to Airwork Services Training to obtain his ATPL (Air Transport Pilot's Licence). While in Perth he was taught by the company's chief flying instructor, Archie Kinch who, as an RAF instructor, had also trained John during his Shackleton conversion course at RAF Kinloss.

One year after starting his course, Chris emerged with his ATPL and immediately applied to join British Airways. He was accepted but again fate stepped in and he received another letter from the airline telling him that he couldn't join them until he had 1,000 hours experience on jets; how he was expected to get the experience without the job was not explained.

After all the hard work and disappointment, Chris applied to British World Airlines at Southend Airport. The company had begun its life in 1946 as Silver City Airways, changing hands and names until it became British World Airlines in 1993[5] and was pleased to employ Chris as one of its pilots, flying the Vickers Viscount. In becoming a Viscount pilot Chris did something that John had never done. Despite the large number of aircraft types that he has flown over his many years as a pilot, John has never flown a turboprop airliner.

By the time he achieved his ambition of becoming a pilot Chris was already a husband and father. In December 1988 he had married Sally Ann Pearson, the girl who had been his brother's school friend. After leaving school Sally trained at the Guildhall School of Music and Drama and, after graduating, became an actress with the stage name, Sally George. She toured with the Royal Shakespeare Company and has appeared in many television dramas.

Sally's mother and stepfather, Ann and Roger Pinnington were friends of John and Sue and so Sally had known her husband's family for some time before the wedding and liked them very much. She said that they were 'great in-laws':

John is a good soul; sensitive and deep thinking. He likes to read poetry. Sue is more exuberant but they are devoted to each other; very supportive and full of energy.

The year after the wedding John and Sue became grandparents to Chris and Sally's first baby, a son they named Timothy George. Sue thought that he was just like his grandfather as he loved eating and sleeping. When Tim began to speak he called John 'Pompa' and Sue 'Ganny'. The names stuck and this is how they are still known to Tim and his two sisters, Rafaella, born in 1995 and Tigerlily, who completed the family in 2000.

# Chapter 17

# Change

*For time and the world do not stand still. Change is the law of life.*
*And those who look only to the past or the present are certain to miss*
*the future.*

John F. Kennedy, 1917–1963, 35th President of the USA

As 1989 drew to a close John received news that he had been elected
a Fellow of the Royal Aeronautical Society and declared himself to be:

> … extremely proud to have been honoured in such a way by this
> learned body and it made a wonderful New Year present for me.
>
> I think, perhaps, that the Fellowship belongs as much to that
> beautiful aeroplane Concorde as it does to me but, nevertheless,
> I must admit that it was one of the proudest moments of my life.

This honour followed one that he had received just over a year before
from the Court of the Guild of Air Pilots and Air Navigators (GAPAN).

The Guild had been formed in 1929, just 10 years after the first scheduled passenger flight began, transporting passengers between Hounslow
Heath in Middlesex and Le Bourget, Paris. It had become clear early in
the history of passenger transport that regulations surrounding the ever
growing number of flights were patchy and uncoordinated and a small
group of commercial pilots decided to address the problem by forming
a company along the lines of the City of London Livery Companies.
The first master of the Guild was the Director of Civil Aviation, Air

Vice-Marshal Sir W. Sefton Brancker, but his tenure was short-lived as he was killed on 5 October 1930 in the R101 airship disaster in Beauvais, France. However, the Guild itself flourished and, in 1956, was granted the status of a Livery Company becoming the 81st to be established in the City of London in 800 years.[1]

John, as a pilot, was eligible to apply for membership of the Guild and did so in 1983 becoming a Freeman on 7 July. The Guild quickly became a very important part of his life and this was recognized when, on 26 September 1988, he became a Liveryman, an honour that can only be conferred by the Court and is limited to 600 members who have made significant contributions to the Guild and to aviation in general. In the coming years John was to make many more noteworthy contributions to aviation and has remained an active member of the Guild ever since. His son Chris, although no longer a commercial pilot, is also a member.

The beginning of the new decade was a difficult time for John as he knew that he would soon have to retire from British Airways. He would be 55 years old in April 1992 and, at that time, this was the maximum age that the airline permitted for its pilots. He dreaded the day when he would no longer be in control of Concorde but had plenty of activities with which to keep himself busy.

In 1990 he was invited to become the third member of a syndicate that owned an aeroplane – an Auster Aiglet, G-AMZT. The aeroplane had been owned by the Cranfield College of Aeronautics and was used to give air experience to would-be pilots. When the college had no more use for it, it was put up for sale and was bought by David Hyde, a British Airways director and research fellow at Cranfield and John Saull, head of Operational Standards at the Civil Aviation Authority, who had been a student at the college. John accepted the invitation and became the third member of the syndicate, which offered a better utilization of the aeroplane and also cut the costs of ownership. As John says, he very much enjoys flying the Auster but doesn't use it enough to justify the cost of owning one outright. It is not a particularly straightforward aeroplane to fly as it has a springy undercarriage and is easy to ground loop:

> You need to give it a lot of attention and, in a way, that's part of the pleasure of flying it.
>
> Its speed is slower than that of the average family car and,

having flown at Mach 2 in Concorde, it is rather humbling to be overtaken by a car on the motorway below.

John is still part of the syndicate but, to further improve the utilization of the Auster, they have now taken on a fourth member – also an ex-British airways pilot – Hugh Dibley.

By January 1991 Concorde had been flying for 15 years, having clocked up 90,000 hours in the air. John himself completed 5,000 hours on the supersonic aeroplane later that year, a figure which unbelievably was the equivalent of 208 days and nights, and one that his friend, engineer Bill Brown, also achieved the following day. John commented at the time that: 'I believe I am correct in saying that Bill and I are the only ones to have spent so much time on Concorde. Mind you, it has been time very well spent.'

In May John was chosen as one of the Concorde pilots to take the Queen and the Duke of Edinburgh to the USA for a state visit. They flew to Andrews Air Force Base near Washington DC, where the Royal couple visited President George H.W. Bush and from there went on to Miami to board the Royal Yacht *Britannia*. John and the crew flew Concorde to Macdill Air Force Base near Tampa, Florida where they had two free days. John spent most of his free time sailing but also managed a visit to the Epcot Center which he enjoyed very much, marvelling at the way the staff managed to organize the huge crowds of visitors that Epcot attracted.

The next stage of the trip involved a flight to Austin, Texas, landing at Bergstrom Air Force Base, where they stayed for one night before going on to Ellington Air Force Base near Houston and another free day for the crew. For John this was the highlight of the trip as they were invited by NASA to take a private tour of the Johnson Space Center where they were treated as VIPs. With astronaut Ken Bowersox at his side in the Space Shuttle simulator, John landed the craft which he said felt like 'bombing the runway' because the Shuttle comes in at a very steep angle, quite different from a Concorde approach. There is only one chance at making a safe touchdown in the Shuttle as there are no means to abort a landing and make another attempt. After visiting Mission Control and seeing a full size mock up of the Shuttle and the Space Station, it was time to leave. John said of that visit, the last of the trip: 'It was absolutely fascinating and I know that we all felt very privileged and honoured to have been given such a warm welcome.'

Her Majesty the Queen did not return to England with the Duke of Edinburgh, but went on to Lexington for a private visit with friends. The Duke returned on Concorde however and, after a short flight from Ellington Air Force Base, they landed at Washington's Dulles International Airport to refuel before taking-off for London. The Duke was on the flight deck for the landing at Dulles and, as a pilot himself, was very interested in the operation of the aeroplane. John said that the trip was the highlight of his flying career and was an unforgettable experience.

Earlier that year John had been asked by the Guild of Air Pilots and Air Navigators if he would organize an air show for them. The show had a dual purpose. It was to celebrate the 60th anniversary of the Tiger Moth and to raise funds for the Lord Mayor of London's nominated charities, the MacMillan Cancer Relief Fund and the Great Ormond Street Hospital for Children. John set about his task with great enthusiasm. Because of the uncertainties of British summer weather, he contacted the Meteorological Office to see if there were any dates that were predicted to give the best weather of the summer. Having been told that the weekend of 22-23 June looked promising, the air show was arranged to take place on Sunday, 23 June at North Weald in Essex. The airfield, an important fighter station during the Battle of Britain in the summer of 1940, had a long tarmac runway and so was an ideal venue.

There was a friendly, happy atmosphere as the show was opened by the Lord Mayor of London, Sir Alexander Graham, accompanied by the Master of the Guild, David Mauleverer, a British Airways 747 pilot and one of John's friends. Thereafter, the day went downhill as the Met Office had been completely wrong in its forecast and the rain poured down. Many of the display aircraft, including the Red Arrows, were unable to fly but one display, the most memorable for John, was that of a flypast by a Concorde accompanied by an Avro Vulcan. He recalled that: 'The sight of the two great Deltas and the sound of their Olympus engines had me jumping about in excitement.'

Only a few of the aeroplanes that had been due to fly that day managed to take part. After all the hard work John had put into organizing the event it was a huge disappointment to him that what would have been a spectacular display had been ruined by the weather. However, what there was of the air show did make a big impression on the ticket holders, who attended despite the rain, and it is still talked about by Guild members as being a day to remember.

A month after the Guild air show, John was back to his commentating role for the BBC at the Royal International Air Tattoo at Fairford in Gloucestershire. For that event the weather couldn't have been better – there was bright sunshine for the entire time. John was delighted to see a display by Hawker Hunters, one of his favourite aeroplanes, performed by the Patrouille Suisse and a stunning aerobatic display by the Red Arrows but was particularly impressed by the Frecce Tricolori of the Italian Air Force who, he said, combined '… faultless flying with imaginative and exciting choreography'.

Between 7-9 August, John attended the Airshow Canada Symposium which was held at the Vancouver Trade and Convention Centre. His presence there was due to the friendship that he and John Burley had formed while the latter was the British Airways Manager USSR, in Moscow.

After 8½ years in the same position John Burley wanted a change but he had been so valuable to British Airways in Moscow that they refused to let him go. Faced with the airline's complete intransigence John Burley resigned and, with his wife Liz, retired to Vancouver where he started an aerospace trade show, Airshow Canada, the Canadian equivalent of the Farnborough Air Show, and recruited his friend, John Hutchinson, as its UK agent, drumming up business for the show by persuading British companies to exhibit there.

Part of the 1991 Airshow Canada Symposium was an international student design competition called Seeking Wings that Work, whose objective was to choose a heavier than air design which pre-dated the Wright brothers' aeroplane and to make working models of the chosen machine which would fly for a minimum of 15 seconds. Ten teams from Canada, Japan, Australia, Britain and France took part and John had been asked to help judge the competition. The machines that the students chose included Adler's Eole and Kokichi's Monoplane. The British entry was a model of Henson's Aerial Steam carriage, an aeroplane designed in 1843 to carry passengers, but which never managed to become airborne because of the weight of its steam powered engine. The model, described by John as having been 'beautifully constructed', was made by students from Imperial College London who were sponsored by British Airways and came third after their entry crashed, having only managed to remain airborne for two seconds. French students from the Ecole Nationale Superieure d'Enginieurs de Construction Aeronautique were the winners with their model of the Penaud and Gauchet submersible aircraft.

John remained the UK agent for Airshow Canada for some years but, although he enjoyed the shows themselves, which were held on alternate years to those of the Farnborough Air Show, he was less enthusiastic about his role in trying to sell the idea of the show to British companies. Sue believes that, 'John was not cut out to be a salesman. He used to find it quite frustrating and difficult.'

In the spring of 1992 John and Sue went to Scotland for the wedding of their nephew, David Noyes and his fiancée, Trina Purves, both of whom were employed by British Airways. The wedding itself was a very happy affair but John spent part of the reception at the Borders General Hospital. When one of his sisters arrived at the reception she discovered that her car had a flat tyre and John offered to change the wheel for her. He jacked up the car and was just replacing the wheel when the jack collapsed and the car fell onto his left index finger. He was rushed to the hospital where the staff had been warned to expect his imminent arrival, and found three nurses and a doctor waiting to attend to his nasty injury. It was done in no time at all and John was relieved to be able to return to the reception, hardly missing any of it.

Sadly, John remains as accident prone as he was in his youth, although he rarely makes much fuss about the things that happen to him. Both his sister Mary, and his neighbour Sid, recalled another accident that could have had a far worse result.

John and another neighbour had bought a lot of wood from a local farmer that they intended to chop into logs for burning in their fireplaces. All went well until John decided to take a short break from cutting up the wood and leant the chain saw he was using against his leg, absentmindedly forgetting that he should turn it off first. The inevitable happened; the chain saw slipped and very nearly amputated his leg. He was rushed to hospital and says that, but for the skill and dedication of the Malay Chinese doctor who attended to him, he may well have lost his leg. The doctor spent a long time cleaning, stitching and dressing the wound and the leg was saved even though he does have a rather nasty scar to show for his lapse in concentration.

As the day of John's retirement approached, thoughts turned to how the event would be celebrated. Flight engineer Bill Brown remembered the British Airways gathering very well. It was usual on such an occasion for a group of colleagues and friends to have a drink with the person who was retiring in The Crown, a pub on the north side of Heathrow Airport. John's farewell drink was, however, rather different. The British Airways staff at Kennedy Airport had arranged a party for him on 23 March, the month before his birthday and actual retirement date, which was attended not only by the men and women at JFK who had become very fond of John during the time he had been flying to New York but by several of his colleagues from London who flew out to the USA solely to be there for the special event. Bill Brown could recall only one other time that a pilot was honoured in this way by the British Airways team in New York and says of his friend: 'John got along well with everyone. He was popular with all the staff and with the managers too and, of course, he was a very good pilot.'

Allan Jacobson, who worked with John on both scheduled flights and the Concorde charter programme in New York, agreed with Bill's assessment, saying that John was, '… great to work with'. Allan, who was known as AJ, also recalled that often, when in New York, John would go out for dinner with some of the British Airways ground staff and was 'fabulous, jovial and great fun to be with; a happy, positive person'[2]

The party, as the photos show, was a riotous affair but John was also given a lasting, unique gift from his New York colleagues in the form of two beautiful red albums filled with photos, anecdotes, newspaper cuttings and personal messages from his friends, one of whom wrote the following poem:

*Dear Captain Hutch.*
*This isn't very much,*
*It's just a little way*
*For all of us to say,*
*We wish for you the very best,*
*Good luck, long life, much happiness.*
*Of things we wish, there's quite a list,*
*And it's for sure, you'll sore be missed.*

*Woe, woe and woe*
*We don't want you to go,*

*And we know that to retire,*
*Is not what you desire …*
*But please, dear Hutch, don't be too sad,*
*For being retired won't be so bad.*
*You have so many things to do,*
*The Beeb, the Guild and much more too!*

*A funny world we live in,*
*Everything considering –*
*If half the staff at JFK*
*Were able to, we'd quit today!*
*One day our turn will come,*
*One day we'll all be done,*
*Then memories will come to mind,*
*Of our friend John who is so kind.*

On his last flight from New York as a Concorde pilot, John had the welcome company and support of his son Chris and of his friend Bill Brown. Retirement was definitely not what he wanted and, in his reaction to his enforced departure from British Airways, he was quite clear:

I was dragged away from the aeroplane kicking and screaming and protesting. It was the last thing I wanted. It was awful, absolutely awful. I didn't want to retire. I was loving the aeroplane; loving the job. I can honestly say I've never worked in my life. I've been paid to enjoy my hobby but the ultimate part of enjoying the hobby was flying Concorde. It was just an extraordinary aeroplane, absolutely extraordinary. It was a wonderful aeroplane to operate and the spirit amongst the crew was second to none. I've never known anything quite like it – it was brilliant.

Sue also arranged a retirement party for John, which was attended by their family and friends. When the party was in full swing she asked for a moment's silence, saying that she wanted to make a short speech. What she said shocked some of the guests, most especially her son. Patrick Cliff remembered:

Sue insisted on standing up and saying something. She said that she'd known that John had had a mistress for some years. And I was looking straight at Chris and his jaw dropped. He hadn't heard about this and Sue had known that John had had a mistress for 15 years! She was sleek, fast, had a droopy nose and … it was Concorde! But to see Chris's jaw drop was a sight to perceive!

Ruth Cliff added:

We all wondered what was coming next but she just had to say 'fast and sleek' and we knew it had to be Concorde. John was in love with that aeroplane.

# Chapter 18

# No End to the Adventures

*We live in a wonderful world that is full of beauty, charm and adventure. There is no end to the adventures we can have if only we seek them with our eyes open.*

Jawaharlal Nehru, 1889–1964, first Prime Minister of independent India

Not one to linger long over the regret he felt at the loss of his beautiful 'mistress', John found that he had plenty of things to fill the time that his retirement had provided.

He continued to appear on aviation programmes for the BBC and was asked to present a piece about the de Havilland Dragon Rapide for the Radio 4 programme *Going Places*, that involved a flight in one of the vintage aeroplanes, belonging to the Classic Wings company, from Duxford in Cambridgeshire. The Dragon Rapide had first flown exactly three years to the day before John's birth[1] and he was delighted to be having a flight in what he described as '… a rare and precious aeroplane' as at that time there were only a few still flying in Europe. On his return to the airfield at Duxford, which had been a fighter station during the Second World War and is now home to the aviation branch of the Imperial War Museum, the owner of the aeroplane, Trevor Butcher, asked John if he would like to fly it himself. He didn't need to be asked twice and so Trevor left the pilot's seat to make room for him as there is only one set of controls in the Rapide and, having given him a very thorough briefing, sat behind him in the front of the cabin while John taxied across the grass and then took-off. He had only a short flight but described it as:

> … a wonderful experience. Once we had taxied in and shut down the two Gypsy Queen engines, I got out feeling as excited as I did the day I went on my very first solo flight back in 1956! I had a grin from ear to ear and have completely fallen in love with this marvellous Gentleman's Aerial Carriage.

After having made a successful first flight on a Dragon Rapide John was asked if he would like to join Classic Wings as a pilot taking passengers on pleasure flights around the Duxford area and sightseeing trips across London. He was very tempted by the offer and did make one or two more flights but because of his other numerous commitments couldn't spare enough time to work the roster that the company required.

One of the commitments that John had made was to be a guest lecturer onboard cruise ships. After his success in speaking about Concorde on the *QE2* to promote the joint venture between Cunard and British Airways, he was contacted by an agent who asked if he would be interested in lecturing on other ships and, since he enjoyed speaking about his favourite aeroplane, he agreed. Sue joined him on the cruises and over the years John has made yet another very successful career as a lecturer; they have sailed all over the world and continue to do so. This change of direction came at a good time for John as the BBC was beginning to reduce the number of its aviation related broadcasts and eventually stopped covering air shows completely. Although John does still give both radio and television interviews, usually about Concorde, they are now sporadic and certainly would not keep him busy, unlike the role of consultant to various American companies such as Boeing, Honeywell and NASA who were involved in the High Speed Research Programme, that he undertook after retiring from British Airways.

After its failure to produce an aeroplane to rival Concorde, the USA planned to produce a next generation supersonic aircraft that would be bigger, faster and with a greater payload than the Anglo-French aeroplane. John's task as consultant was to inform them of the sort of issues that they needed to be addressing if they were ever going to build a supersonic airliner.

One of these issues concerned the way the crews were able to see where they were going and what obstacles there were, when coming in to land and while on the ground. Since the shape of the new aeroplane would be very similar to that of Concorde, long and thin, with limited vision through the cockpit window, it was at first thought likely that the American airliner would have the moveable nose section that the Concorde had. Boeing however, believed that this would add too much extra weight to their aeroplane and so investigated the possibility of using Synthetic and Enhanced Vision technologies, already being used on military aircraft. Synthetic Vision projected a computer generated picture of the topography onto a screen on the flight deck allowing the crew to see what physical features were around them without having to look through a window. Enhanced Vision gave an actual display of the same area created by infrared imaging sensors or by millimetre-wave radar[2] – the technology also used by the controversial airport security scanners that created such an uproar when it was revealed that they produced nude images of those being scanned.

The new Boeing HSCT (High Speed Civil Transport) as the aeroplane was known, was anticipated to be in service by about 2005 and John spent a lot of time going backwards and forwards between London and the giant Boeing main assembly plant near Seattle on the west coast of America. He also had a fascinating time flying many different simulators at NASA Ames Research Center at Moffett Field near San Francisco, California and at NASA Langley Research Center in Hampton, Virginia where he met many interesting people: 'I did a lot of presentations to fairly high-powered boffin-type audiences and that was a huge privilege.'

Unfortunately the High Speed Research Programme suddenly came to an end when Boeing found they were going through lean times. They were laying off lots of employees and to have a rather exotic programme which didn't appear to have any relevance in the short term wasn't a good idea so they just pulled out of it. Since they were the main contributors to the programme it effectively meant that it came to an end.

The lessons that had been learnt from the research that was undertaken were hopefully noted and stored away somewhere to be resurrected at a future date.

John believes that the aviation industry as a whole has gone about as far as it can with jet engines, jet fuel and aluminium alloy construction and that in the future there will be a breakthrough in new power plants and fuel that conform to airport noise regulations and exhaust emission standards:

I think it will happen but it's going to be a long time in coming. It's not going to happen with the technology that we've currently got. It'll be different technology in whatever shape or form that comes.

Maybe we're looking at sub-orbital flights where you fly from London to Sydney, or New York to Tokyo, in a matter of three or four hours. That will transform the world; it really will.

In the early days of their marriage when money was tight and they had small children to consider, John and Sue had taken short holidays to places fairly close by. When John became a BOAC pilot they were able to holiday farther afield; not only were travel arrangements a little easier, they also had a number of friends and family members who were living overseas at that time with whom they could stay. After John's retirement when time was not so much of a problem as it had been when he had been flying, they were able to take long holidays to exotic and remote destinations. They discovered a travel company in Seattle, Zegrahm Expeditions, that arranged special trips to places usually off the tourist trail and had visited the Galapagos Islands, Easter Island, Tahiti and Fiji, exploring the habitats of the birds and other wildlife; had been scuba diving which they both enjoyed, and had also visited South Georgia and the Antarctic. Then, in 1994, they took a trip, accompanied by two of the company's co-founders, Peter Harrison and Shirley Metz as guides, to the Falkland Islands, South Georgia again, and on to the Torres del Paine National Park in Chilean Patagonia. They flew first to New York then on to Miami, Santiago and Punta Arenas where they took a small charter aeroplane for the final leg of their flight to the RAF airfield at Mount Pleasant on East Falkland. At Port Stanley they boarded a Russian research ship, the *Akademik Sergey Vavilov* and spent two days cruising around the Falkland Islands of which there are more than 740.[3] At the western end of the group of islands they visited Steeple Jason to see the largest colony of black-browed albatrosses in the world and then set sail to the east for the 1,000 mile trip to South Georgia. Their previous trip there had been marred by terrible weather which had prevented them from landing or seeing any of the island's wildlife and they were hoping that it would be better the second time around. It was; compared with its usual Antarctic climate it was almost warm and the first sight of South Georgia was spectacular. John, quoting penguin expert Frank

Todd, said: 'If God ever wanted to take a holiday, it would be on South Georgia. Sue and I would certainly agree.'

They spent 10 days cruising around the island observing the many varieties of penguins and albatrosses, skuas, sheathbills, prions, Arctic terns and giant petrels as well as elephant and fur seals, and loved every moment in this wild island with its impressive mountains and glaciers, and its important breeding grounds:

> It made us feel very humble indeed to be surrounded by wild nature in all its pristine glory and we have been left with a million memories. I think for me one of the most unforgettable was the sight of an Elephant seal in the middle of a King penguin rookery surrounded in every direction by thousands of nesting birds. The seal decided it wanted to go walkabout and the penguins most certainly did not want him to. Seeing a penguin fearlessly holding tons of bellowing Elephant seal at bay is a truly impressive spectacle. My other enduring memory was the visit to the cave (little more than an indentation in the cliff, in reality) where Sir Ernest Shackleton first landed after his epic voyage in an open boat from Elephant Island in 1916. Cave Cove, as it is known, is by Cape Rose on the south shore of the entrance to King Haakon Bay. To stand there was an intense and powerful emotional experience.

After leaving South Georgia, John and Sue, along with a small number of fellow travellers, and their guides Peter and Shirley, went on to Patagonia to visit the spectacular Torres de Paine National Park. They stayed at the Explora Hotel on an island in a lake, with stunning views of both the mountains and the glaciers. Having spent three days walking, horse riding and bird watching, several of them decided they wanted to go fishing. Peter suggested that they might like to take a boat trip on Lago Grey in the morning and go fishing in the afternoon and they agreed.

They went first to visit the huge Grey Glacier that flows southward into the lake and on which they were able to walk, and then boarded a tourist boat; a new, well equipped vessel, with a captain and cabin boy, on which they spent a pleasant morning. They all enjoyed the trip but the wind was against them and as they turned to return to shore were battling against very choppy waters and ever increasing winds, while having to keep watch for ice and small icebergs that were bobbing around in the water.

Suddenly the engine stopped, the propeller having been fouled by a rope left trailing from the bow. With no power they drifted backwards for some time before crashing into a cliff face and becoming jammed between rocks and icebergs. Unable to either restart the engine or disentangle the rope, although Peter manfully dived into the icy water to try with the help of a Swiss Army knife, it was obvious the boat was in imminent danger of breaking up and would have to be abandoned. Peter again dived into the water, swam to a ledge, hauled himself out and managed to climb to the top of the cliff. Securing a line to a small tree, he helped the heaviest man on the boat up to the clifftop and they secured the rope he brought with him. Each passenger in turn was then tied to the other end of this and jumped off the bow at the top of the boat's rise and fall to climb to the top. It was a daunting prospect but eventually everyone made it to the clifftop, even a lady with cancer and another who had arthritic knees. Sue recalled how they managed to cope with the situation that they faced:

> It's very interesting when you're in a tight squeeze. You know you are in a life threatening situation and yet, funnily enough, perhaps we are just lucky. You become very calm. We were very lucky with the group we were with. Apart from one girl who started to scream, everyone was very calm.

The last person to leave the boat was its captain but he misjudged the jump he had to make and fell heavily back into the vessel. Although everyone at first thought that he had broken his back it soon became clear that he was not badly injured – just winded – and he too reached the comparative safety of the cliff top and then ran away, never to be seen again.

There was still a long way to go before they were really safe and back in the hotel. They had not brought any food with them nor did they have much water but they divided everything that they did have equally so that everyone had something even if it was only a piece of an apple or a sweet. John and Sue had become friendly with a couple from Seattle called Nancy and Ham (Hamilton) and, while Sue and Nancy talked as they walked, John and Ham helped the lady who had cancer. With one on either side, they each supported her and John kept her mind off what was happening by telling her stories of his flying with British Airways. The strategy worked and she was amazed, later that night, to find that they had reached the lake in which their hotel was situated without too much trouble. They managed to contact the hotel with a mobile phone and the small motorboat that belonged to the Explora was sent over the water to fetch them and bring them to safety. Unfortunately their ordeal wasn't yet over. It was a very small boat, too small really to take the number of people that squeezed onboard and John and Sue were the last two. They had just started off across the lake towards the hotel when there was a huge bang. They had hit a submerged rock and, as John looked down at his feet, he suddenly realized that they were getting wet; the motorboat was taking on water. The girl who had made such a fuss when the first boat got into trouble became hysterical again and started to scream, stopping only when John told her to pull herself together and smacked her face. Although the boat was holed and leaking they eventually managed to get to the island, very thankful to have survived. Staggering into the hotel they adjourned to the bar where, according to John, '… we all went off and got pissed on Pisco sours'. They stayed in the bar for most of the night, leaving in time to catch the early flight the next morning that took them on the first stage of their journey home.

The group felt that Peter Harrison's heroic efforts to save them should be recognized and so each wrote an account of what he had done. Although he lived in Seattle, Peter was not American but British and John put his name forward for a British award, using the other passengers' accounts to back-up his application. Peter was eventually awarded an MBE, not for his bravery but for his wildlife conservation work as it was felt that this would be more beneficial to him.

After having had a near-death experience on this trip, the following year, instead of taking a holiday in a less dangerous location, John and Sue again decided to test themselves and went to the Grand Canyon where they had what John described as, '… one of the most amazing holidays of my life', white water rafting along the Colorado River. They had heard about the trip from Nancy and Ham but were told that it was always booked up two years in advance. Then the following year they received a call to say that two people had dropped out of the next trip and would John and Sue like to take their place. They jumped at the chance but just before they were due to leave, Sue's father had a stroke and died. They considered cancelling the trip but there didn't seem to be much point and so about three weeks after his death they set off for Phoenix, Arizona from where they took a small aeroplane to Flagstaff to join the tour.

Because Sue had had only two weeks after her father's death to clear his belongings from the sheltered flat in which he had spent his final years, she had not had much time to plan what they would take to Arizona and they arrived with some large suitcases filled with their clothes. They were given two small waterproof bags each and told that one was for their tent and sleeping bag and the other for their clothes and other necessities. It was a huge shock to discover that they would spend two weeks in the same clothes which were wet most of the time and that their only dry clothes would be those in which they slept. During the day they wore swimsuits which were covered by special cotton pyjama-like suits that prevented sunburn as they were not allowed to use sunscreens which would wash off into the water. Every scrap of rubbish had to be taken out of the canyon with them when they left and this included the contents of what John described as the 'thunderbox' which was set up each morning for all the group to use in turn. Sue believes that there must have been something added to their food as they were all as regular as clockwork which was very important as they had to use the facilities during a one hour time frame early in the morning.

They travelled down the Colorado River, five to each rubber boat, one of whom was an experienced guide. Some of the rapids were small and fairly inconsequential but when they reached the larger, more dangerous ones they took the boats out of the river and walked down to the rapids to work out the best line to take, which would avoid rocks near the bank and also those on the riverbed. The weather was brilliant and the daytime temperatures were generally over 38 degrees Celsius (100 degrees Fahrenheit) although the water temperature was considerably colder. Each day they had to drink at least 2 litres of water to guard against dehydration. If anyone suffered from dehydration or any other medical condition, one of the guides would have had to contact a passing aeroplane on a VHF radio and ask the crew to alert the emergency services. The canyon is so steep and narrow that mobile phones and even emergency flares are completely useless. Happily, although one of their party did suffer mild dehydration, they were able to rectify the situation without having to contact any medical services by making her drink a large amount of water while immersed in the river itself.

At the end of each day everything was pulled up onto the bank. Although they each had a tent, all but one of the group slept outside on the riverbank. The exception was John who, every evening, put up his tent and slept in it saying that he had read about scorpions and rattlesnakes and wasn't going to allow either to get into his sleeping bag.

According to John, approaching the rapids was like: '… Heathrow in the rush hour, and a roaring noise would swell up the canyon.'

Having worked out the best route they climbed back into their boats:

> … and out onto the river again before plunging over the edge of the world into a raging storm of white water, hanging on for grim death. It was always an amazing ride.
>
> And if all that excitement isn't enough to satisfy you, there is always the view. To say it is stunning is a big understatement. It is a spiritual experience that leaves you feeling a sense of awe at the wonder of nature. The majestic scale is almost impossible to comprehend and the colours constantly change with the light. It's also a sharp reminder of the very short time human beings have inhabited the earth. The oldest rocks in the Grand Canyon are 1.7 billion years old while human history goes back only 10,000 years.

When he wasn't dicing with death on exotic holidays, lecturing about Concorde on cruise ships or acting as consultant to various American companies, John was working hard for the Guild of Air Pilots and Air Navigators. In 1999, the Guild's 70th anniversary year, John received the ultimate accolade when he was elected Master. Each Master serves for one year and presides over a number of functions as well as undertaking the Master's Tour of the Regions, visiting members in Australia, New Zealand and Hong Kong. At the time of John's election, the Guild had not yet reached Canada. However, largely thanks to his efforts, both as Master and as a Past Master, the Canadian Region was established and, in 2010, it was expanded to include members living in the USA. It is now called the North America Region.

Having been installed as Master in March 1999, John took aviation safety as his theme for the year and, in the Master's Message of the Guild News, wrote:

The Guild has an immense depth and breadth of knowledge and experience within its membership and I believe that we must harness that wisdom to promote the cause of safety through our committees, through conferences, through representations to Parliamentary Select Committees and through alliances with other organizations such as the Royal Aeronautical Society. In short, we must take every opportunity we can to make our own contribution to the future of safe aviation.

His first few weeks were very busy as he attended the Lord Mayor's Banquet for Masters, and visited RAF Lyneham in Wiltshire and RAF Cranwell in Lincolnshire to present Master Air Pilot and Air Navigator certificates.[4] Sue had already organized a tea party for Guild members' partners which was held at the RAF Club on 25 March and was a great success.

When considering what event to host in the summer of his year as Master, John decided to have a summer ball. It was an ambitious project and Gina Benmax, the wife of one of the Guild members, was asked to be chair of the organizing committee. She did a magnificent job. Another committee member was a senior RAF officer who suggested that they hold the ball at Bentley Priory, famous as the headquarters of Fighter Command during the Second World War, and a wonderful summer venue as it had beautiful grounds as well as being an imposing building. The ball took place on 7 August and, because of the history of its setting, had a Second World War theme. Tickets were in the form of ration books and there was a band playing Glenn Miller music, a jazz quartet and a disco; guests were greeted by John and Sue to the strains of a harp, and a string quartet played until the buffet dinner was served. This was done with three sittings in the Officers' Mess, with the first course being served in a marquee, the Seafood bar, because there were too many guests to fit into the dining room. Dessert, cheese and coffee were available in an ante-room.

Apart from the dancing there were other attractions – a casino with roulette wheels and blackjack tables, and bumper cars in the grounds to the front of the house. Sue particularly enjoyed the latter and when she and John flew off to Vancouver the next day on Guild business she was horrified to find that she had large bruises on her legs, a result of her competitive driving the night before.

The ball was a huge success; the weather was perfect and everyone had a wonderful time. The only item that had to be abandoned was a flypast by a Spitfire from the Battle of Britain Memorial Flight at Coningsby, due to bad weather on its route from Lincolnshire to Bentley Priory, but the event was judged by everyone to have been a night to remember.[5]

John's claim to fame during his time as Master was that he was the one under whose watch the Guild was taken into a respectable office building. The original headquarters were situated in what John described as: '… a rather grotty office building at the top end of Gray's Inn Road, very close to King's Cross where our Grand Master probably wouldn't be seen dead. I don't think he ever visited us there.'

The person of whom he spoke was HRH The Duke of Edinburgh, a man for whom John has great admiration, who had been the Guild's Grand Master since October 1953 and was a very enthusiastic supporter of the Guild and its affairs. In 2002 His Royal Highness relinquished the role of Grand Master to his son, HRH The Duke of York, becoming the Guild's Patron himself.

John was delighted to have been able to get the Guild's headquarters moved to the other end of the road, to a very pleasant office at Warwick Court, close to Chancery Lane tube station, describing it as one of the highlights of his time as Master.

The move took place at the beginning of December 1999 while John and Sue were in Hong Kong on the final stage of the Master's tour. They arrived back in London a few days later to mountains of post and several Guild functions to attend, one of which was the annual carol service held at St Michael's, Cornhill on 14 December. John was very proud that the third lesson in the service that year was read by his 10 year old grandson, Tim who, he said, '… read quite beautifully in spite of the fact that he had flu and was feeling ghastly!'

Just before John's year as Master came to an end, HRH The Duke of Edinburgh visited the new premises to formally unveil the plaque commemorating the opening of the new offices at Warwick Court. In his final letter as Master, John wrote in the Guild News:[6]

On behalf of the Guild I would like to say how grateful we are to him for his support and I thank him most sincerely for finding the time in his busy schedule to join us … it was the happiest of occasions.

When his time as Master came to an end John handed over the reins to his friend Arthur Thorning. Arthur, an engineer, who holds a private pilot's licence, had worked with the Civil Aviation Authority and this, in John's opinion, illustrates one of the great strengths of the Guild, that it represents all air pilots and air navigators not just those who fly with airlines or the Armed Services. The Guild remains a very important part of John's life:

> The Guild is wonderful because it's an organization that embraces the whole spectrum of piloting from military fast jets, to commercial airline pilot, to corporate pilot, to general aviation pilot, to balloon pilot. The binding common theme with all these people is that they love the air in whatever shape or form.
>
> It's a super organization whose objectives basically are to promote flight safety, promote high standards of training in aviation and we also have a benevolent fund for distressed aviators or their widows or families.

Despite the enormous amount of work that John undertook in the years after his retirement, he was always ready to take on more and his expertise proved invaluable when he offered his services as an expert witness in aviation related court cases. He has appeared in court on many occasions and enjoys the scope and variety of the work although it does involve a lot of preparation before he is able to testify. Although he can be called for any number of different reasons, having been a pilot himself he is particularly keen to support other crew members, both flight deck and cabin, if he feels they have been wronged.

John continued to be the UK agent for Airshow Canada for several more years. It later became Aerospace North America encompassing the USA as well as Canada. The first event of the new organization was due to take place at the Convention Center in Seattle in September 2001 and John Burley had spent two years preparing for it. John flew to Seattle to be there for the opening and stayed with the friends, Nancy and Ham, that he and Sue had met while on their Patagonian adventure.

At 6 a.m. on the day the show was due to open, Ham knocked on John's bedroom door and told him to get up immediately and come and look at the television. John fell out of bed and hurried into the living room just in time to see an aeroplane hit one of the twin towers of the

World Trade Center in New York. He was stunned, and was even more shocked to learn that it was the second aeroplane to fly into the towers. He immediately called John Burley at his hotel and gave him the news. Although his friend was worried about the impact that this would have on the show, he was much more concerned about his daughter and son-in-law, both of whom were financial traders working at the World Trade Center. He waited all day for news until at last he heard from his wife, Liz, that they were safe.

Both men struggled through the remaining days of the trade show but it was a disaster. After what had happened no one was interested in aviation; the nation, along with most of the civilized world, was in a state of shock at the atrocity that had been committed. After all the work that John Burley had put in to make the show a success, it was this act of terrorism that destroyed it. It was the first and last time that the event was staged and after all the effort that had gone into the show, its founder was out of work. He and his wife wanted to remain in Vancouver although John was sure that he could find something for his friend to do in London. Instead John Burley eventually became a yacht broker and John involved him in the Guild when the Canadian Region came into being. He is now chairman of the North America Region.

In 2005 John was invited to join the Air Squadron, an organization founded in 1966 by a group of aviation enthusiasts who all flew light aircraft. The membership, which is by invitation only, is strictly limited to ensure that it remains a small group of likeminded people who all have aviation qualifications. Most members also either have a share in an aircraft or own one outright, and these are flown to Air Squadron events all over the world.

As well as just having a great deal of fun, the Air Squadron members support the aviation branches of the Armed Services, presenting trophies to outstanding air cadets both here and abroad, and have their own charity, the Geoffrey de Havilland Flying Foundation, which helps young people who want to fly.

When John accepted the invitation to join the Air Squadron he became part of an exclusive organization whose members have included Sir Douglas Bader, Sir Hugh Dundas, Tommy Sopwith, Bruno Schroeder, Adrian de Ferranti and the Astors. He sometimes wonders if he was invited to join because the members wanted to have a Concorde pilot in the organization.

Even if this were true, and he can offer no evidence to support the theory, there were other Concorde pilots who could have been invited but were not; they chose John.

In 2006 the Polish Air Force invited Air Squadron members to Warsaw and John flew to Poland in the Auster with his friend, GAPAN Past Master David Mauleverer. They made the long journey to eastern Europe in easy stages across France and then on to Germany where they landed at Berlin's Tempelhof Airport, just 20 minutes away from the Brandenburg Gate, in the heart of Berlin. John thought that Tempelhof was a 'wonderful airfield'. It was the oldest commercial airport in the world, having been built in 1923 and, until 1934 when the Pentagon was constructed, its elegant Art Deco main building had been the largest in the world. John was very pleased to have been able to visit it before it finally closed on 31 October 2008 amid protests from many Berliners who remembered the airport's role in saving them from starvation during the Airlift, 60 years earlier.

Having left Berlin they flew on to Warsaw where the Polish Air Force had arranged concerts, memorial services and a flypast for their guests. They then went to Cracow from where John visited the Nazi death camp of Auschwitz. He didn't want to see it but felt that he had to:

> Not going would have been ignoring an inconvenient truth so I had to confront it. It was beyond description. It reduced me to complete rubble. It was just appalling. You go round and see something like that and you just cannot credit man's inhumanity to man.
>
> It was absolutely shattering to see these great display cases filled with human hair – just awful. Then another with spectacle frames that had belonged to Jews or gypsies. And another with little things like children's pots, or flower vases that, at one time, had been very useful or precious to someone.

John also reflected on how the camp commandant, Rudolf Höss, could have lived there with his wife and four children:

> The camp commandant's married quarter was just outside the fence from one of the ovens. What did he say to his wife about what was going on? Did he tell her the truth? What did he say to his children?

After what had been both an entertaining and yet a shattering visit to Poland, the following year John attended another Air Squadron event which was completely different. This time he and Sue drove to northern Italy where they met up with other members of the Air Squadron and were entertained in great style in villas owned by members of the Italian aristocracy. At Lake Como they attended a function on a private island owned by an Italian nobleman and his family. Everywhere they went they received amazing hospitality and thoroughly enjoyed their visit.

John says that Air Squadron events are wonderful, including those within the UK, such as the yearly visit to an RAF station where members are treated as very special guests. He modestly admits that he sometimes feels out of his depth among the illustrious members, but he is proud of his membership of the Air Squadron and believes it to be a 'great organization'.

# Chapter 19

# A Beautiful White Bird

*Without doubt, Concorde died yesterday at the age of 31. All that will remain is the myth of a beautiful white bird.*

*Le Figaro* editorial, 26 July 2000

On 25 July 2000 a party of wealthy German tourists was due to travel on an Air France Concorde charter flight, AF4590, arranged by the German travel agency, Peter Deilmann Reederei, from Paris to New York where they would be boarding the MS *Deutschland* for a two week cruise to the Caribbean and South America via the Panama Canal.[1] The aircraft on which the 100 passengers were to have flown was Concorde F-BVFC but when the aircraft that was scheduled to take the regular Air France flight, AF002, to New York that day was found to be unserviceable, F-BVFC was switched to the scheduled New York departure and the charter group was allocated the reserve aircraft, F-BTSC. This aircraft also had a technical problem; the thrust reverser on the No. 2 engine was not working and the captain refused to take the flight until the problem had been fixed. Because of the changes and the maintenance issues, the flight was two hours late in leaving Paris.

The captain that day was Christian Marty, a 54 year old sports fanatic who loved skiing and had windsurfed across the Atlantic some years before.[2] He had been an Airbus pilot before joining Air France's Concorde fleet and had 317 hours flying the supersonic airliner, 284 of which were as its captain.[3] With 2,698 hours, the 50 year old first officer, Jean Marcot, was the most experienced on the aircraft type and 58 year old Gilles Jardinaud, the flight engineer, had a total of 937 hours on Concorde.[4]

When, eventually, the aircraft was ready for departure Marty called air traffic control to ask for clearance. He spoke to controller Gilles Logelin who remembered:

> I gave him the clearance for take-off and as it is a very nice plane that I like very much I was watching the plane getting on the power on the runway. Suddenly I saw a flame behind the aircraft. This happened in a few seconds after the initial clearance for take-off. As soon as I saw this flame I opened the mike to inform the captain that there was a fire going on behind the plane. The pilot just answered me 'Roger'. I knew that the situation was critical after maybe two seconds. Then I heard a voice on the radio that told me, 'That's it!' … [5]

Only a minute or so after taking-off, the Air France Concorde crashed into a hotel in the suburb of Gonesse, killing four people on the ground, the three flight deck and six cabin crew members, and all 100 passengers.

Firemen from Le Bourget, the airport Concorde had tried in vain to reach, were the first to arrive at the crash site in Gonesse but found that the aircraft was burning so fiercely that all they were able to do was to try to contain the fire while they waited for the reinforcements from the Rescue and Fire Fighting Service that arrived soon after from Charles de Gaulle Airport from where the Concorde had taken-off. They brought with them 12 vehicles, half of which had foam fire fighting systems. There were also reinforcements from local fire brigades. The blaze was eventually brought under control after three hours, during which time 180,000 litres of water and 3,800 litres of emulsifier had been used.

When news of the accident broke in the United Kingdom John was contacted by the BBC and interviewed for the *PM programme* on Radio 4 that evening. He told listeners:

> It's terrible news and I think that for anybody involved with Concorde it's a shattering piece of news. And I would certainly like to express my great sympathy and sadness for all the Air France crew and the German passengers who died in the crash. It's a shattering accident.

Asked about the safety record of the aircraft, John replied:

> It is in my view, and remains so in my view, the safest aeroplane that is flying in the skies today, for two reasons.
>
> One, is that it's a very tough aeroplane; it's built in a very robust manner, and secondly it's got tremendous reserve capacity, by that I mean it's got a huge excess in capacity and power on the engines, all that sort of thing.
>
> So it's a very, very safe aeroplane. And in my view, in spite of this accident, it remains so …
>
> It's a beautiful aeroplane to fly, it's a responsive, thoroughbred of an aircraft.
>
> It is the most beautiful aeroplane out of all the 70 aeroplanes I've flown in my life; far and away the most beautiful aeroplane I've ever flown.[6]

Five days later John was again in demand for his opinion about the Air France crash when he appeared on the BBC *Breakfast with Frost* show. Television journalist Peter Sissons was standing in for David Frost on this programme and began by saying:

> It's been a nightmare week for the aircraft that was everyone's dream machine, a lot of bleak words in the Sunday papers as well, how do they strike you?

John replied:

> I think in terms of a lot of the technical content, you know, I wouldn't argue with much of that. I think the sort of gloom and doom apocalyptic spin that's been put on it has been grossly over-hyped. I mean Concorde is an aeroplane and sadly aeroplanes do crash from time to time. I particularly took exception at something in the Mail on Sunday where it says essentially it is a controlled fire – this is talking about the reheats, of the afterburners – but one that risks becoming uncontrolled, as happened in the crash. There's no evidence at all to suggest that the reheats have led to an uncontrolled fire – nothing at all. I've seen no evidence to support

that theory at all – and it then goes on to say two engine failures on the same side will inevitably lead to disaster; that is not true either. But aside from that, by and large, the technical content has been reasonably accurate, it's just the spin that's been put on it.

Peter Sissons asked if the aircraft was designed to take-off if two engines were to fail on take-off, to which John answered:

> I've practised it in the simulator. I'm not going to pretend it's an easy situation to be in, particularly if the aeroplane's at a full load – but it is a containable situation. And the thing I would emphasize is that there is no aeroplane – Concorde's no exception here – there is no aeroplane that is certificated with the requirement that it can fly at max take-off weight with two engines out on the same side, whether we're talking about a Boeing 747, an Airbus A340 or Concorde.

Peter Sissons wanted to know if John had begun to have any thoughts about the actual cause of the accident having seen the numerous pictures of the crash and read the details that had been appearing in the newspapers. John believed that the cause was becoming a little clearer:

> Yes I think it is narrowing down and I have to say I take my hat off to the French authorities. I think they've been very good about releasing hard facts and information as it has become available to them. And I think this actually contributes towards the cause of aviation safety and I think it also cuts down the scope for speculation. I mean it seems to be becoming clear, from the evidence that we've had so far, that obviously a tyre, or maybe two tyres, actually blew during the take-off run. What caused those tyres to blow up, we have yet to find out – it could have been debris on the runway.[7]

When the final report of the enquiry was published and cleared Air France of any blame whatsoever, even though some of their staff had made several serious mistakes, John would be less complimentary about what the French had to say about the accident.

The French air investigators of the Bureau Enquêtes-Accidents (BEA) had immediately started work on an enquiry to determine the cause of the crash. In accordance with the arrangements that were put in place as part of the joint Anglo-French Concorde agreement, the British Air Accidents Investigation Branch (AAIB) also took part in the enquiry. The joint preliminary findings were that while making its take-off run along runway 26R at Charles de Gaulle Airport, the Concorde had run over a small sharp piece of metal which had cut through one of the tyres on the left main landing gear, shredding it. The pieces of rubber from the tyre had pierced a fuel tank located in the wing and the fuel which escaped had caught fire and caused the crash.

This initial report, agreed upon by both the French and the British investigators, made a recommendation on 16 August 2000 that:

> The Certificates of Airworthiness of Concorde be suspended until appropriate measures have been taken to ensure a satisfactory level of safety as far as the tyre destruction based risk is concerned.

The recommendation was accepted by the airworthiness authorities in France (DGAC) and the United Kingdom (CAA) and the Concorde's Certificates of Airworthiness were suspended. Air France had stopped its Concorde operations immediately after the crash but British Airways continued flying Concorde until the suspension of the C of A.

These preliminary findings followed a narrow path from which the final report did not deviate, except to elaborate on the basic premise that the crash had been caused by the aircraft hitting a piece of metal which burst the tyre and sealed the Concorde's fate. There were, however, several other factors which the investigators examined but whose significance they seemingly failed to appreciate. The British investigators also complained that they were not allowed access to much of the evidence by the French authorities. Meanwhile the enquiry continued for many more months until the final report emerged the following year.

The demise of the aircraft in Paris motivated much discussion in the media about the safety of Concorde and opinions varied considerably. The aircraft was described as possessing both '… the most remarkable safety record in aviation history'[8] and as having '… the highest fatal event rate … 12.5 fatal events per million flights'[9] which does perhaps prove the assertion of financial author, John Rothchild that 'Statistics are like prisoners under torture: with the proper tweaking you can get them to confess to anything.'

Other sources such as America's *Cable News Network* dredged up accounts of all the incidents that had occurred during the long history of Concorde as if it were the only aircraft type ever to have had problems.

It was to be another 15 months, during which time major modifications to the aircraft such as Kevlar linings for the fuel tanks, and tyres that shredded into small pieces when they burst, were undertaken, before normal services were resumed on 7 November 2001.

When, the following January, the final report on the crash was published it did detail most of the 'hard facts and information as it has become available' for which John had commended the investigators on 30 July 2000, but he was horrified to learn that it had ignored the implications of the hard facts and had laid the blame for the crash solely at the feet of Continental Airlines. The small strip of metal that had been on the runway and which BEA claimed was the only reason the aircraft had crashed, was found to have come from a Continental Airlines DC-10 which had taken-off five minutes before the Concorde.

Air crashes are seldom the result of just one thing and, in John's opinion, the investigation was wrong to focus on a single cause. He highlighted several incidents, the significance of which the investigators chose to ignore. These were:

An overload of fuel.
Extra last minute baggage.
A change in the weather conditions.
A missing component in the undercarriage.
A below minimum take-off speed.
A breakdown in crew discipline.

One of the most significant points that John made about the crash was that of the fuel overload. The maximum capacity of each fuel tank had a built in safety allowance for a small air-filled space amounting to approximately 5 per cent of the tank capacity. However when extra taxi fuel had been called for and put onboard, the tanks had been completely filled, leaving no space for movement. And, by the time the Concorde reached the end of the runway ready to commence its take-off run, there were still

1.2 tonnes of extra fuel that had not been burned, making the aeroplane overweight. Tank number 11 in the tail of the aeroplane was a transfer tank which allowed the crew to change the centre of gravity for take-off, the fuel having been moved to tanks numbers 1-4 supplying the engines. Fuel should not be transferred during the take-off run but it has been suggested by several sources that it was still being pumped as the Concorde began moving down the runway.

In addition 19 pieces of baggage, not accounted for on any of the aircraft documentation, had been brought out to the aircraft just before departure. Since the bags had not been shown on the paperwork, there had been no calculations for their extra weight or for the change in the centre of gravity of the aircraft – both vital in ensuring a safe take-off.

The change in weather was significant because it meant that the Concorde took-off, not into the wind as is normal, but with the wind behind it. The information about the meteorological changes had been passed to the crew who could have dealt with the problem quite easily by simply requesting clearance to taxi to the other end of the runway to be able to take-off into the wind. But no such request was made and so the aircraft took-off with a tailwind.

By ignoring the speed and direction of the wind the crew ensured that the weight of the aircraft itself was magnified, making it behave as if it were much heavier than its actual weight.

As John points out about this type of take-off:

It's OK. You can do that but you have to compensate for the tailwind by reducing the weight of the aircraft.

Basically it means that the aircraft would have accelerated down the runway more slowly. It would also have had to get to a higher speed on the ground, because of the tailwind, before it was able to lift off. So everything was working against the crew.

The missing part, a spacer, although only a simple component, was vital in keeping the wheels in alignment. Because of the stresses on the undercarriage, certain parts were regularly replaced and, on 18 July, Concorde F-BTSC had been taken into the hangar where a maintenance crew replaced the horizontal tube through which the wheel axles pass. In error they left the spacer attached to the part they had removed. Although the aeroplane had made four flights with the spacer missing before its final take-off run on 25 July, the wheels were still properly aligned. It was only when one of the tyres burst that, with no spacer in place, they became unbalanced and skewed around. It was one of a team of British Airways engineers who had gone to Paris to help with the investigation who discovered that the spacer was missing and pointed it out to the French authorities at the scene of the crash in Gonesse. It seemed obvious to John that the carelessness of the Air France engineers, who had done the work on the aircraft the previous week, had put the lives of the passengers and crew at risk from the moment the aircraft started to move.

As it began its take-off run it started to veer towards the left side of the runway. This was proved after the crash when an inspection of the runway was made and photographs were taken. It was clear from the tyre marks on the surface, and the smoke damage, that the pilot had been unable to keep the aircraft straight. The excess weight from the extra fuel and baggage, coupled with a take-off in a tailwind made the departure precarious enough but not being able to control the path of the aircraft along the runway made it extremely dangerous.

It was at this point, a few seconds after the start of the take-off run, that the aeroplane hit the piece of metal identified as coming from the Continental Airlines DC-10. The tyre was badly damaged and a large piece of the rubber flew upwards, hitting the underside of the wing where the fuel tanks were housed. It did not pierce a fuel tank directly but as it hit the outer surface it deformed the skin, causing a shock wave through the liquid within. Since the tank was full there was no space in which the shock wave could dissipate and it pushed out the inner surface of the tank which ruptured at its weakest point. Another piece of metal found on the runway, was identified as being from the underside of tank 5 and showed signs of having 'petalled' outwards from the inside of the tank which had caused it to rupture allowing the fuel to escape and a fire to start. There is also evidence that:

> … tank 5 had its inlet valve override switch set to open. This enabled the valve to stay open no matter how full the tank was. Coupled with this the rear tank 11 de-air pump would be set to 'on' pressurizing the lefthand fuel transfer pipes and so tank 5 was under great pressure when it was struck by the tyre.[10]

John believes:

> ... that the unbalance that was caused by the tyre deflating combined with the spacer being missing was very significant. I think that led to the wheels skewing around and dragging the aeroplane off the side of the runway.
>
> You can see from the pictures very clearly that the aeroplane has been dragged off the side of the runway. And that then led, of course, to the captain lifting the aeroplane into the air at too slow a speed because he could see himself going off the side of the runway and no pilot wants to go across the grass at a very high speed like that.
>
> ... The correct speed for rotation [actual take-off] on that flight was 198 knots and he lifted the [nose of the] aeroplane into the air at 183 or 184 knots – about 15 knots or thereabouts, below the correct speed.

There was a second reason which may have made the pilot anxious to get the Concorde into the air as soon as possible. The cockpit voice recorder revealed that the first officer had shouted, 'Watch out' and, although no explanation of this warning was given, it was extremely likely that it had been made because the aeroplane, as it veered to the left, was heading terrifyingly close to an Air France Boeing 747 which was waiting on a taxiway to cross the live runway. The 747 had just arrived from Tokyo and among its passengers were the French head of state, President Jacques Chirac, and his wife Bernadette, who were returning to France after attending the G7 summit in the Japanese capital. By taking-off when he did Captain Marty missed the 747 by a matter of metres, a fact confirmed to John by retired Air France Concorde pilot, Jean Marie Chauve.

As the first officer made his alarm call the air traffic controller, Gilles Logelin, was informing the crew of the fire he had spotted. Eleven seconds later the flight engineer was heard to say: 'Shut down engine two.'

Shutting down an engine without reference to the captain was not within his remit. It should have been Captain Marty who decided if or when the engine was shut down but he did not challenge the flight engineer although the engine was shut down at a speed that was too slow and when the aeroplane was at a height that was too low for it to have been safe to do so.

It was hard to reconcile the opinion voiced in the final report of the crash that it had been caused by the piece of metal from the DC-10 and that neither Air France nor any of its employees was to blame in any way. The maintenance which had taken place just four days before the crash had not been done properly and a vital part of the Concorde's undercarriage had been left behind in the hangar when the aircraft went back into service. The amount of taxi fuel had been miscalculated leading to the aircraft being over its maximum take-off weight and its tanks being completely full. The person who had completed the loadsheet had failed to add the details of the extra baggage which contributed both to the overload and the unsafe centre of gravity at take-off. Nor had the flight deck crew behaved in an appropriate manner. The captain had been unwise to ignore the change in weather conditions which had been reported to him by the air traffic controller and the flight engineer should not have made the unilateral decision to shut down an engine. In addition, although there was no suggestion that this had anything to do with the crash, the report also showed that the first officer's medical certificate was out of date and, therefore his licence to fly was invalid. Jean Marcot's details, on page 12 of the preliminary report, show that his last medical had taken place at the CPEMPN (Centre Principal d'Expertise Médicale du Personnel Navigant de l'Aéronautique Civile) in Paris on 17 January 2000. At the foot of the page is a note which says:

The Captain's and First Officer's licences are covered by the FCL1 regulations (July 1999), the type rating renewing the licence as long as the medical certificate is valid. For those over 40 years of age, the medical certificate is valid for six months. Unlike the previous regulations, its validity runs from a specific date to a specific date rather than to the end of the month.

This meant that the 50 year old first officer's medical certificate had run out on 17 July 2000, eight days before the fatal Concorde flight, thus invalidating his licence to fly. Since the entire flight deck crew had to have up-to-date licences for the flight to be properly licensed, this meant that the operation of flight AF 4590 was invalid from the moment Captain Marty and his crew took control of the aeroplane.

John is certain that this would never have happened on a British Airways' aeroplane as staff were always reminded in good time that their medical certificates were coming up for renewal and had to have the new details noted on their files before they were allowed to fly again. For a company which was supposedly blameless, this did suggest that Air France had a rather cavalier attitude towards regulations and the laws which governed them and it is incomprehensible that the official enquiry should absolve the airline of any of the blame when its staff had made so many mistakes. As John reflected:

> I think that the final report basically glossed over the realities that led to the crash. It was economical with the truth.

On 10 April 2003, 16½ months after Air France and British Airways had resumed their Concorde services following the return of the aircraft's certificates of airworthiness, they announced that Concorde would make its last passenger flight that year; Air France on 31 May and British Airways on 24 October. Heavy maintenance costs and a fall in passenger revenue were cited as the reasons for the decision. British Airways' chief executive, Rod Eddington, said that the grounding of its flagship fleet marked '… the end of a fantastic era in world aviation'.

Once more Concorde was making headlines but this time there was genuine sorrow that the world's only supersonic passenger airliner was coming to the end of its life.

The first of the Air France Concordes to retire made its final flight from Paris to Washington Dulles Airport on 12 June 2003 when it went to its new home, the Steven F. Udvar-Hazy Center, part of the Smithsonian National Air and Space Museum. During the same month the other three Air France Concordes that were still flying after the crash of F-BTSC also went to their new homes; F-BVFB to the Sinsheim Auto & Technik Museum in Germany which became the only museum to have examples of both the Concorde and the Tu-144; F-BTSD to the Museum of Air and Space at Le Bourget while F-BVFC returned to the place where the French Concorde had been built and had made its first flight, Toulouse. On board the short flight from Paris was French test pilot André Turcat who had been at the controls of the very first Concorde to take to the air.

Having decided to fly for a short while longer than their French counterparts, British Airways began to retire its Concorde fleet on 31 October

2003 when G-BOAC flew to Manchester where it now resides at The Runway Visitor Park. Five days later G-BOAG took-off for Seattle via New York and its new home at the Museum of Flight. The museum's President, Ralph Bufano, said of the museum's latest acquisition, 'We are delighted to be able to share Concorde with the public here in the Pacific Northwest and with our visitors from around the world'.[11] G-BOAD followed it to the USA five days later to become an exhibit at the Intrepid Sea Air Space Museum in New York. When it had been announced that there would be a Concorde on display in New York, David Noyes, Executive Vice President Sales and Marketing, British Airways, North America, and John and Sue's nephew, said:

> We are extremely proud that Concorde has been our flagship for the past 27 years – during its tenure, it became a defining icon of our age. Concorde is bowing out in style, with dignity and affection, and we can be especially proud that the legacy of Concorde will have a place of honour at the Intrepid Sea Air Space Museum and that millions of people visiting New York City will be able to marvel at this wonderful aircraft.[12]

On 17 November G-BOAE took-off for Grantley Adams International Airport, Barbados. In the late 1980s a winter service had begun to the Caribbean island and it had proved to be so popular that Barbados became a regular part of the Concorde's winter timetable. It was logical, therefore, that one Concorde should make the island its final resting place and it now has pride of place at the airport's Barbados Concorde Experience, where visitors can sit in a room based on the Concorde lounge at Heathrow, fly an aircraft simulator and find out many facts about Concorde before boarding the aircraft itself. In February 2011 while on a trip to Barbados John gave a very well received lecture at the museum.

The final flight, made by British Airways Concorde G-BOAF on 26 November 2003, was to Filton near Bristol from where the first British Concorde had taken-off on 9 April 1969.

British Airways dispatcher, Jeremy Haslett, describes the very last departure of a Concorde from Heathrow:

> Wednesday, 26 November 2003 turned out to be a wet grey day.

This was not a start you wanted for what was a most momentous occasion – the very last Concorde flight.

Both Darren Kennelly and I walked out to Concorde G-BOAF that was parked on stand D58 in Terminal 1. It was for this reason, and this reason alone, that I was involved in this movement. I was an aircraft dispatcher based in this terminal so I involved myself in engaging with all the departments that were required at aircraft side that came from the central area. Darren was the main dispatcher from Terminal 4 who dealt with these aircraft on a regular basis and it was his signature that appeared on the very last load sheet.

At around 1 hour and 30 minutes before departure, the 11 crew appeared at aircraft side. A photo session took place. Security had to be tight and we were told not to allow anybody on board who was not directly involved with the movement – many were turned away.

The weather unfortunately proved to be a downer in that it drizzled most of the time. The coaches that brought out the 100 staff passengers staggered their departure from the terminal so that when they got to the aircraft, there was time to allow photos to be taken. At this stage I was in great demand in taking people's pictures, mainly as they boarded up the steps. I was always aware that this was the most popular place to be on the airfield and seeing so many people there suggested that the rest of the airline's operation could wait.

The next phase for me was the most memorable; with load sheet signed, we both stood at the top of the steps posing for photos and then witnessing the departure's final moments; closing the door, steps taken away and the final pushback ever.

I then went out with the airport marshallers as we followed the aircraft to its departure runway. A traditional send off by the fire service – a cannon of water forming a crown over the aircraft – and then a slow taxi, followed only by an American Airlines B777 and nothing else.

As G-BOAF operating BA9020 to Filton took-off from runway 27R on full power with 42 tonnes of fuel on board, the rain stopped and a small window of blue sky appeared through the clouds. It was to this that Concorde headed and the last view you had was that of the aircraft appearing on a blue background that was encircled by an otherwise cloudy sky – a magical moment not to be forgotten.

Despite the inclement weather over 1,000 people watched as the aeroplane left Heathrow and many more turned out to see Concorde on its way to Filton. Crowds had begun to gather long before the departure time along the coast at Weston-super-Mare, Portishead and Clevedon. Others waited at the Clifton suspension bridge spanning the Avon gorge for the last sight of Concorde as it swept low over the bridge before turning north to make its approach to Filton; for many of those waiting, the rain masked the tears that they were shedding. A crowd, estimated to be more than 20,000 people, waited at Filton, among them HRH The Duke of York who received the aeroplane's technical log from Concorde Chief Pilot, Captain Mike Bannister. Describing Concorde as, '... the icon of the 20th century' the Duke went on to say that:

Today is one of the saddest days in aviation history ... but it is a day to reflect on the glory of what the United Kingdom can achieve.

# Chapter 20

# A Warmth and Richness

*Keep love in your heart. A life without it is like a sunless garden when the flowers are dead. The consciousness of loving and being loved brings a warmth and richness to life that nothing else can bring.*

Oscar Wilde, 1854–1900, Irish writer and poet

On 25 October 2008 John and Sue celebrated their golden wedding anniversary. They had arranged a party at their home with a marquee in the garden but found that there just wasn't enough room for the number of people they wanted to invite and so had to host two parties, one for family members and the other for friends. Many more people attended the two parties than had been at their wedding. It required a lot of planning to ensure that all went smoothly but at least Sue knew that this time her husband would definitely be attending, unlike the uncertainty she had gone through in the days leading up to the wedding 50 years before when she was not even sure that John would be in the same country.

The years since the wedding have not always been kind to them and they have suffered much more heartbreak and worry than they deserved. The near fatal experiences that they have been through and the tragic loss of their eldest son could easily have destroyed them but they remain together; supporting each other through their troubles and thanking God for the good times they have shared. When John suggested calling this book *The Wind Beneath my Wings* it was not just as a reference to his aviation career.

Chris and Sally Hutchinson are no longer together but Sally still speaks fondly of her former in-laws. Chris is grateful for the support he received from his parents and says of John that he has never been judgemental but has always been calm and conciliatory:

> He's not flamboyant or an attention seeker. He is a modest, self-effacing perfectionist with a pride in his work and he has always understood his luck in his career. He has a simple approach to life and he has fabulous friends from all over the world.

John and Sue remain enthusiastic and, sometimes, indulgent grandparents. Some time ago when they acquired two cats, their granddaughters were allowed to name them and Ginger and Posh[1] are much loved members of the family.

Now grown up, their grandson Tim attended Manchester University where in 2010 he graduated with a degree in English and Drama Studies. As modest as both his father and grandfather before him, he simply said that he had passed, omitting the fact that he had actually gained a First.

When asked about his grandfather, Tim wrote:

> *My grandfather, or Pompa John as he is known to his grandchildren, is a much-loved, characterful member of the family. He takes a keen interest in all our trials and tribulations and this is always evident in his response to the latest news of our endeavours. I can recall his genuine sense of disappointment and unrest when I have telephoned him about any small struggles at school or university; his enthusiasm and glee when he hears of the good news is equally palpable.*
>
> *I am slightly too young to properly remember Pompa as a Concorde pilot although so strongly does his passion for aviation emanate that I cannot help but think of him in this way. His precision and orderliness, no doubt honed during his days flying Concorde, are admirable qualities – expressed in his own unique manner. For example, while at my grandparents house only the other week, I got a call from my Dad who was driving over to The Maltings from work and needed the Transport for London telephone number in order to pay the congestion charge. So, I asked Pompa if I could use his computer to search for the number online but before I knew it he had opened a supremely organised*

*filing cabinet and located the number amid a spread of papers under the heading: 'CAR'! I can also remember countless times when we have arranged to meet and he has asked on the phone: 'What's your ETA, Tim?' ETA? I pause and think for a moment. Oh yes, my estimated time of arrival!*

*If I had to identify one of Pompa's allegedly 'weaker' qualities, it would be his tendency to raise his stress-levels! This often provides great comedy value, particularly in hindsight when the stressful situation has been dealt with or rectified. As a child, I remember being at my grandparents house when Pompa had misplaced a cable for his digital camera or some other piece of technology. For a few moments, Pompa's wonderfully dramatic reaction was frantic and desperate. However, the cable was soon found and he was gently teased by my sisters and I for ever so slightly over-reacting! It seems that I have inherited this propensity for stress from Pompa's genes and, for both of us, a carefully managed dose of 'healthy stress' actually appears to motivate us in getting things done, controlling situations and even fulfilling our dreams.*

*As anyone will tell you, Pompa is a fanatical traveller and has a rich bank of tales to tell from his journeys across the world. His photography too is the subject of much admiration; not only does he witness an array of the world's wonders but he brings these home in the form of stunning photographs which, as a child, I remember gazing at in awe during the slide-shows he would present at The Maltings.*

*Pompa is kind, reliable, loving and eager-spirited. Being a grandfather certainly didn't put Pompa and Ganny off riding on all the wild rides and roller-coasters at Disneyworld a few years ago. There were no other grandparents so keen to hop aboard the stomach-churning contraptions. In 2010, Pompa is as brilliant a grandfather as ever and shows no signs of slowing down.*

Although still at school, Rafaella and Tigerlily are both accomplished actresses. Rafaella has appeared in several television dramas including *Doctors*, *New Tricks*, *Wild at Heart* and *Life on Mars*. She also appeared with her younger sister in *Blind Eye* in 2007. Tigerlily worked with Emilia Fox and Charles Dance in *Fallen Angel* and appeared in *Burn Up* with Rupert

Penry-Jones. In 2009 she played a young Pope Joan to much acclaim in the film of the same name.

Like their elder brother, both Rafaella and Tigerlily are extremely fond of their grandfather, as the following accounts show. Unsurprisingly, Rafaella chose to begin with one of John's most favourite things:

*Pompa loves Concorde, the house is full of plane models of all different sizes, pictures, books and both Ganny and Pompa always wear little gold Concorde brooches.*

*I remember when I was small enough to sit on Pompa's lap and he would take out his front tooth and it would land on his plate of crumbs left over from some cake, because Pompa loves a bit of cake, and he told me the story about how he lost his tooth and it's very heroic … so every time I saw him after that I would make him take out his tooth again just to remind me that my Pompa is the Bruce Willis of Hertfordshire.*

*Holidays with Ganny and Pompa are always fun, they took me and my brother to Florida; we swam with dolphins, took a ferry to the Bahamas, went to the NASA space centre and stayed with a few of their amazing friends. There will be friends of Ganny and Pompa's in pretty much every country, they love their adventures around the world and they love making friends. While we were on this trip Ganny and Pompa delighted me and my brother by taking us to Disney, Pompa particularly enjoyed Space Mountain and it's pretty scary.*

*Pompa's one of the kindest, most interesting and lovable people ever and we all love him to bits.*

Tigerlily also knows what her grandfather likes:

*My name is Tigerlily. I'm 10 years old. I like singing, dancing and acting. I also play the piano. I call my grandpa Pompa. Pompa loves watching me and my sister on television. It's really great and funny watching him on TV.*

*On special occasions my grandpa will wear his Concorde tie and Concorde socks. You may find my grandpa shouting down the stairs looking for his L59S cable for his Canon camera!*

243

*My grandpa is a huge chocoholic! Every year on his birthday it is almost a tradition that we make him a chocolate cake!*

*Pompa is a great photographer he is especially good at photographing animals.*

*I have flown in a plane with my grandpa as the pilot before. My dad sat next to him and I was in the back in charge of looking out for other aeroplanes.*

*I know he is a really good pilot but he is not a bad grandpa either.*

John and Sue are extremely proud of their three clever and talented grandchildren, and are equally proud of their son, Chris.

Despite the struggle he had had to become a pilot, Chris was not destined to remain one. He flew for British World Airlines for some years before being offered a job with Air UK. This would have involved a move and Sally did not want to relocate so she asked her stepfather if he could find a job for her husband. Chris again changed his career path when he joined Montanaro, an independent specialist fund management company in the City, as a fund manager. He excelled in this role and was head hunted by Unicorn Asset Management where he remains today as a very successful investment manager.

John has an aversion to both exercise and salad but remains generally fit, although he has recently had surgery for eye problems. While convalescing after the first operation, he had to remain on his stomach for two weeks doing absolutely nothing. Remarkably for someone as active as John, he stayed surprisingly cheerful during the enforced rest. The other operation, to repair a detached retina, was carried out in typical dramatic style when he was airlifted from a cruise ship in the Indian Ocean off the west coast of Australia, taken by the Royal Flying Doctor Service to the hospital in Broome and then transferred to Perth for the operation, which was a great success.

In 2011 he is still nursing his shoulder which was i njured when he fell while escorting a party of cruise passengers in Rome but which is slowly improving. Although obviously still rather accident prone he has taken steps to ensure that he no longer has the car accidents that plagued his youth, or the speeding convictions:

I have changed! I'm now a boring old fart – I actually drive at speed limits and do stupid things like that. I never used to; speed limits were for all the other people.

The urge to speed has gone from me now. After 15 years of flying at supersonic speed I don't find the need exists in me any longer. I've gone from one extreme to the other.

John is still upset at the demise of Concorde. He continues to believe that it was an extremely safe aeroplane and that its withdrawal from service was the wrong decision. The French judicial enquiry into the Air France Concorde crash whose report was published in December 2010 has done nothing to change his mind. He, along with many, many others is still convinced that the mistakes of Air France on this particular flight, were largely ignored although the airline should have accepted the major part of the blame for an accident which could and should have been avoided.

He is also angry that British Airways has made it almost impossible for the aircraft ever to fly again by draining the hydraulic pipes and disabling the electrical systems on its seven Concordes, which are on display in the UK, USA and Barbados.[2] He is not alone in this. His friend and former colleague Jock Lowe has said:

It was an act of vandalism by BA to drain off all the fluids. It will be embarrassing for Britain if only a French Concorde flies again because it was always a joint project between the two countries.[3]

There are many people who want a British-registered Concorde to fly again even if only to display at air shows or state occasions. Steve Falder, a spokesman for the Save Concorde Group, which is campaigning to return a British Airways Concorde to flight, said in 2006:

We would also have plenty of well-qualified volunteers if only BA would give them the chance. It is disgraceful that these aircraft, an important part of Britain's industrial heritage, are being allowed slowly to deteriorate.[4]

British Airways is not interested in giving anyone a chance to return a British Concorde to the skies. An airline spokeswoman made its rather arrogant position clear when she said: 'It's not debatable because we own them.'[5]

Unless British Airways changes its policy it seems that the attempts being made by a group of French enthusiasts may well be the only chance that is now left to see the Concorde fly again.

Pascal Touzeau a former Air France ground engineer who worked on Concorde has said:

> We are keeping Concorde alive and ready for the time when funding is found to let it fly again. We have no problem finding volunteers with the necessary expertise because they all love this plane. People don't feel the same passion about modern aircraft.
>
> We always felt the British loved Concorde more than the French so we cannot understand why nothing is being done with the British Airways Concordes.[6]

In 2010 the Save Concorde Group and the French group, Olympus 593, began work to see if the engines on Air France Concorde F-BTSD can be returned to an airworthy condition as a prelude to it flying once more.[7]

Nineteen years after he retired John is as busy as he ever was. He still enjoys the Air Squadron, is very active with the Guild and is part of the Flight Operations Group (FOG) of the Royal Aeronautical Society. Another member of this group, Terry Buckland, Deputy Head of Flight Crew Standards with the CAA, says of him:

> Captain Hutchinson has my utmost respect. His legacy to aviation is immense.
>
> He will not remember, but I flew with him 40 years ago as a 'one ringer'. His support and advice has stayed with me over the years.
>
> A true airman.

John continues to have excellent reviews for his cruise lectures and is often amazed to find that some passengers book a cruise simply because they know he is the guest speaker, even though they have heard the lecture before. He speaks on several diverse subjects – the Polynesian voyages across the Pacific between the eighth and tenth centuries, the Chinese treasure fleets of explorer Zheng He in the fifteenth century, the history of navigation, air navigation disasters such as the Air New Zealand DC-10 that crashed into Mount Erebus in Antarctica in 1979, and famous navigators such as round-the-world sailor, Sir Francis Chichester and the 1930s record-breaking New Zealand aviatrix Jean Batten to name but a few.

But it is still Concorde that holds the greatest fascination for his audiences. He believes that his lectures are popular because he speaks with passion about his subject. He also speaks with a vast knowledge and experience of Concorde and he enjoys talking about it. He sometimes finds it quite tiring to be away such a lot and occasionally wishes he could spend more time at home:

> To be honest I wish sometimes that I wasn't quite so busy and I really, really sometimes get so stressed inside that I think, 'If only I just had a week at home with nothing to do'. But things always keep coming up and it does stop you getting bored.

Neither he nor Sue are the sort of people who would be happy pottering about the house or sitting in front of the television every evening and both are thankful that John's lecturing career has enabled them to continue visiting places all over the world and meeting people they would otherwise never have got to know. As John says, 'long may it continue'.

Reflecting on the life that she has shared with her husband, Sue says simply:

> Who would have thought that the shy boy I met at dancing classes in 1951 would be my husband for 52½ years and counting! I certainly would not have believed anyone who predicted it then, and am constantly amazed at our good fortune. I can only be thankful that with his customary tenacity, once John had decided that it was me he wished to marry, he did not give up! I would have missed having the most wonderful, supportive and loving husband; having two wonderful sons, three amazing grandchildren and a hugely loving and supportive family.
>
> John has given me – through his life in flying and his whole love of life – a huge circle of friends, amazing opportunities to travel and explore the world and a life full of unexpected adventures and fun.
>
> Thank you my darling – we have been blessed and I couldn't be more proud of you.

# Epilogue

# 2020

Ten years ago, when John said of his hectic life, 'If only I just had a week at home with nothing to do' he could never have imagined that his wish would be granted in such a dreadful way. The Covid19 pandemic has given him that time and more, and he is now anxious to get back to his very busy life once again. He and Sue are both fit and well and will be celebrating their 62nd wedding anniversary in October.

In December, John is hoping to resume his lecturing career when he and Sue are due to take a cruise on the *Queen Mary 2*. Then, at the start of 2021 he has been booked for yet another cruise, this time to the Caribbean. They both are looking forward to the return of some sort of normality.

Thankfully their son Chris is doing well. He is Senior Fund Manager and a Director of Unicorn Asset Management. They have a portfolio of award winning funds and the office is located in The Charterhouse, a five minute walk from Barbican Underground. The business seems to be thriving in spite of all the uncertainty in the world at the moment.

Their grandchildren are also safe and well and all three of them are now grown up. Tim is 31 and has been tutoring on the internet throughout the Covid crisis. Although he had considered an acting career he has decided that it is not a secure enough profession and, in September, is embarking upon legal training to become a barrister.

Rafaella, now 25, is still an actress and also a musician and singer. She works as a nanny as well to supplement her income. A very creative person, she also designs and produces vintage style clothes which she sells online and through a shop in Peckham.

Twenty year-old Tigerlily will be starting her third and final year at Queens' College, Cambridge in September, where she is reading English with Drama. She is hoping that her final year at university will allow her to return to live tutorials as this year has been quite difficult. She is also looking forward to next year when she is due to go to the USA with the Cambridge Footlights.

# Photographs

John and his mother in Rawalpindi.

John with his much-loved ayah.

Colonel Hutchinson – Royal Indian Army

John aged two learning to ride.

Michael and John in Simla.

Boarding the T-33 at Gimli, Manitoba.

Flight Cadet Hutchinson gaining his wings in Gimli in October 1956.

25 October 1958.

Tim, Bobo and Chris.

The burning wreckage of BOAC 707 'Whisky Echo' on 8 April 1968.

The burning wreckage of BOAC 707 'Whisky Echo' on 8 April 1968.

Captain John Hutchinson and Concorde.

Mick Jagger. (Bill Tidy cartoon)

Athletic Endeavour. (Bill Tidy cartoon)

259

John and Sue with Susan Northcote and Patrick Tisdall,
the owners of the yacht *Severance*.

John with record-breaking aviatrix, Jean Batten, on Concorde.

# Notes

## Chapter 1

1  Documentary produced by Termite Art Productions for Travel Channel, Discovery Communications Inc.
2  ibid.
3  ibid.
4  ibid.
5  ibid.
6  ibid.
7  Transcript from JFK control tower 24 October 2003.
8  Documentary produced by Termite Art Productions for Travel Channel, Discovery Communications Inc.
9  BBC website, www.bbc.co.uk
10  Transcript from United Kingdom ATC, 24 October 2003.
11  *Flight* magazine, 28 February 1946.

## Chapter 2

1  www.the-forest-ashdowns.pwp.blueyonder.co.uk
2  ibid.
3  *Recollections of a Tea Planter* by W.M. Fraser.
4  ibid.
5  www.the-forest-ashdowns.pwp.blueyonder.co.uk

## Chapter 3

1  www.bishopcottonshimla.com
2  Figures taken from *World War Two: Nation by Nation* by J. Lee

Ready. www.nato.int/cps/en/natolive/official_texts_16912. htm?selectedLocale=en

3   Text of Atlantic Charter from NATO website
4   *Raj; The Making and Unmaking of British India* by Lawrence James; *Shameful Flight* by Stanley Wolpert.
5   *Mountbatten* by Philip Ziegler; chapter 28.
6   www.ukpolitical.info/1945.htm
7   Library of Congress interactive exhibition – Churchill and the Great Republic. www.loc.gov/exhibits/churchill/wc-newhome.html
8   Wolpert, op. cit.
9   Viola Hutchinson diary, Wednesday, 10 September 1947.
10  ibid., Thursday, 11 September 1947.
11  ibid., Saturday, 18 September 1947.
12  ibid., Tuesday, 23 September 1947.
13  ibid., Thursday, 25 September 1947.

## Chapter 4

1   Conversation between Michael Hutchinson and the author.
2   *The Independent*, 16 October 2005.
3   www.stgeorges.herts.sch.uk
4   Correspondence between Mary Piachaud and the author.
5   Correspondence between Viola Lawlor and the author.

## Chapter 5

1   Correspondence between Mary Piachaud and the author.
2   *Architect of Wings, A biography of Roy Chadwick* – Designer of the Lancaster Bomber by Harald Penrose.

## Chapter 7

1   These details were taken from John's own account, as he was one of the people who searched for the wreckage of the missing Shackleton. The English language newspaper in Singapore, *The Straits Times*, shows the ship which removed Flight Sergeant Dancy's body to have been the New Zealand Navy frigate HMNZS *Rotoiti* although it also

lists HMS *Albion* as being the vessel to locate the fishing boat whose crew witnessed the crash and buried the body.

## Chapter 8

1   *The Times*, 29 March 1963.
2   *The Sunday Times*, 7 April 1963.
3   ibid.

## Chapter 10

1   For a more detailed account of what happened to BOAC Boeing 707 Whisky Echo on 8 April 1968, see *Fire over Heathrow: The Tragedy of Flight 712* by Susan Ottaway.

## Chapter 11

1   www.montessori.edu/method

## Chapter 13

1   Quoted in an article in *The Guardian*, Friday 17 October 2003.
2   *Concorde – the complete inside story* by Brian Trubshaw.
3   Associated Press report in several North American newspapers, 12 May 1977.
4   ibid.
5   *Chronicle of Aviation*, eds. Bill Gunston and Mark Pyle.
6   Walter Cronkite on CBS Evening News Monday 17 October 1977, reported in Vanderbilt Television News Archive.
7   Gunston and Pyle, op. cit.
8   Trubshaw, op.cit.
9   *North Herts Gazette*, 12 October 1978.
10  Conversation between Jock Lowe and the author.
11  Conversation between Bill Brown and the author.
12  www.elviscostello.com
13  *Daily Mail*, 29 August 1988.

## Chapter 14

1   *A Dual Legacy of Antigua's First Prime Minister Vere Cornwall Bird (1909-1999)* by Lomarsh Roopnarine.
2   Brian Vine, *Daily Mail*, articles entitled *'Terror in Paradise'*, on 16, 17 and 18 July 1984.
3   Ann Leslie, *Daily Mail*, 3 October 1984.
4   ibid.

## Chapter 15

1   Reported in article by Jane Johnston in *British Airways News*, 8 June 1984.
2   Reported in article by Jane Johnston in *British Airways News*, 8 June 1984.
3   Conversation between Chris Serle and the author.
4   Conversation between Sid Batterbury and the author.
5   Conversation between Rick Gardner and the author.
6   *British Airways News*, 30 September 1983.
7   *Vauxhall-Opel-Bedford News*, November 1983.

## Chapter 16

1   www.sthildasharpenden.co.uk
2   *Heathrow Villager*, 3 September 1984.
3   *British Airways News*, 24 January 1992.
4   *The Children's Newspaper*, 4 June 1955.
5   www.fundinguniverse.com

## Chapter 17

1   The Guild of Air Pilots and Air Navigators of London, 1929-2004, www.gapan.org
2   Conversation between Allan Jacobson and the author.

## Chapter 18

1 www.dragonrapide.co.uk/history
2 *Fusion of Synthetic and Enhanced Vision for All-Weather Commercial Aviation Operations* by Randall E. Bailey, Lynda J. Kramer, and Lawrence Prinzel III NASA Langley Research Center
3 www.falklandislands.com
4 *Guild News*, May 1999.
5 Conversation between Gina Benmax and the author.
6 *Guild News*, January 2000.

## Chapter 19

1 http://news.bbc.co.uk/1/hi/business/851115.stm
2 *The Observer*, 13 May 2001
3 Accident report of the crash of Concorde, F-BTSC issued by Bureau Enquêtes-Accidents (BEA).
4 ibid.
5 Television documentary *Concorde: Anatomy of a Disaster*, Vidicom Media Productions for Discovery Communications, Inc. 2003
6 Interview on BBC *PM programme*, 25 July 2000.
7 BBC television programme *Breakfast with Frost*, hosted by Peter Sissons, 30 July 2000.
8 *Washington Post*, 26 July 2000.
9 *The AirSafe Journal*, 1 August 2000.
10 Conversation between Concorde engineer and the author.
11 www.concordesst.com
12 ibid.

## Chapter 20

1 Posh has sadly died but Ginger lives on, although she is becoming very frail.
2 Article by Ben Webster in *The Times*, 19 October 2006
3 ibid.
4 ibid.
5 ibid.
6 ibid.
7 *Daily Mail*, 29 May 2010

# Bibliography

## Books

Ahmed, Akbar S., *Jinnah, Pakistan and Islamic Identity: The Search for Saladin*, Routledge, 1997

Brendon, Vyvyan, *Children of the Raj*, Weidenfeld & Nicolson, 2005

Brooks, Peter W., *The World's Airliners*, Putnam & Company Limited, 1962

Chant, Christopher, ed., *Boeing 707 – Super Profile*, Haynes Publishing Group, 1983

Fraser, W.M., *Recollections of a Tea Planter*, The Tea and Rubber Mail, 1935

Guha, Ramachandra, *India After Gandhi: The History of the World's Largest Democracy*, Pan Books, 2008

Gunston, Bill, *Faster than Sound, The Story of Supersonic Flight*, Patrick Stephens Limited, 1992

Gunston, Bill and Pyle, Mark eds., *Chronicle of Aviation*, JL International Publishing, 1992

Hounsfield, Christopher, *Trailblazers – Test Pilots in Action*, Pen & Sword Books, 2008

Jackson, Robert, *The Encyclopedia of Military Aircraft*, Parragon, 2003

James, Lawrence, *Raj; The Making and Unmaking of British India*, Little, Brown and Company, 1997

Mayo, Katherine, *Mother India*, Jonathan Cape Ltd, 1932

Motum, John, ed., *The Putnam Aeronautical Review [VC10]*, Issue No. 1, Conway Maritime Press Ltd., 1989

Nichols, Beverley, *Verdict on India,* Jonathan Cape Ltd, 1944

Orlebar, Christopher, *The Concorde Story*, Osprey Publishing, 2011

Ottaway, Susan, *Fire Over Heathrow – The Tragedy of Flight 712*, Pen & Sword Books, 2008

Penrose, Harald, *Wings Across the World – An illustrated history of British Airways,* Cassell Limited, 1980

*– Architect of Wings, A biography of Roy Chadwick – Designer of the Lancaster Bomber*, Airlife Publishing Limited, 1985

Radford, John and Farrington, Susan, *Tombs in Tea, Bangladesh,* British Association for Cemeteries in South Asia, 2001

Ready, J. Lee, *World War Two: Nation by Nation*, Arms & Armour, 1995

Simons, David and Withington, Thomas, *The History of Flight*, Parragon, 2006

Sinha, Mrinalini ed., *Selections from Mother India*, University of Michigan Press, 2000

Taylor, Michael J.H. and Mondey, David, *Milestones of Flight*, Jane's Publishing Company, 1983

Trubshaw, Brian, Concorde – *The Complete Inside Story*, Sutton Publishing, 2004

Von Tunzelmann, Alex, *Indian Summer – The Secret History of the End of an Empire*, Pocket Books, 2008

Wise, Michael (compiler), *True Tales of British India*, In Print Publishing, 1993

Wolpert, Stanley, *Shameful Flight – The Last Years of the British Empire in India,* Oxford University Press, 2006

Woodley, Charles, *BOAC An Illustrated History,* Tempus Publishing, 2004

## Articles

Rose, David, *The Real Story of Flight 4590: Special Investigation*, *The Observer*, Sunday 13 May 2001

## Magazines

*British Airways News*
*Flight magazine*, 28 February 1946
*Guild News*, March and May 1999, January and March 2000
*Vauxhall-Opel-Bedford News*, November 1983

## Newspapers

*The AirSafe Journal*, 1 August 2000
*The Children's Newspaper*, 4 June 1955
*Daily Mail*, 16-18 July and 3 October 1984
*Heathrow Villager*, 3 September 1984
*The Independent*, 16 October 2005
*North Herts Gazette*, 12 October 1978
*The Straits Times* [of Singapore] December 1958
*The Sunday Times*, 7 April 1963
*The Times*, 29 March 1963, 19 October 2006
*Washington Post*, 26 July 2000

## Private Papers

The diary of Viola Hutchinson (1947)
The diary of George Hutchinson
Letters from John Hutchinson to his parents, brother and sisters
Letters from Colonel and Mrs Hutchinson to John Hutchinson
Letters from John Hutchinson to Sue Roe, later Hutchinson
Letters from Sue Roe, later Hutchinson to John Hutchinson
Letters from Sue Hutchinson to Colonel and Mrs Hutchinson

## Report

Accident report of the crash of Concorde, F-BTSC issued by Bureau Enquêtes-Accidents (BEA).

## Websites

www.bbc.co.uk
www.bishopcottonshimla.com
www.concordesst.com
www.concorde-jet.com
www.elviscostello.com
www.falklandislands.com
www.fundinguniverse.com

www.gapan.org

www.loc.gov/exhibits/churchill/wc-newhome.html

www.montessori.edu/method

http://tvnews.vanderbilt.edu/

www.nato.int/cps/en/natolive/official_texts_16912.htm?selectedLocale=en

www.save-concorde.co.uk

www.stgeorges.herts.sch.uk

www.sthildasharpenden.co.uk

www.stmichaels.kent.sch.uk

www.the-forest-ashdowns.pwp.blueyonder.co.uk

www.ukpolitical.info/1945.htm

# Index

271

# Acknowledgements

When the subject of this biography was broached, John Hutchinson was not keen on the idea. He was of the opinion that no one would be in the least bit interested in what he had done but I knew that there would be many people who would find his story fascinating.

Having finally decided to let me write the book both John and Sue have been wonderful in the help they have given me. They have allowed me access to private family papers and put me in touch with colleagues, friends and family members. All this has been done with great good humour and patience despite their incredibly busy lives and the frequent trips overseas during which they have kept in touch by e-mail and telephone. I really couldn't have asked for more.

My thanks are due to Anthony Butler, John Haslett and Liz Randall for their help in contacting people; to Jeremy Haslett for his account of Concorde's last flight; to Richard Hamond for his photo of Whisky Echo and to Ian Ottaway for his help in the production of some of the photos and for his advice in aviation matters. I am very grateful to John's friends and colleagues, Ricky Bastin, Sid Batterbury, Sheila and Derek Bell, Gina Benmax, Bill Brown, Terry Buckland, Liz and John Burley, Ruth and Patrick Cliff, Rick Gardner, Allan Jacobson, Jan Knott, Jock Lowe, Chris Serle and Arthur Thorning for the information they have given me. Thanks to family members Michael Hutchinson, Viola Lawlor, Pippa and Roger Noyes and Mary Piachaud, and to Sally Hutchinson, for sharing their memories with me.

To John's grandchildren Tim, Rafaella and Tigerlily for taking the time to write the accounts of their grandfather, despite their university, school and acting commitments, and to Chris, John's son, for agreeing to share with me his memories of his childhood, and his brother Tim, and for his insight into his parents' lives.

Special thanks to Sue Hutchinson for her piece about her husband and for telling me about the loss of her son, Tim, although I know that the latter was a difficult thing for her to do.

My thanks also to Lord Tebbit for the splendid foreword. I really appreciate his taking the time to write it despite his very busy life and numerous other commitments.

Last, but by no means least, my thanks to my partner Nick, without whose constant help and support this book couldn't have been written.

Susan Ottaway 2011

Ingram Content Group UK Ltd.
Milton Keynes UK
UKHW040752070423
419815UK00005B/249